> "If your number's up, your number's up. Doesn't matter if you're on a plane or a bus."
>
> Ronnie Van-Zant, Oct 20, 1977

RESTLESS ARTISTS

RESTLESS ARTISTS
Copyright © 2011 Ron Eckerman
Copyright © 2014 Ron Eckerman, Carolyn Day

First Edition released October 2011
Second Edition released in August 2014 in memory of Ron Eckerman

ISBN: 1500711438 ISBN-13: 9781500711436
Cover Photo by Ben Upham – for more info and to view his photography collection: www.magicalmomentphotos.com
Photos by Neal Preston with permission.
Photos by Craig Reed and Karen Griggs used with permission.
Publication Editor: John Neal

Special thanks to Craig Reed and John Neal for your contributions and your loyal friendship with Ron.

Special thanks goes out to Artimus Pyle for offering to help with bone marrow donation after Ron was diagnosed with leukemia in 2013.

AVAILABLE on Amazon in PAPERBACK, KINDLE,
and
AUDIO BOOK narrated by Ron Eckerman in 2011

TURN IT UP!

My years with Lynyrd Skynyrd

Love, Life, and Death, Southern Style

by
Ron Eckerman

In October of 2011, Ron Eckerman released this book in memory of Ronnie, Cassie, Steve, and Dean.

In August 2014, this book has been re-released in loving memory of Ron Eckerman, 1951-2014

Ronnie Eckerman
Gone but not forgotten.

All proceeds from the sale of this book will be donated to leukemia research.

Please promote Leukemia Awareness
Please donate blood or platelets at your local hospital whenever possible to help someone with leukemia. Please register at *www.bethematch.org* and become a bone marrow donor.

CHAPTER 1

I heard a loud explosion on the left side of the plane, followed by a couple of screams, and then silence. Looking back over my left shoulder, I caught a glimpse of a bright reddish-orange fireball just as it dissipated, leaving a cloud of thick black smoke trailing behind. It was about ten feet in diameter and disappeared completely within seconds. The engine sputtered a couple of times, the propeller spinning sporadically before it locked up. Quickly moving to the other side of the aisle, I squeezed into a space where I could see out of a window on the left side of the cabin. I'm not sure who I was climbing over, but they didn't seem to care. They were staring into space, their eyes already glazed with fear, their lips moving in silent prayer. I made it to the window just in time to see a smaller fireball explode from the other engine. Both engines had flamed out. The propeller spun sluggishly for a few revolutions and then it, too, locked into place. The propellers weren't spinning – they certainly weren't propelling, and the cabin lights were flickering on and off, creating this surrealistic "B" horror movie atmosphere. We were quickly losing altitude, and then everything went into slow motion, the way it happens in the movies, when you get ten different angles of a brief moment that stretches into five minutes. As I glanced around the cabin, I captured each of those angles, and they burned themselves into my brain, never to be forgotten.

1974 / 3 years prior

From a corner of the stage, well out of the way, I watched as the stagehands and roadies quickly peeled off the line of amplifiers after the opening act finished, stripping the stage of any evidence they were ever there in a matter of minutes. Drums were slung quickly to the side and manhandled to a forklift turned freight elevator, where they were lowered to the venue's floor. Beefy gray-haired stagehands then slung them out of the way while a roadie, the 'essential' roadie, in faded jeans and a tour t-shirt, blond hair down to his shoulders, was desperately trying to keep track of everything. This was a classic set change: an exercise in choreographed chaos.

It wasn't rocket science, these set changes, but if things weren't set up properly and it took too long, the audience could get dangerously rowdy, leading to expensive repair bills. It's funny how a mob reacts. Once the chairs start flying, everyone gets into the act. This had happened a few times over the years during a lengthy set change. Concession stands were torched and stages shelled with beer bottles and anything else that could be thrown. Ole Sarge (Cliff), a barrel chested, gray-haired Houston Police Officer, taught me a few of the rules years ago. He always had my back, but at the time I never realized it. After all, he was a police officer - the enemy! This was 1974 - you could be thrown in jail for ten years or more for possessing a single joint. Yet, in spite of the smoke-filled venues we booked, there were rarely any busts. Our patrons would really have to get crazy before that happened. I have to thank Sarge for that.

A very important lesson was learned at one of those monster stadium events when I was seeking his help. The audience had gotten completely out of control and the stage was being pummeled by anything and everything that wasn't fastened down. When I pleaded with Sarge, he told me none of his men were going out there.

"No way. It's in your hands," he said, his heavily creased eyes gazing calmly out at the destruction. "You better get someone on stage as fast as you can. A performer would be preferable." Easy for him to say, hidden backstage behind the line of motor homes we used as dressing rooms. He added, "Don't fire up the fans and make them wait. Drunk fans just shouldn't be left with idle time on their hands."

It was Sarge's golden rule, which I was presently

learning the hard way. I bravely crept up to the lone microphone set up center stage to make an announcement to try to calm the audience down. Before I got a word out, someone nailed me with a beer bottle. I woke up a short while later in one of the motor homes with a big goose-egg blossoming on my temple. I wasn't sure how I had gotten there, but later found I had wandered in under my own power. They also let me know everyone had thought I was drunk or stoned, or worse.

We were in San Antonio, in the music hall of a local college, and this was the first of a number of shows I was handling as stage manager for Wild West Productions, a growing concert promotion firm in Houston. I rarely slept more than a few hours a night during a run of shows like this, and it was light sleep, barely qualifying as a nap. Wild West was doing about twenty to thirty shows a month throughout Oklahoma, Texas, Louisiana, and Arkansas, so I was constantly on the move, meeting new artists and their crews daily. Very few of them made any impression on me.

That was before I ran into the Lynyrd Skynyrd bunch.

I waited until the stage was clear and the Skynyrd crew had just about completed setting up the band's gear. Not much to it really... the amplifiers were already set so it was just a matter of rolling the drum riser out, resetting a few cymbal stands that had fallen over during the move, and rolling out the grand piano. The keyboard tech was quickly performing some last minute tuning, and the guitar techs were all busy hitting a chord or two on each guitar and brushing microphone stands to make sure there were no surprises. Most of them had learned not to grab a stand while holding a guitar. The small shock on the back of the hand was much more preferable than getting the full 120 volts running through you. It's impossible to release your grip once that voltage grabs your muscles. I had both witnessed and experienced it. That was just one of many hazards the roadies and performers faced.

Once the Skynyrd crew gave me the okay, I went back to

summon the band. I'd never met them before and hadn't had time to introduce myself. They weren't really a welcoming bunch. The dressing room was about a hundred feet from the stage, down a rather narrow light grey corridor of poured cement lit by harsh industrial lights, and by the time I got there, they were on the way out. Evidently one of their crew was a few paces in front of me.

The band exploded from the room, forcing me back against the wall. I just flattened myself against it. There was really no choice - there was nowhere else to go. They charged past me, one by one, intense, intimidating, and focused on the stage with precision tunnel vision. I don't think they even noticed me yet I was so close I caught a draft as each one raced by. Not a one of them so much as gave me a glance. I blended in with the wall in the hall, and that song of Willie Nelson's popped into my head: *Hello Wall*.

Leading them was their personal assistant and resident bartender, Dean Kilpatrick. A wiry fellow was following closely behind Dean. Once he took the stage and leapt to the drum riser I knew who he was – drummer Bob Burns.

Next in line was a short fellow. Since he carried a bass guitar it had to be the bassist, Leon Wilkeson. I wouldn't have known that much if I hadn't studied their photos on an album cover the night before. I had to at least know how many people were in the group, and I memorized as many of their names as I could. I didn't know a single one of their songs, at least not by name, but I'm sure I'd heard them on the radio. I had to have. Evidently they were one of the hottest upcoming bands around.

Closely chasing Leon was Allen Collins, a tall, lanky individual with long flowing blond hair and a mean scowl on his face. I had to take a second look – his double had just passed me seconds before. Like Dean a few seconds earlier, Allen slipped past me without so much as a nod. It was odd, Dean and Allen, as they were close to identical twins. Both moved the same way, both dressed in similar outfits.

Next out was a character with long, flowing black hair and deep set eyes. Gary Rossington, one of the guitarists.

Ronnie Van Zant followed. I was surprised to see he was barefoot. That was a dangerous practice at concerts. Heavy equipment was being thrown about and the rough plywood decking on the stage was far from splinter-free. Ronnie was relatively short and a bit stocky, not really out of shape, but more like an athlete who liked his beer. He evoked a feeling of power and confidence as he strode by. There was no doubt in my mind who he was. He had to be the singer, and the main cog that kept the machine operating.

Another guitarist about the same size and build as Ronnie followed closely behind - Ed King. Bringing up the rear was Billy Powell, the keyboardist.

So there you had it. They were followed by their road manager, Gary, who was walking with a cane due to a recent injury. He was followed by another member of their crew, Craig Reed, who looked really stoned. I'd met Craig earlier in the day and found him to be a hard worker who had been with the band for quite a while. They had picked him up early in their career. In spite of his stoner appearance and easy-going attitude, he was highly professional and took excellent care of the band. At the time I didn't know exactly what Craig did – he was definitely a lead man on the crew and he took care of whatever was needed. Most crew members were specialists of a sort, assigned to take care of one member of the band. Craig seemed to kind of float around and see to everyone's needs rather than being attached to one single musician like the rest. And don't let that stoner appearance fool you – he was always on top of his game... and he was, more often than not, really, really stoned. My hat's off to anyone that can pull that off.

I was racing behind, trying to jockey into a position so I could get in front of the band and hold them back before they entered the stage area and the audience's view. I managed to squeeze in front once we made it out of that corridor, and I immediately stopped them in their tracks, which surprised me, as I was expecting to get flattened again, this time against the floor. I gave the house light operator the cue to dim the lights and then waited. The group waited impatiently with me, many of them shifting their weight from foot to foot. Then the house lights went down, the crowd roared, and a half dozen flashlights popped on from all around us, helping as we navigated our way to the stage. The band took right to it, targeting in on pre-show chores, plugging up their guitars and hitting a lick or two, tweaking the tuning, then repeating. Bob banged a couple of rounds on his drums as Allen waved excitably at the crowd, already working them, another trademark of his that he'd repeat over and over during the show. Aside from playing a stinging guitar he was apparently their on-stage cheerleader. And the crowd loved it, responding to his every move. Satisfied he had done his job, he, too, plugged in and checked his instrument.

I waited in the wings, as aside from being the stage manager I also emceed the shows, something I wasn't overly fond of. I was in my usual state at this point, nervously running my lines over and over in my mind, even though I always blew it and said something completely different once on stage. I never knew what would come out of my mouth when I was in front of that microphone. I hated the chore as I always had a bit of stage fright, but someone had to do it, and that someone was inevitably me, so I waited for a nod from the band (their first acknowledgment that I existed), then approached the center stage microphone.

"*Good evening... Ladies and gentlemen, boys and girls. Put your hands together and give a warm welcome... from Jacksonville, Florida... the hardest working band in music... Lynyrd Skynyrd!*"

It was my standard introduction. Every band is the best or the hardest working, or, as in the case of Blue Oyster Cult, the "shortest band in the world", but I never introduced them with that. It was my personal observation, something I noticed on the very first show I did with them.

"They're a bunch of fuckin' midgets," I confessed to my coworkers. "How am I going to keep a straight face introducing a bunch of midgets?" I was laughing so hard when I introduced them I didn't feel a bit nervous. Got right to it.

My task done, the band kicked in hard before I could get off stage, and the crowd went absolutely berserk. I scurried off as quickly as I could, dodging a drum stick - Bob was a damned good shot. Moments later I found out what all the excitement was about.

The band opened with a full tilt boogie woogie number enhanced with their own Southern touch, and they were off like a freight train powered by a rocket. They just kept on building steam – a multi-stage rocket. Ronnie was sauntering around on stage more or less directing his band of warriors, draping an arm around a guitarist, resting his foot on the drum stand, where he'd gaze at the drummer for a moment, that little menacing smile on his face. Then he'd stroll back to his microphone, grabbing the stand and yielding it like a weapon, never threatening anyone, just holding on to it as if he was going to use it at any second - on his band, the audience, even God almighty. He wasn't like any singer I had ever seen. No posing, no fancy moves, and certainly no dancing. He just assumed the position of commander-in-chief, prompting his foot soldiers, moving from one to the other as their solos came up. He'd step back on occasion when the three-guitar army charged to the front, beaming proudly from behind like a new father as they worked the audience. These guys kept up this energy throughout the performance, a fast moving freight train, one threatening to run off the tracks at any moment, stopping only for a slug off that ever present bottle of Jack Daniels. Powerful fuel.

Allen was playing his ass off, slinging that vintage Firebird this way and that, aiming it at the crowd, a sniper's threat when he fired off a round or two from between his legs, then letting it swing freely as he swung an arm out in a grandiose movement, directing everyone's attention to Billy. Billy would let it fly, squeezing every ounce of honky-tonk out of the piano. And so it went, that freight train building speed minute by minute until they had whipped the crowd into a frenzy. And then they were done, and I had about forty five hundred fans on my hands, all waving lighters and matches, screaming their lungs out for more.

So I waited... and waited... and waited, and the crowd grew louder and louder. Then the chair banging began as the audience began stomping their feet.

After looking back from the stage and not finding the band anywhere, I started feeling the heat. It crept right up my backbone and settled in my head, my whole nervous system going electric. With feet and hands tingling, my mind flashed back to the incident in the stadium, to the words of Sarge, and I started wondering when the chairs were going airborne. Their crew, for the most part, were waiting like the rest of us and I found myself wondering if they were waiting for the houselights to go up so they could tear down the stage.

I ran toward the dressing room and for the second time that night, found myself pushed back against the wall as the band raced back towards the stage. The audience, which had managed to reach painful and illegal sound levels, somehow doubled their volume when the band hit the stage, and it took a moment or two before the band could even start. Then, miraculously, in unison, they calmed right down. Ronnie grabbed the mic stand, leered at the crowd, and then asked,

"*What song is it you wanna hear?*"

The crowd went nuts. Then Billy began this beautiful classical piece on the piano, and the crowd went completely silent. Once they recognized the song, *Free Bird*, the roar came back, but again only for a moment, then they took their cue and quieted down for the opening.

Then the band cut loose in one of the most frenzied instrumentals I'd ever heard, and the crowd exploded. And that freight train got to rolling once again, sucking every bit of energy out of every single person until they could finally leave the stage in peace. The audience howled in appreciation, then filed out for a drink or sat and waited for the next band, knowing, as every Skynyrd fan knew, they wouldn't be returning after *Free Bird*.

Shortly afterwards, the stage had been reset for the next act, and I wandered backstage to thank the band. It was one of those duties that came with the job. I always thanked the band, even the assholes. This time I faced two security guards in jeans and t-shirts at the dressing room door who refused to allow me entry. I heard a bit of yelling from inside, so I politely excused myself and got the hell out of there. I'd seen this before. I had better things to do anyway, and three more shows before I'd be home again. Lynyrd Skynyrd wasn't on any of them.

I didn't expect to see them again, at least not for a while, as our calendar was full for the rest of the year and I wasn't that sure we'd have them back anyway... not after shelling out an extra $3,000 dollars for the damage done to the dressing room that evening.

CHAPTER 2

It was October 20, 1977, and knew this was going to be a bear of a day as soon as my eyes popped open. There was trouble with the limo drivers the night before. Our limos, as often the case in small towns, came from a couple of local funeral homes. Needless to say they weren't very well prepared for a bunch of dope-smoking, pill-popping drinkers literally pouring themselves into the cars after the show. Although the band had cut down their consumption substantially so far this tour, they still had the reputation, the behavior, and attitude from the past. It was in their blood. I'm not sure what we'd done to offend them (any more than normal), but they didn't show up this morning for the trip to the airport. I had twenty-six anxious and somewhat hungover individuals milling around the hotel lobby waiting for cars, and there were no cars. Gene and I called every cab in the city, walked outside so we could watch for them, and waited impatiently.

December 1975

I was sitting in my office in Houston when the call came in. Mary, my secretary, quickly put the call through.

"Ronnie, would you be interested in helping me out with Lynyrd Skynyrd?"

It was Allen Arrow, a powerful music industry attorney, and an acquaintance of mine from New York whom I had met through a mutual client, Fleetwood Mac.

"What do you have on your mind, Allen?"

He explained that the band needed a new tour manager, and laughingly told me that they had evidently "broken" the last one. I remembered the guy, Gary-on-a-cane, who was quite a hell raiser himself. I couldn't really imagine him managing a band, especially this one.

"They broke him?" I asked. I was definitely off script. I thought he meant they had forced him into bankruptcy or worse. My thoughts went to another friend of mine who had killed himself after losing all of a band's earnings in Las Vegas. The guy had been horribly drunk and wouldn't quit playing until he had lost everything, both his own money and the band's. He went to his room, drew a bath, and slashed himself a few dozen times with a razor blade. It had been quite traumatic to everyone that knew him.

"No..." Allen laughed, "I mean they physically broke him."

That didn't sound good. I remembered that he walked with a cane the last time I saw him. Thus his name, *Gary-on-a-cane*, and I knew from my own experience that they were the very definition of redneck.

"Physically broke him?"

"No, no, no – I meant to say they mentally broke him. They bankrupted his damn mind."

"Oh hell, Allen, I don't know. I've got Frampton going out on the road, and the Mac is gearing up, but they're kind of mad at me right now, so I don't know how that's going to go. Clearlight is prepping three tours."

He turned on the charm and sucked me right in. "You're the only one I know that can handle this group. Seriously. You are the only one. I'll help you find someone to take care of Frampton. What's going on with Fleetwood Mac?"

"Same old thing. Anti-management. They've been screwed so much by managers they don't trust anyone. I don't blame them. Then this magazine article came out about me managing them. Really pissed 'em off. I did an interview with one of the trade magazines and they printed this crap about how I was taking over management."

"I have the same trouble. Just keep your mouth shut."

"An interview is an interview. They ask questions, I answer them as best I can."

"Ever heard of *no comment?*" Allen asked.

"No comment."

"So what do you think? Can you do it?"

"I guess so. Maybe for a few weeks." I was toying around

with the phone, trying to get the cord unwound, not really thinking about the commitment I had just made.

"Great! I'll be in Houston next week. I'll give you a call when I get in. We can finalize everything and get you settled in with the band."

"Next week? It's New Year's."

"I should be in by Wednesday."

"The band's coming?" I asked.

"No. I just need to update you on them. They're a handful."

"And when does the tour start?"

"Week after that. I've got to go. I'll call you as soon as I get in." He hung up before I could get another word in.

I sat back in my chair, feeling a bit hoodwinked. Allen had worked me over pretty fast, as was his fashion. He could swoop in, close a deal, and exit before you could even gather your thoughts. I wasn't that concerned, though. He had always treated me right, and it was only for a month or two. In a moment I shrugged it off and dove back into the lighting design I had been working on.

The week passed quickly, and I was still trying to finish the same lighting plot I had started the week before when Allen called.

"I made it," he declared when I picked up the line.

"You're in town?"

"I'm at the Whitehall."

The Whitehall was an older hotel in Houston where we had once had offices. We had slowly been transforming it into a rock and roll hotel over the past few years, referring it to every group that asked about accommodations.

"Can you make it by?" he asked.

"Yeah, I can come over tonight... about nine?"

"Let's make it in the morning – how does ten sound?"

I woke up the next morning with a trace of a hangover. There were always tons of people dropping by my house unexpectedly, and the night before was no exception. They started arriving at eight, with a steady flow of arrivals until about ten. I guess I was throwing a party, I just wish someone had let me know about it! It was around eleven that the tour bus pulled up, parking right in front of the house.

This house, the Holcombe House, as it was known, was a large, two story on the west side of Houston. Since I was on tour most of the time, the other residents, which included my wife, friend and ex-neighbor Linda, her daughter Mona, my brother Rodney, a couple of lighting technicians/designers, and a variety of others (depending on who was in town) would rotate in and out on a regular basis.

I was always surprised when I got home from a tour – I never knew who had taken up quarters. This week's cast of characters included my best friend, Curry Grant, and Christine McVie from Fleetwood Mac, who was staying with us in Houston in between tours. They were in love. That's another story, but John McVie has blamed me for his breakup with Christine for years. I had nothing at all to do with it.

I checked out of the party sometime around one in the morning so I could get some sleep before meeting with Allen. Of course there were several visitors before I went to sleep. Inevitably, right as I was fading away, someone would barge in with a drink. I kept turning them down and pulling the covers over my head. Finally the disturbances tapered off, but only after the police showed up. Apparently they didn't like tour buses parked on the street.

Answering the calls from downstairs, which were somewhere between frantic and comical, I climbed out of bed, threw on some clothes, staggered down the stairs in a sleepy haze, and answered the door. Everyone else had gone quiet and had moved to the back room – they had all looked out the window and knew who was at the door. I opened the front door and realized there was a thick cloud of marijuana smoke (or so it seemed), stepped out, and shut the door quickly behind me. My heart began to race as I began assessing the situation as I knew I could be facing serious trouble.

One officer stood back a few feet, the other was right in my face.

"May we come in?" he asked politely.

"No sir," I answered, just as politely.

"Okay," he said, looking over my shoulder, trying to see into the house through the little window in the door. "You can't park that bus on the street."

"Not a problem, sir. I'll have it moved immediately."

"Okay... you behave yourself now... and don't call me sir. I hate that," the officer told me as he turned toward his car. I detected a faint hint of amusement in his eyes, but there was no wink.

It was that brief. They left, I behaved, the bus left, and then everyone else left, and I crawled back up the stairs to my room. I fell asleep worrying if they were going to return with a warrant.

I awoke fairly early the next morning, showered quickly, and began rummaging around in my closet for something to wear. I was meeting Allen at a fairly swanky downtown hotel and I had never seen him without a suit, so I picked out my best and pulled it on. After three or four attempts at getting both tails of my tie proportioned right, I was done. I took a quick look in the mirror, and was out the door.

Allen said he'd meet me in the restaurant, so I strolled in, all suited up, feeling very professional, and found him at a corner table in a t-shirt and jeans. It knocked me back to reality – this is rock and roll; suits are not worn. His t-shirt was nice and crisp, as well as his jeans, and he had a nice jacket over them. But still, we had reversed our normal attire.

We had a good talk about the group, how they were doing, and where they were going. I was convinced in very little time that they had explosive potential and even more explosive personalities. We also discussed the band's manager, Peter Rudge, whom Allen was convinced was one of the best in the business. He described Peter as "brilliant", having first worked with Peter during the 1974 Stones tour, of which I had stage managed one of the shows at The Cotton Bowl in Dallas.

I had worked three days straight without sleep in preparation for the event, so on show day I was found fast asleep in The Eagle's dressing room. When I awoke, The Eagles had landed and they were being extremely quiet and were speaking in whispers so I wouldn't be disturbed. I soon discovered that the show had begun hours ago, my work having been completed by various friends and employees. I came around quickly, thanked the guys for letting me sleep, and excused myself from the dressing room. They had to be relieved, it must have been impossible to prepare for a show when you're tip-toeing around.

It took a while to reorient myself and figure out where we were in the schedule, and I was shocked to discover I had slept through about half of the performances. It was damn near time for the Eagles to perform, followed by the Stones.

The Eagles brought the crowd to their feet. Although I enjoyed the band, their music was a bit too tame for my tastes, so I wandered around backstage checking security, dressing rooms, and a host of other things during their set.

Bill Graham, who was co-promoting the show, had arrived so things got even tighter and, true to form, extremely tense. Bill always made people tense. He was a legend... and a bit of a bully. He always got what he wanted.

I had just finished securing the ramp leading to the stage and was turning around to climb back up to the dressing rooms. It was a hundred yards or so back to the top and I had only managed about fifty of it when I saw some clown in a purple cape twisting and turning, dancing his way towards me down the ramp, evidently intent on reaching the field where the stage was set up. I figured he was some stoned-out hippy who had managed to sneak by security, so I silently crept up from behind and grabbed him, full force, in a bear hug. I was willing to physically remove him – he was small enough - and figured I could simply carry him out. I wasn't going to take the chance of him getting away.

So there I was, my arms wrapped around this character, holding him tighter than a steel trap, about to lift him from the ground, and he turned his head and looked me in the eye. I instantly released my grip and apologized. He stepped back, looking both angry and confused, then broke into a wide smile.

"Well that's a bit rude."

"I don't throw out that many performers."

"I'm not the first then?" he asked, his feet starting to move, getting back to some rhythm only he could hear.

"No, I threw Van Morrison out once."

"Me and Van? Honorable company at least."

"I guess so, Mick. Sorry."

"It's alright, mate. Can I go now?"

"Absolutely," I laughed, and watched as he spun his way down the ramp until he was just out of the audience's sight. I looked up to see the rest of the band starting down, so I proceeded to the stage in front of them, making sure there weren't any other loonies like Mick Jagger that might be waiting in the shadows.

I walked away from the meeting with Allen with a packet of information on the band, their current itinerary, and a strong word of warning:

"Do not, under any circumstances, let Dean Kilpatrick (their personal attendant, who would be my assistant) hold money, your briefcase, or any other important document, or anything else which you wish to keep."

He handed me my airline tickets to Jacksonville, wished me luck, and we parted ways.

January 1976

I boarded a plane for the long flight from Houston to Jacksonville, touching down at 11:00 that evening. I looked around for Dean, which wasn't easy, as I had no idea what he looked like. He was supposed to meet me, so I assumed he would have a sign or something, but after thinking about what Allen had said, I soon realized that was way beyond expectations.

The luggage area emptied quickly, so I sat on one of the concrete benches that were scattered around the perimeter and started digging through my briefcase to find the hotel address. After locating my booking info, I raced to the only car rental counter still open and saw a chain mail fence slide down over it. But there were still phones to the hotels, and the shuttles and cabs were still running... I hoped.

As I picked up the phone to the hotel, a skinny fellow with sunken eyes and long blond hair approached me.

"You Ronnie?" he asked.

"That's me."

He extended his hand, "I'm Dean."

I shook his hand, smiling, somewhat relieved. We grabbed my bags and exited the airport. He had parked at the curb, so there wasn't much of a walk, just a blast of hot, wet air as the humid Jacksonville climate struck. January in Jacksonville, 85 degrees and 100% humidity.

We quickly threw my bags in the car, a faded blue Cougar, cranked down the windows, and took off towards the city. He didn't have a lot to say, so I followed his lead, talking as little as possible as we headed into town.

Even though it was nearing midnight, I expected to meet with the band. After all, this was the quintessential southern rebel band, and I was sure they'd be up practicing and/or partying before the tour. Instead, he drove me straight to the hotel, which was actually a relief – I was dead tired from the flight.

The next morning, bright and early, my eyes popped open. I hated it. I had this internal alarm clock – it always went off on time, and usually with ample time to spare. After a quick breakfast I sat, waiting, and quickly skimmed through the pages of a newspaper someone had left on an adjacent table.

It was a fairly nice place, actually, a Hilton that was, as I found out later, convenient to nothing in which I was involved. In fact, there were no decent hotels convenient to either the band or the airport other than some run-down family motels, so I should have been counting my blessings.

Dean and Kevin Elson, their sound man, a radical departure from this motley crew, picked me up at 8:30, right on time, and the four of us (Dean had a friend to drive his own car back) sped out to the airport and rented three large station wagons – our transportation to the first gig.

I was really surprised at Kevin – he wore the normal t-shirt and jeans, but they were wrinkle free, and he was clean cut, with short, dark hair, and a strong sense of intelligence about him. Like a lot of engineers and producers, he was a bit geeky for rock... he just didn't capture the whole rock and road warrior stereotype.

We caravanned over to Allen Collins' house, Dean's friend leading in his car, Kevin following closely behind in one of the rentals, Dean following next, and me trying to keep up with them in the last of the Ford Country Squires. Dean had little respect for speed limits, stop signs, or common road courtesy. He was bent on keeping up with the lead car no matter what.

After a frightening drive, we made it all in one piece and pulled up to Allen's house in the Jacksonville suburbs where the band had assembled. They were scattered about in the cool morning sun with their friends and families: some tossing a football, some a Frisbee, others talking in small groups, saying goodbye to wives and girlfriends.

We double parked in the street. There were cars everywhere and we had a lot of luggage to load. Kevin quickly slid into the shadows. I suspect he knew what he was doing as he neatly avoided assisting with the luggage piled up in the driveway. That air of intelligence I sensed proved to be right.

I leaned against one of the cars, my arms folded, surveying the scene, trying to match faces with names, figuring out which of the women were paired with which of the men. Leon was the first to approach me.

"Ron," he said, staring at me with a curious smile. Since there was no hand extension, I continued leaning against the car, trying to match his smile.

"Ron Eckerman..." he said.

I realized my lifelong name had just been shortened from "Ronnie to Ron."

"Ronnie Eckerman," I said, extending my hand. "You're Leon, aren't you?"

"That's right, Leon Wilkeson, bass," he said, finally extending a hand. "Um...I gotta tell ya somethin'," he said in his low, monotone way of speaking, "Ronnie isn't gonna work, you know. We already have a Ronnie. So you're Ron."

"Okay, Ron then." I shook his hand as other members of the group began assembling around us. I stood up straight, preparing for intros. It was a macho thing and a natural reaction – I was dealing with rednecks. We all froze for a moment. They checked me out, I checked them out. We stood in that moment of awkwardness sizing each other up – it was weird, like we were going to fight.

Then I broke the silence. "I'm Ron Eckerman, you guys ready to hit it?"

"Hell yeah!" Allen answered, "The real question, Ron Eckerman – are you ready to hit it?"

"Well, hell yeah. I was born ready."

Everyone broke into laughter – a couple of them a bit suspicious, more of a sarcastic smirk, then they began introducing themselves and we all shook hands. It appeared I'd been accepted into the pack.

Allen leered, "Born ready... we'll see about that, Ron Eckerman."

I hated everyone using my first and last name, but I found out quickly I'd better get used to it. It was said with a quick, melodic flow, with no pausing between my first and last name. It was Roneckerman, to everyone in the band, except for one person who always called me Ron.

Ronnie Van Zant overheard us — I caught his gaze — a moment later he was introducing himself,

"Hi, Ron. I'm the real Ronnie."

We both had an uncomfortable chuckle and he moved on to more introductions — the girls. Ronnie personally introduced me to each one, in a good imitation of a Southern gentleman, with all the charm associated with the stereotype.

"These are my girls," he said, "The Honkettes I'm gonna call 'em." And so the back-up singers were given a name right there on the spot. "This is Cassie Gaines." I gently shook the young woman's hand. She was a sweet girl, fairly good looking, with long, light brown hair, full lips, and a matronly vibe about her. She was someone you could trust. I liked her instantly. She was definitely the leader of her sisters, which consisted of Leslie Hawkins, a petite brunette with a cute face, a great body and as I was soon to find out, an extraordinary voice.

And then there was Jo-Jo Billingsley. Ronnie introduced her with the same charm as the other two, then whispered to me, "You gotta keep your eye on her." I was unsure what he meant but had my suspicions. Jo-Jo was dressed in a Janis Joplin style outfit — very fitting — and she also carried what I imagined was the same attitude. I soon discovered she could probably drink Janis under the table. It was easy to see why I thought of her as Janis incarnate, and I soon found she sounded a bit like her as well.

I met Kathy, Allen's wife, and Stella, Billy's wife, and of course Ronnie's wife, Judy. They were all sweethearts. We had an instant and mutual respect for each other. Truth is, these women weren't hard to love, and even easier to respect. Not surprisingly, they were strong women. They'd have to be to put up with their road-warrior husbands.

Final goodbyes were made, the luggage loaded, and seats were called. Dean would be driving the lead car, with Gary riding shotgun, Artimus and Allen in the back. I was nominated to drive the second one, with Ronnie riding shotgun, and Billy and Leon in the back. Kevin and the girls filled the last one.

We were soon winding through the neighborhood heading towards I-95 on our way to Savannah, Georgia. Once on the freeway and out of town, I settled into my temporary role as chauffer and began enjoying the lush greenery on either side of the road. There were thick woods on both sides of the interstate, with thicker undergrowth, all healthy, all green, creating a primeval forest.

It was beautiful, and even though I'd traveled the road many times in the past, it was always as a passenger, most of the time in a tour bus, so I'd never been able to enjoy the wholesome beauty of the area. The sun was beaming, clear blue skies – the day couldn't have been nicer, and it was warming up quickly. Ronnie had found a good station on the radio, and I was bobbing my head to the beat and slowly picking up speed to keep up with the car ahead of me.

We hit about 65 miles an hour, and as my eyes flicked back and forth between the beautiful scenery, the car in front, and my rear view, I noticed a growing flurry of brown hair whipping around outside the left rear passenger window of the wagon in front of us. At the same time I could hear Billy and Leon giggling from the back seat. I glanced in the rear view at them, then turned my attention to the activity in front. As my eyes narrowed in, focusing, I could feel them bulge. I wasn't quite sure if it was an optical illusion or my imagination. A second later, I found out it was neither.

That mass of flying hair was followed by Artimus' head glancing back at our car to make sure we were watching. I wasn't sure if he could see us as his hair was whipping around like Medusa. No, much worse than Medusa – there was so much of it and it was so wild, not like a head growing snakes at all – it was a hurricane. I glanced down at the speedometer to see that we had crept up to 70, and Artimus' shoulders and arms had cleared the windowsill.

Billy and Leon were going crazy in the back seat. I shot

them a look and glanced over at Ronnie just in time to see him cup his forehead in his fingers. Focusing my attention on the car ahead, I saw the growth on the side of the car blossom into a full human.

Artimus had managed to pull himself completely out of the window, climbed on to the roof, and was now pressing himself down and hanging on for dear life at 70 mph. He rode for a few seconds like that, body flattened against the car – brown shoots of hair whipping around like a fire in high wind. And then the dismount - he inched his way slowly to the driver's side of the roof. His left leg dropped over the side of the car, flailed for a split second, then was pulled back and replanted on the roof.

He began manipulating his body away from the alignment with the car until he was stretched in a diagonal. Then that left leg snaked out again, searching for a foothold. He couldn't quite get it, so he dropped the right leg down with it.

Ronnie and I were watching in disbelief while Billy and Leon cheered him on. And on he went, sliding his legs around until everything from the waist down was blowin' in the wind, and everything from the waist up was pressed so hard against the body panels he had formed an airtight seal. I don't think he had calculated the dismount, forgetting that legs only bend one way at the knee, and turning around so he was belly up would turn him into a kite.

Somehow he managed to find the rear windowsill, and soon had the major portion of his legs firmly planted inside the vehicle. We couldn't see, but I'm sure the other passengers had lashed on to his legs by now with the tenacity of bulldogs, no doubt, and they weren't about to loosen up until he was safely inside.

As I watched, his body became more and more flexible. He inched his way down, sliding back into the vehicle slowly until his shoulders and that mass of hair were the only things visible. Then he hung there for a moment until his head disappeared, leaving only the dark brown hurricane of hair, then zip... everything went back in. It was like watching someone suck in a strand of spaghetti. There was still a small mass of hair whipping around, then that organism slipped back inside as well.

Ronnie looked over at me inquired, "Ron, you certain you're born ready?"

"I thought I was. Now I'm not so sure."

He gave me a big grin, tugged on the brim of his hat, removed it, and rested his head against the window and said, "Wake me up when we're there."

We arrived in Savannah a short while later and rushed to the hotel, where I checked into the fifteen rooms we required. It was quite an ordeal as the desk clerk had not pre-registered us, so it was taking some time.

The band members were milling about impatiently in the lobby, and time was something I didn't have. Sound-check was scheduled in less than half an hour. As soon as I had a room registered, I yelled out the occupant's name, gave them each their keys and instructions: "Come right back down for sound check." It was a slow process. I kept reminding everyone that they only had fifteen minutes. Fifteen minutes later, I was still handing out keys and still reminding them they only had fifteen minutes. It wasn't fair at the end when the remainder of the group really only had about two minutes.

Finally, I got the hotel squared away and went to my own room, where I immediately began calling everyone to assemble in the lobby. Another fifteen minutes, and I was in the lobby myself, only to find that some of the band members had ordered food at the coffee shop, and the rest were at the desk complaining about their rooms. Either a TV didn't work, a room wasn't clean, or they didn't like the view. It went on and on. After a while, I snapped, ordering everyone to the cars. We then proceeded out the door, leaving Dean to follow us with the remnants of the group.

We rolled into the venue a short time later, me in one car with half the group, Dean following behind in another. He had been complaining about the luggage, as he hadn't yet had time to go to his own room, since he had been far too busy distributing bags. As I drove, he never appeared in the rear view, but I figured he had to be on the way...or so I hoped.

Backstage at the cavernous coliseum, I was assaulted by the crew. Craig was first, with Joe Barnes, our production manager, standing beside him, but Craig was speaking for both of them. As soon as we shook hands it started:

"Ron, we need our per diem."

I told him that they'd have to wait until after the show, because I wasn't carrying much cash. He was wearing his ever-present smile, but I could tell he was upset and I didn't blame him. I didn't want to face the crew without their per diem either, but there was nothing I could do. I wouldn't have any funds until I settled the show that night. There was some rumbling, and all of the guys copped an attitude, and then the late-arriving band members chimed in, Allen first,

"Roneckerman, where's my per diem?"

I went through the whole speech, again and again as members of our entourage approached me. I may as well have been talking to a wall. They wanted their money. No doubt they had found a few tour essentials. Pot, nose candy, etc. - all vital materials necessary to keep the group going on these long, arduous runs.

We were scheduled with about five back-to-back shows at a time and there was minimal sleep in between venues, especially for the crew. Any sane person would never enter this business. I had succumbed to the insanity years ago.

I survived the per diem gauntlet only to get hit with the next challenge. Leon, always the first in line, approached me.

"Roneckerman, I need some backstage passes for my friends here." I glanced over at his friends. They were standing beside him, two guys and a girl, all young, all looking at me with expectant and hopeful eyes. I reached into my pocket and peeled off three passes, initialed them with the date, and handed them over.

"Can you give me a few more... just in case?"

"Afraid not," I told him. "We can't have a zoo backstage. Write their names down and I'll leave them tickets at the box office."

"But I need passes. These are real good friends."

"What are their names?" I asked.

"Uhh, hold on," he replied, rushing off with his "real good" friends. Apparently the names had escaped him.

A short time later, I was approached by Artimus, again needing backstage passes. He was followed by Billy, Allen, Gary, and Ronnie, and then the crew began their requests. By the end of the night I was wondering if we'd have more fans in the audience or backstage.

We had initiated a routine that would be repeated countless times over the next few years: we rushed to sound check, the band rehearsed and worked out technical bugs, I visited the box office to check ticket sales and call local radio stations and record company reps, then we all rushed back to the hotel in time to change clothes, and then it was back to the gig – show time!

The guys ripped through the set, and they were on fire. I hadn't seen many groups explode with such energy. Usually you'd have the normal ebb and flow in a concert, these guys just powered through until they incited this explosive mass orgasm in the audience when they hit *Free Bird*. I knew I was on to something. Thank you, Mr. Arrow.

CHAPTER 3

I sensed the hesitancy of everyone as we boarded the plane, yet no one said a thing to me. In fact, I hadn't heard much from anyone about flying on the plane this morning. After the experience on the last flight, I certainly understood why people were afraid to fly – that backfire was pretty frightening, so it was fine by me if anyone flew commercial. But from what I'd heard, Ronnie had been pretty insistent that everyone stay together on the plane. That was typical. Over the year I found I was always the last one to know about any incidents or complaints unless someone wanted money. No one ever had a problem approaching me for money, or backstage passes, or tickets. But there was no end to the activities and discussions that they tried to hide from me. I had become a father figure, and my children weren't about to rat out their own brothers and sisters.

January 1976

Things had settled down a bit as we boarded the cars bound for Asheville, N.C., a four hour drive. Our bus had a problem and wouldn't make it until Asheville, so we were driving one more leg.

Leon was bored, stooping to low brow humor. "Hey Billy, look at this!" He bobbed his head a couple of times to some imaginary beat, managing to make it look really strange, and then asked, "Who's this?" He'd hesitate a few moments, then bob his head erratically again, "It's Roneckerman."

So the battle began. There was always a bit of strain between the band and management. I would bounce back and forth between being on the band's side or management, I never knew which. It depended on the band's attitude at the moment.

I was actually hired by the band; they paid me, but management tapped me as well. It was push-pull most of the time. At the moment I represented management, so the band was lashing out.

"How do you book these tours, anyway?" someone would ask. And then they all would throw in their two cents. "A blind man throwing darts at a map?" "Is it booked by the alphabet? Atlanta, Boston, Chicago, Denver?"

Truth is, it's quite the game to figure out bookings and I didn't book the band anyway. Every date was subject to a number of factors: venue availability, travel distance, amount of shows in a row, etc. I didn't envy the agents.

I sat calmly, biding my time, as I'd be off the tour in a few weeks anyway. Evidently, no one had told the band I was leaving, but I had mentioned it to Allen Collins the night before and he had spread the word. Now, everyone was pissed off and challenging. They had been told I was there for good... if I passed the audition. If the audition was Artimus' little escapade in the car, I thought I had passed.

And so this love/hate relationship began. It was mostly love, I have to admit, but when it turned to hate... well, I knew there were some difficult days ahead.

We made it to Asheville in record time, but it took its toll. We were definitely dragging by the time we got to the hotel. Already tired, and it was only the second show in the run.

Sound check was interesting – they were correcting a few technical problems from the night before, and some of the corrections headed south. There was a grounding problem and most of the amps were producing an annoying and loud buzz. Ronnie took it in stride, patiently waiting while the crew got things squared away. Gary didn't seem to be fazed either, but Allen came unglued, firing demands at the crew, yelling at them. By the end of sound check, the buzzes had been eliminated, Ronnie had been able to get in a few lyrics, and everyone was fired up and ready to go.

When we returned to the hotel, everyone vanished in seconds. I couldn't find any of the band, just the girls, which was fine with me. I did have a sweet spot for the girls. This was one of the first of many mysteries I was to encounter. Where the hell did the band go?

They resurfaced a couple of hours later. I found them roaming the hotel halls in small groups, so I issued the warning,

"We're leaving for the gig in an hour."

They let me know we wouldn't be leaving for two hours, which was cutting it close but we'd still arrive at 8:30 or so – plenty of time for their 9:30 stage call.

We entered the dreary concrete locker room converted to dressing room in the Coliseum at about 8:45, and the band and crew quickly settled in to their routine. Dean was mixing drinks, Chuck, Allen's guitar roadie, was putting the final touch on tuning, Joe Barnes was drinking a beer while twiddling with one of the guitars, and Kevin was schmoozing. Joe, who'd been with the band a number of years, had no qualms about approaching me for anything, and confided in me with anything that came up. We hit it off from the start.

Chuck was another story. He'd been with the band for a while, too. He was short, about 5'3", with straight blond hair that damn near reached his waist, and he had a huge Hitler complex. Short but tough (or so he thought), he'd challenge everyone he met, especially after a few drinks. He drank a lot, but it was usually when he was off, and he was a mean drunk. At the gigs he never even touched a beer. He rarely said a word to me, passing any comments to Craig, our liaison.

Craig had laid into me earlier that day, complaining about security, or the lack thereof. He said that Chuck was really upset that one of the many wing-hangers (that crowd of onlookers standing on the sides of the stage) had knocked one of the guitars off its stand. So now I had to deal with John Butler, our so-called security chief.

John and I hadn't hit it off from the start. He seemed shady to me. There was something in his face, in his eyes, that didn't sit right. He had razor thin lips, reminding me of a Nazi officer in the movies. If he had worn a monocle he would have been perfect. His blond hair just reached his shoulders and it was slicked back a bit, and he was a smart-ass. He looked the part, the security chief, but he really didn't secure much, although he did know how to clear a dressing room when necessary. And it was necessary every night. The band always invited a load of friends into the dressing room; they always played the good hosts. But we all had orders from them: clear the room a half an hour before the show. The band would pretend they knew nothing about it as John, Dean, and I would come in and escort everyone out the door. We were always polite, but very forceful. When it was time to go, it was time to go.

The band used this time to do final checks on tuning and to get hyped up for the show. Ronnie would usually sing a bit – running scales and testing lyrics, warming up with the girls. Billy and Artimus (keys and drums) would simply get hyped, Artimus beating the hell out of anything that would make a sound. Billy would drink - always a Bud.

Once again the band fired it up that night. The crowd was outrageous. While there were no panties thrown on stage, I did notice from my view from the wings that there was plenty of flashing going on. The band got to look at a sea of tits on a good night, and they always returned to the dressing room talking about the audience.

"Did you see that girl in front of me?"

"No, did you see that other one? Man, they were just bouncing... right in time."

The audience came to see the band, and act out; the band came to see the audience, and perform. Sweet! And a fair exchange, at least for the band – they got paid.

We moved on to Macon, Georgia, the next day for a performance that night. Macon was one of the few cities I had never visited, and I had a keen interest for a number of reasons: it was one of the birthing grounds for Skynyrd, it was revered by the Allman Brothers, and it was a legendary music city, spawning such greats as Leanna Horne, Otis

Redding, Little Richard, and James Brown. If you were into music, you had to be into Macon. We had a show that night and four days off afterwards, and I would have liked to spend a couple of days there, but we were leaving early the next day for Knoxville so I knew I wasn't going to be able to see very much.

The friends, wanna-be friends, and posers started showing up at sound check. Peter Rudge even came down from New York. It was a very important gig, not due to the size of the show, but because we were so close to the industry. There were so many music insiders popping in and out of Macon, Peter wasn't taking any chances. He knew too well the dangers of letting another manager get too close to the band. After all, that's how he had stolen them from their former manager, Allen Walden. He didn't really steal them... Allen was paid, but you see what I mean.

Although I had been talking to Rudge daily by phone, it would be the first time officially meeting him, other than a very short introduction at a Who show in San Francisco a couple of years ago. That was the infamous show where Mooney (Keith Moon) fell right off his drum stool during the show... twice. The first time, after a couple of moments of crew induced resuscitation, he got back up and played. The second time, he was out for good. A stone cold, alcohol induced visit with the tooth fairy. Roger Daltry called out for a drummer from the audience, and the band continued a few minutes later. The kid that volunteered was a surprisingly good drummer, but he wasn't Mooney, so after a song or two, the band gave it up.

"I'm afraid we're finished for tonight," Roger announced. "We're just not The Who without Mooney. And it's not fair to you to continue. We'll return," and the show was over.

The remainder of the band took their bows and exited the stage, and the surprisingly well-behaved audience began filing out. Personally, I would have been mad as hell if I'd bought a ticket, but I never buy tickets... to anything. If I'm not invited, I don't go.

Peter stayed in the background for the most part that night, observing, as I denied and granted passes to the appropriate guests. There were a few local producers and engineers there, as well as musicians, a lot of whom wanted to "jam" with the band, and our agent Terry Rhodes showed up, and they all wanted access to the band, all demanding backstage passes.

Each band member needed at least a couple of passes, so that accounted for 18. The crew needed 8 for their guests, and we had about 30 unplanned guests. In all, it came to 114 backstage passes, and every one of them wanted access to the stage when the band performed. This was totally unacceptable, and by the time the band went on we locked down the stage – backstage passes didn't work. We knew exactly who was supposed to be on that stage, but we did end up allowing a few more than normal, resulting in a shoulder-to-shoulder crowd in the wings. That's when Peter lost it and started throwing everyone off stage – it didn't matter who they were. I got a stern lecture, and we decided right then and there, that from then on, absolutely no one except band and crew was allowed onstage during a performance. We'd see how that worked.

After the show, per the band's wishes, I locked down the dressing room. It was a bit strange, since I was new with the band, but I had orders to keep Rudge, Terry Rhodes, and even the crew out. Reactions were stranger still. Everyone thought I was pulling a power trip in retribution for Peter's earlier stage lockdown. The band just wanted some time alone. They knew the amount of guests they had to face, the same crowd that was there earlier, plus a few. I stood outside the door with John Butler, arms folded, and simply turned everyone away. It was a "Godfather" thing.

An hour later, the beer, Jack Daniels, pot, coke, and God knows what else were flowing steadily. It was getting louder and louder as it grew later and later. The crew had packed the gear, the trucks were loaded, the maintenance crew was cleaning the building, and we were still stuck in the dressing room. Finally, we were thrown out by the building management and the promoter. The party moved to the hotel and after hanging for a while, I gave it up and retired.

I managed to get up the next morning to visit a couple of diners that claimed some fame in the local music scene. I just wish we had been able to visit some of the local clubs, but it was obvious we needed to get out of town. There were too many influences in this one. I had this dream of "discovering" the next big act there, breaking out my management career like so many others. So much for dreams... they always remain just that. Dreams.

Peter Rudge caught up with me before we left town. He wanted to pick up receipts and review the rest of the tour with me. He also engaged me in their long-range plans, something I really wasn't interested in at the time. He explained that they'd be working in Europe in February, and were going to record a live album in May, followed by an extensive tour of the States lasting through the year.

I told him I'd need some time to think about it, and quickly reviewed the tour accounting and itinerary with him. He didn't look pleased when he left. He also assumed I was there for good, but he maintained a stiff upper lip and was quite cordial.

We were in Knoxville stuck in a Holiday Inn, nobody's favorite. In fact, we all hated Holiday Inns. Not that they didn't provide good clean rooms, we just viewed them as family vacation spots which meant... well, families. And Lynyrd Skynyrd was a bit X-rated while on the road and sometimes while at home. Leon, meanwhile, had scoped out every bar in the city by nightfall and was arranging an outing to a local rock club that evening. He knew the band there.

I got a call from Joe Sullivan, our Knoxville concert promoter, as soon as I settled in, and he was pissed.

"Ron, what do you mean ordering limos for the evening?"

"I didn't order any limos," I told him. "What are you

talking about?"

"My drivers just called and told me you guys were going out tonight and needed cars."

"It wasn't me, Joe."

"Well, someone ordered the cars. You've got two limos heading over there in an hour, if I don't cancel them."

"I'll call you right back."

I called around the rooms, finally locating Billy. He knew all about the evening, and suggested Leon had ordered the cars. Leon had jumped back into one of the limos as soon as we checked in and spent a while looking for clubs and making friends, so it all made sense.

Leon answered on the first ring. "Cheng-Wa Fireworks," he answered, or something like that.

"Leon, did you order a limo?"

He copped to it immediately, explaining that most of the band was going. I read him the rules on hiring cars, making them up as I went, of course, and told him that the band wouldn't pay for them.

"It's okay, the promoter will pay for it."

"I just talked to the promoter and there's no way he's going to pay for this."

"Cheap bastard," Leon replied. "I'll pay for it myself then."

I called Joe and told him not to worry, we'd take care of the cars. It was settled for the moment, Leon would be paying for the car, but as the night went on the deal came unwound.

Somehow, I was talked into going out that night. After all, it was with the whole band. Once the full assembly started in on me and I had downed a few drinks, I didn't have a choice - it was a band decision. The band picked up the tab for the car. So much for my rules.

Turns out, Leon didn't know the band playing in the club at all, but had run into them earlier that day. They weren't bad, but I couldn't say they were that good. Of course, the later it got, the more we consumed, so by the end of the evening they were sounding pretty damn good. As usual we had to put up with all kinds of tactics to coax one of the Skynyrds up on stage. All were game from time to time, but none ever made it. The result of my outing? I felt absolutely terrible - I don't do hangovers well. So much for going out with the band.

We took it easy for the next couple of days. Everyone had laundry to do and we were all worn out from recent outings.

A couple of days later, after a sell-out in Knoxville and another in Nashville, we were rested and headed for a club as soon as we left the gig. So much for not going out with the band.

This time it was well worth it, and besides, how could I not go out in Nashville? After all, there are thirteen hundred and fifty two guitar pickers in Nashville. We settled into a nice little hole-in-the-wall, with a small stage to one side and a superb sound system, which was very unusual for most clubs of this size. It couldn't have seated over a hundred shoulder to shoulder. A quartet was on stage: guitar, bass, drums, and keys, and they were hot. We had blindly run into some amazing talent. But from past experiences in Nashville, you could do that anywhere in the city.

We pulled a couple of tables close. They were round so we couldn't fit them together, but we settled in. The music was awesome. They were mixing it up: some oldies, a few current hits, a bit of blues, a bit of jazz, and country thrown in for a good mix. These guys didn't miss a lick, and our tables were abuzz. As the evening wore on, Allen began calling out to the band, praising them, egging them on, and shouting and clapping at the close of each and every song. The rest of the band joined in from time to time.

Finally, after both of our tables were littered with glasses, Allen yelled out,

"You guys are great! I bet you didn't know we have one of the best vocalists around sitting right here!" I'm sure the band thought one of the Skynyrds would join them, but once Allen was acknowledged, he shoved Jo-Jo out there. "Really!" Allen shouted, "She's fuckin' unbelievable!"

Jo-Jo was in no condition to sing, but then again, I'd seen a ton of performers sing their best when they could barely stand up. Jo-Jo staggered to the stage, thanked the band, and tested the mic with a little do-wop. Then she and the band discussed a couple of songs, deciding on Me and Bobby McGee.

The band ran the intro and got into a groove, waiting for her to start. Jo-Jo was standing at the mic stand silent, not quite figuring out where to come in, so they re-started the intro. I have to admit that it was a very unique intro – it was impossible to recognize the song.

On the second try, she missed the entry again. When she missed the third time, the guitarist/singer came in and sang the first verse, then Jo-Jo sang with him, but when he dropped out she lost her place and they had to stop one more time.

I looked around the table. From what I could see in the low light, everyone was staring at the stage intently. I didn't envy Jo-Jo. She was so flustered, I figured she was going to walk, but she didn't. They did the intro again, their singer starting in the right place so she knew where she was, and he had to join in again when she drifted, which was often, but she finished it. We applauded and then got the hell out of there. It was too much, and we were too embarrassed.

The desk called me at seven sharp the next morning. It was always some cheery voice on the other end, someone fresh that had just started their shift. It was annoying when you had little sleep. I'd much rather hear someone with a bit more anger in their voice. The cheerfulness just didn't work for me when I was up early, and was so tired.

After an hour or so of talking to promoters, stage managers, our management and agent, I began calling each band member.

"The bus is leaving in an hour. Time to get up."

One by one I called them and, as usual, I got more agitated with each call. Not a single one of them would place wake-up calls with the operator. They relied on me to wake them up every single day. And to top things off I had about a 50/50 shot at them answering their phones. The ones that wouldn't answer required a walk down to the room, where I pounded on their doors until they were up. It was the most ridiculous of my chores, and it angered me on a daily basis. There's nothing like waking up angry every day. I discharged those duties to Dean that day. I'd had enough.

While I was eating breakfast I heard the bus pull up to the front of the hotel - that unmistakable diesel shaking the ground, the fumes permeating the air, the sound transferring through the walls, then band members began accumulating and mulling about. A few of them sat down for breakfast. Most just grabbed a cup of coffee to go.

I finished up and began checking out as Dean and a bellman pushed a luggage trolley overflowing with bags through the lobby. Soon all the cats were corralled and on the bus, the luggage was secure, and we were off.

Allen must have gotten a good night's sleep, because he was loud and boisterous, making fun of everyone, trying to get a rise out of someone, just pursuing his favorite hobby - mischief.

Not to be outdone, Leon was digging in, and pretty soon everyone was either laughing in the front or sulking in the back, depending on how well they could handle the relentless needling. We had a day off between gigs, but a long drive ahead of us, as we were moving out of the East and heading West, eventually ending up in Monroe, Louisiana. It was a long trip, plenty of time for tempers to flare.

For the time being, though, we were one big happy family. It reminded me of the great American vacation, a couple of adults in the front seat and a bunch of kids in the back. The only thing was the number of kids. I had a dozen of them, and I was the only adult (and Ronnie, if he wasn't playing with his best friend, Black Jack). But even if he had been drinking, he didn't really make it in the kid category. He was more like the distant rich uncle, the one the rest of the family didn't officially recognize, but would pop up from time to time and bestow a gift on you. You'd love him for a time, at least until he got drunk and wailed on you.

Whenever things started to get a bit hot in the bus (and I'm not talking temperature) we pulled over for something to eat and to stretch our legs. It was usually a truck stop, as the driver would have to tend to fuel and maintenance. This time it was one of those mega stops with restaurant and gift shop and it was quite surprising how easy it was to lose people in such a confined area. People would literally disappear. It was amazing. Houdini had nothing on some of these guys.

I finished my lunch and left the group I was sitting with - they patiently waited in the booth, staring out the window at our bus, waiting for that black flume out of the exhaust which meant we were ready to load. Ronnie, Gary, and Billy were left at the table.

Leon was trying on hats, having found a huge rack of them in the gift shop. He was rapidly whipping them on and off. These weren't caps, although there were plenty of them as well, but hats, and strange ones at that, so he was in hat heaven.

Cassie and Leslie were looking through a rack of cassette tapes while Artimus was sitting at the counter in the restaurant with Kevin, talking about the band's stage sound.

That's when a group of genuine Southern redneck truckers strolled in wearing their trademark plaid shirts, insulated vests, and baseball caps, looking for trouble and amusement, and a few long-haired hippies must have been their favorite target. In spite of a counter full of empty seats, they sat right next to Artimus.

I saw them immediately and prepared for the worst, locating Dean and telling him to round up the troops and get them on the bus... fast! He glanced around, saw what I was worried about and began moving, but I had made a fatal error. I had sent Dean to the restaurant and his hair was the longest of anyone's. I began rounding up the people in the gift shop and looking for the ones that had disappeared while Dean hurried to the restaurant.

In moments, the trouble began. The truckers had already started picking on Artimus, who was at heart a peace-loving hippy... but with a temper and a wild side. Luckily enough, Kevin was with him so we at least had a clean-cut, rational being in the mix, but Ronnie was watching the proceedings from a booth with an eagle eye and it wasn't long before he decided to move to the counter, followed by Gary and Billy. They never got that far. I heard it all the way from the gift shop – so did the lady at the check-out stand. The truckers started in lightly, talking just loud enough to ensure everyone could hear, as they started complaining about how hippies were ruining the country. This escalated quickly and they began commenting about how something "smelled bad" in this diner.

"Oh, it must be those damn hippies."

In moments the truckers had squared off with Artimus and Kevin. Everyone was off their barstools and standing nose to nose. One of the truckers took a swing at Artimus, which he somehow ducked, while Kevin faded back a few steps avoiding the trouble.

I heard a huge crashing noise a moment later. It sounded like a gunshot, as Ronnie had picked up the closest projectile, a bottle of ketchup, and threw it at one of the truckers at point blank range. He missed, but the bottle exploded against the counter and ketchup went everywhere. It was quickly mistaken for blood, the lady behind the counter started screaming, the truckers were frozen in confusion, looking at their ketchup-stained clothing, trying to figure out if they had been shot or cut, and the band exited in a hurry as no one really wanted any trouble in the first place.

I managed to get everyone out of the gift shop and into

the bus. In seconds we were gone, with everyone laughing hysterically, prompted by Leon and Gary.

"Did you see that? That was outrageous," Leon hailed.

Ronnie was still bristling, claiming, "I don't know how I missed 'em, at least one of 'em oughta be on that."

A few minutes passed before I whispered into Ronnie's ear, "You meant to hit that counter, didn't you?" Ronnie looked at me from under his hat, grinned, and said

"You know, I'm a pretty damn good shot."

And down the road we went... but not very far.

We were a little ways own the road when someone noticed the flashing lights behind us. They were approaching rather quickly. By then the whole bus was thick with smoke as everyone had, as usual, turned to some magic herb to relieve anxieties and wring every bit of humor out of the truck stop episode. We were given a heads-up by the driver, and within seconds, all of the joints were extinguished and someone had found some Ozium and was spraying it everywhere.

We felt the bus slow, and then heard the rattle of the shoulder under our wheels. In a moment we were parked. I looked around the bus and saw a bunch of angels sitting there, all sitting straight up, minding their posture, ears pricked, all looking to the front of the bus. The group had transformed itself into a religious congregation on the way to the next revival.

Our driver opened the door and you could feel a communal gasp as everyone saw the thick cloud of smoke billow out the door. The officer took a step back and politely asked if he could enter. Sam, our driver, was quick with a response.

"You got a warrant?"

"No," the officer responded, "but I can get one."

"Well, I tell you what. You get that warrant and I'll be happy to let you in." Sam wasn't taking any shit. "In the meantime, I've got a tight schedule to keep."

You could barely hear the patrolman as the door was

closing, "I'll have that warrant…" and then the door slammed shut, cutting him off. Sam put the bus in gear and began moving forward at a surprisingly fast clip. I was hoping we weren't going fast enough to spray the police car with pebbles. Luckily the bus didn't have anywhere near that much zip, otherwise I think Sam would have done it.

We were off again, but this time, instead of everyone lighting up their celebratory joints, everyone was searching through their bags and pockets, pulling out baggie after baggie of illicit material, and they had it all: pot, coke, speed, the whole enchilada. It was all collected and dumped, one bag at a time, until we had a bus as clean as a whistle. We were never stopped again that night. I'd have to assume that things worked out exactly as the officer had planned. The usual party atmosphere in the bus had definitely been subdued and there were some very pissed off passengers once they figured out they had dumped their stash for no reason.

After Monroe we would be in Austin, Texas, and I had a healthy crowd up from my hometown of Houston. My wife Alice and brother Rodney showed up, as well as my secretary Mary, our roommate Linda and her sister Judy, and Albert Pike, who ran Clearlight for my brother Rodney and me.

I had started the company a couple of years back and it had been growing ever since, and brought Rodney in recently to help out with a Peter Frampton tour I could no longer do. My parents were ready to kill me when I talked him out of going to pre-med school and hitting the road, but I had set him up with Peter Frampton, who was finally inching his way into the big time, so there was little they could say. Rodney had been extremely lucky to fall into the gig with Peter as he released the Frampton Comes Alive album a few months after he joined the tour. It was going to be really thrilling to see everyone, as it seemed like I'd been on the road for months - it had only been twelve days.

When we arrived, we proceeded directly to the hotel.

Upon checking in I found that my wife Alice and our housemate Linda had already managed to check into my room, but none of my other friends and family had shown up.

I finished checking in the band, they disappeared to their rooms, and I headed for the elevators, looking forward to seeing Alice. I didn't see her often, as I had been on the road nine out of twelve months for the four years we'd been married. It wasn't that I didn't love her. After all, she was my high school sweetheart. I just had different priorities than your average husband. My career came first, that was all there was to it. I made that very clear to her before we were married. And even if she didn't agree or particularly like the situation, she kept her mouth shut. After all, she was living the good life and only had one thing she was into: partying. That she attacked with gusto. Since it was her single goal in life and she had no responsibilities, she practiced and practiced until she got it right. This also made her the most problematic of all my charges. I went through life keeping people out of trouble… and taking care of their money. Those were, ultimately, my main functions in managing these bands. And they were all headed for trouble, as the boredom of being on the road, spending every moment with the same people, and the repetitive nature of the game led to incidents of one person or another "acting out" and it was usually internalized within the band. This happened with every band I had ever worked with – it was an occupational hazard.

So, as a tour manager, it wasn't all about the money, the music, or even the fans. Sure, all of that was of extreme importance, but the main goal is to keep people in line so they could perform. Naturally, with the onslaught of family and friends and having a great deal of business to review with my secretary, I was having some serious apprehension about the whole affair in Houston. But, as human nature has it, I was also conflicted, as I was very excited at the prospect of seeing my friends and loved ones.

The band had a totally different view of any "special occasion." They simply handled the pressure by getting drunk... very, very drunk, and they augmented the alcohol with a variety of substances most of which were, of course, highly illegal, which leads to another priority: keeping them out of jail.

The more I thought about it, the more I disliked it. I simply didn't need all of the various factors in my life coming together at one geographic location and time.

I quickly put two and two together and went to the bar. Alice was first to see me and shouted my name from across the darkened room. Allen and Billy saw me, but continued to look around somewhat bewildered, because they were looking for Ronnie Van Zant – he's Ronnie. I, on the other hand, had become used to my new moniker, *Roneckerman*. Alice rose from her seat, steadied herself by grabbing the back of her chair, and rushed over, throwing her arms around my neck and giving me a big kiss and held on to me as I ushered her back to the table.

"We've been getting to know your wife," Allen said, "She's been filling us in on you."

"I'll bet she has."

"Why didn't you tell us anything about her before?" asked Billy, "She's a hell of a character! Our kind of people."

Alice was sitting close to me, and she scooted her chair even closer as we went through this idiotic true love ritual. I sat still.

"You guys getting started a bit early, aren't you?"

"Hell, it was your wife that wanted a drink!" Allen exclaimed.

"Yeah, yeah," I replied, "she loves to party, I can promise you that."

"My kinda girl," Allen sat forward.

"Well, I like her," Billy added. "We don't see all that many smart women on the road."

I winced at that. She was, in fact, quite smart. The type who could unload a mountain of trouble when you least expected it. Ah Billy, I thought, if you only knew.

"Listen guys, we haven't even done sound check. It's not too cool to show up at sound check drunk."

"I'm not drunk," Allen replied indignantly.

"Me either," Billy said, attempting to mimic Allen's attitude, but he couldn't pull it off.

"Yeah, you aren't drunk… yet. Just give it time," I told them.

They lost their righteous indignation.

"I guess you're right." Billy quipped as he got to his feet, he too grasping the table for balance. "I'll be in my room."

Allen wouldn't give in as easy, so he started down Belligerent Avenue.

"I can handle my drinking. You can't tell me when I can drink or not. You aren't my mother, Roneckerman."

Alice chimed in at that point. To my surprise she was actually defusing the situation.

"Let's go to our room," she told me. "I haven't seen you for ages."

"It's only been two weeks."

"That's what I said. Seems like ages." Maybe she wasn't lying after all.

With that we all went to our rooms. I went directly to the bathroom to freshen up. By the time I got out of the shower, Alice was sound asleep. I didn't bother her.

For a fleeting moment I recalled our wedding night, when she ended the evening passed out on the stage at the post wedding party. She never fully awakened on our wedding night – it was a lonely night for me. The moment quickly faded and I sat at that silly little round excuse for a table where I would begin my never ending phone calls.

I was in the lobby, waiting for everyone to assemble for sound check. I announced that we would be leaving right after the gig. I was barraged with complaints. It was a change of schedule and caught everyone off guard. Everyone had already made plans after the gig, and everyone was in 100% party mode that evening, which was the primary reason for my decision. In the end we made a compromise: we'd leave at 2:00 am, giving everyone plenty of time to visit with their friends, and we would still get out of here before anyone could get into too much trouble. I figured everyone would need at least thirty minutes to pack and thirty minutes to shower, leaving only an hour or so to party.

That night the band was fairly loose with their dressing room rules, and Alice mixed right in with them all the way to show time. I think they relaxed their rules for Alice's benefit but I didn't really know. It didn't seem to irritate anyone but me.

During the show I made sure Dean was looking after Alice while I settled the box office. This time it took forever to settle the receipts. I wasn't sure what was wrong, but I sensed something was way out of whack. It was a daunting task, settling the box office with a pocket calculator and a handwritten spreadsheet.

When I walked into the back room of the box office I saw huge stacks of tickets. They were key to getting paid properly, both those unsold tickets and the certified ticket manifest.

Here's the kicker – all those tickets, the "deadwood", had to be counted and verified. Once that was done, you compared the tickets left unsold (the deadwood) to the manifest and that resulted in the number of tickets actually sold. When I saw a large stack of deadwood it meant a long night of counting. And when the show was obviously sold out, or close to it, gauged by a visual on empty seats, and there's a large stack of unsold tickets, something is obviously wrong. That's why I was alarmed: there were huge stacks of deadwood, unsold tickets, and by my calculations and from what I'd seen of the audience, we were sold out, or extremely close to it.

When I first pointed this out to the promoters, nobody stepped up. They actually let me count a good portion of the tickets. At that point, which I suspected was a test to see what they could get away with, one of them pointed out that there were actually two sets of tickets. One was a misprint and had the wrong date on it. So now I had to go back and look through the tickets to ensure the bad ones were separated from the good and then do a recount.

Once done, which took hours, I was satisfied and returned to the empty backstage area. Everyone had gone, leaving me stranded. After a short, angry wait, one of the limos appeared – it had been sent back from the hotel for me by Dean.

By the time I got to the hotel, everyone had pulled their disappearing act, including Alice, and I was too exhausted to run around searching for them. So I pulled out the books and dug in, working until I passed out. At some time during the night or morning Alice climbed into bed but didn't wake me. Maybe she was getting a bit smarter. Maybe she was just too drunk.

We left for Corpus Christi before she could explain or argue, thank God, leaving her to find Linda and return to Houston.

Corpus Christi was an exceptional gig for a number of reasons. The first was that the band simply blew it out – as fine a performance as ever. The second, Billy Powell had some distant relatives there that came to see them. And the last… well, that happened after the gig when Ronnie called me to his room. He had a bottle of champagne and a glass waiting for me, which he instantly filled.

"Ron," he whispered, leaning in close like he had some big conspiracy he had uncovered, "I'm gonna have a baby. Judy's pregnant."

"Congratulations," I said cheerfully. "I'm really happy for you." And we toasted, emptying our glasses.

While Ronnie was refilling them he added a couple of more thoughts.

"This is gonna change a few things, and we really gotta clean up this band. Sooner or later somebody's gonna die."

"I know what you mean. This band seems to live on the edge."

"Live on the edge?" Ronnie asked. "Hell, we live off the edge, we're just hangin' on by our fingertips when we're on the road. And if it don't stop, like I said, someone's gonna end up dead. The point is, you gotta tighten the reins on these guys."

We talked until we finished the champagne and Ronnie asked me not to tell anyone about Judy's pregnancy, and I returned to my room with the satisfaction that Ronnie had confided in me. That was damned cool in my book. But tightening the reins? I was the new guy, I didn't know how much tightening I'd be able to do.

During the swing to Amarillo, Leon started getting bored again and was teasing Allen to no end. Allen and Jo-Jo were resting comfortably, with Jo-Jo's head resting on Allen's shoulder, and Leon kept using Jo-Jo's feather boa to tickle Allen's nose. After the third or fourth time, Allen had an eye open and caught him and threatened to shut him up for good.

Leon began singing a new song he had just created, repeating it over and over until we were all sick. He was very proud of his new creation, "Billigan's Bus", based on the Gilligan's Island TV show tune. It went like this:

"I'll tell you the tale of a bus on tour
On bad highways at night
With Ronnie front and center
And Allen played to his right
There was also Gary and Artimus
Roneckerman and his wife
Leslie, Jo-Jo, and Cassie Gaines
Here on Billigan's Bus...."

By the time he had sung it a couple of dozen times, we were ready to throw him under the bus. Of course that didn't faze him so he continued until he was threatened by Ronnie, Gary, and Allen. No one could take it anymore.

Leon finally quit singing when Allen exploded out of his seat. Ronnie caught Allen's arm right before he could launch a punch.

The tour wound up in San Antonio, the last gig on the run. I had expected quite a crowd of friends there so I was surprised that Alice and Linda didn't even bother to show up. Not so much Linda, because she had a four year old daughter to take care of. But Alice, my wife? I guess she was too busy, or maybe it was the fact that I would be home the next day, or maybe she was pissed at my sudden announcement the previous day: "I'm going to New York the day after tomorrow."

The band's tour was over… I was just getting started.

CHAPTER 4

This hesitancy, just a feeling, was the first time that I realized how reluctant and scared everyone was after the backfire we had experienced. I don't blame anyone. It's terrifying enough flying in private planes with all the famous accidents in which they're involved. No one had approached me with their misgivings, but it was evident a mutiny was in the making. Still, I had been assured by our last pilot that this was one of the safest planes ever made – we could easily glide to a landing without any power at all. I trusted that man, Les, and he certainly had the credentials to make the statement. He had been flying Jerry Lee Lewis around in our plane for years, and had made it through hurricane force winds and many a storm without incident. And there were also Ronnie's comments...

February 1976

Peter Rudge asked me to New York to assist in putting the band's next U.S. tour together. That was normally Lynn Volkman's job, but the office was so busy with the Stones that they needed help. I arrived somewhat overjoyed in New York late the next evening.

I loved New York. I think it was the culture – nothing remotely close in Texas. The cab dropped me off at the Mayflower, the current rock and roll hotel, an older establishment that had musty hallways and mustier rooms, and about twenty coats of white paint on the walls. In spite of it, it always felt like home. I'd been staying there on and off for years. I ordered room service, which actually came from a deli down the street, made myself comfortable, and went to sleep early.

I arrived at SIR Productions first thing the next morning. I was surprised to see Mary Beth Medley there when I first walked in. Mary Beth and I had worked together for years but I had no idea she was working for Peter. She was a fellow Texan, transplanted to New York and loving it. We had worked together with the Stones and many others over the years but I never put two and two together. It only made sense that she worked here.

She showed me around, introducing me to the staff, and then escorted me to Peter's private office. It was huge, with a twenty foot high ceiling and a library cove above the entrance reachable by a beautiful antique spiral staircase. He had a basketball net hung at regulation height from the cove safety rail, and the whole room was covered with thousands of dollars of art, mainly huge portraits of Mick Jagger by Andy Warhol, which I later found were gifts from Andy himself. It's a wonder any of them survived near that net, as few visitors to that office could shoot a basket, but everyone took a shot, and Peter always kept a basketball handy.

Peter and I talked for a while before escorting me to the small office he had carved out. Then I met my assistant. Selma was wonderful, a young girl afflicted with a disease or genetic defect of some type. It affected her hips so she struggled daily – sometimes she could barely walk, but she was always cheerful and enthusiastic - it never got her down. Selma did such a thorough job, she made my work in preparation for the tours fairly easy. She always sought out the best hotels that were within our budget and still allowed the band in, figured out the best travel arrangements, and even had an attorney and doctor secured in each city in case of trouble.

I wandered through the office and met Jenny, a beautiful petite brunette with long, dark hair she wore combed back so it flowed down to her waist. She had that distinct Manhattan style about her that enhanced her Mediterranean features, and she was a real sweetheart. She was also quite young, in her early twenties, and had a huge amount of responsibility - she was the office bookkeeper. Her office was piled high with paperwork which she buried herself in daily, a job I didn't envy, but she always appeared happy. She rarely questioned any of my books, at least she hadn't yet. I kept a daily log of everything, and always had a receipt book in my pocket. I never let a dime out without recording it somewhere. The problem was where. After a few days of back to back engagements, I had receipts stuffed in every corner of my briefcase, luggage, and scattered throughout pockets in my clothing, so I spent most days off tracing and reconciling the books. I also discovered that the band went through an enormous amount of "group supplies" which were very difficult to account for, as suppliers of those goods didn't give receipts.

Peter would call me into his office frequently while I was visiting. I would sit across from him at his large glass desk, occupying a small percentage of real estate in the corner of that grand office space. It was designed to impress, with gold and platinum records lining the walls, and awards and assorted memorabilia covering every inch of wall and desk space. On occasion, when he really wanted to hype me up on an event or stunt, we'd move to one of two sofas that faced one another in the center of the room, separated by a large square coffee table. It was much less formal there, and we could talk a bit more intimately under an air of comradeship: the two of us, and Mary Beth on occasion, sharing plans for the band. Stadium shows in the summer, lengthy runs in small intimate theaters - it was all planned out. Based on marketing reports from the record company, radio reports, and ticket sales figures from promoters, we knew which markets were hot and which weren't, and we'd plan the band's activities accordingly. It was exciting, being there with Rudge, taking an active role in their career. For the first time, I felt a bit more than a tour manager.

The group had a new album coming out, *Gimme Back My Bullets*, which the band had just finished mixing during a break in tours, and everyone was fairly excited. The guys even called me and had me fly to the studio to hear it once they completed the final mix. Kevin Elson had his hand in the production... barely, and although the legendary Tom Dowd (Derek and the Dominoes, Eric Clapton, The Eagles, the list goes on and on) was producing, Kevin was involved in the process, adding a few ideas here and there, yet staying out of the way for the most part, biding his time. He was a smart man, always acting in the shadows, keeping to himself.

I had known Tom Dowd for a while, and was used to his style and work ethic – it made it easy for me to visit the studio - he frowned upon outsiders at sessions. We were definitely on the same wavelength. There would always be an interruption of work flow that could take hours to recapture when visitors dropped by, so I slipped in unnoticed and parked myself in a dark corner. Tom seemed happy with the record and the band, and they were certainly enthused about working with the "master."

Once I had heard the record, I returned to the office in New York and started working the phones, calling our publicist and firing him up, talking to management to coordinate interviews while on the tour, and generally talking up the album to whomever would listen. I was on the phone with the record company, and calling their various reps around the country, trying to ensure that they were working on promoting our record, as they always took some nudging - they had a lot of product to promote. MCA had hundreds of artists and it was easy to get lost in the shuffle. Luckily Leon Tsillis, our champion at MCA, was on the case.

When I left the office a few days later, I thought about New York a lot. As a Southerner born and raised in Houston, I was caught off-guard by my sudden attraction to the city, but it faded quickly, as I had to save face, and my heritage forced me to tell everyone how much I hated it there. I just couldn't admit to my Texas brothers that I had gone Yankee on them. That simply would not go over well in Houston. So I bit my tongue, denounced New York, and steadily prepared myself for the road. It was looking like a marathon tour, with dates being added daily, and I was looking at a good three months of road work ahead unless I bowed out early.

Upon my return to Holcombe House in Houston, Walter was the only one that met me, his thick tail wagging his whole body, his doggy tap dance going complete James Brown. He was a sight to see. He was barking - no, whistling, excitably. Walter couldn't bark, but he could whistle. Rather curious, but that's what he did. My welcoming party of one.

I had been trying my best to enjoy three weeks off as the band toured Europe and Britain. It wasn't really time off for me since I still had my hands full with other groups: Clearlight lighting clients, and three bands to which we provided tour management services. We were extremely busy - it was our busiest season yet, and we had a full crew working non-stop to package our touring systems.

Albert, our manager, was in full gear. He was a great manager who had given the road a short stint, but found it wasn't for him, so he had settled comfortably into his role at the company, turning out lighting systems for tours on time and in budget, except for once, when he sent a rig to the wrong city. Who would have known there were two St. Pauls? We sent the rig for Wishbone Ash to the famous St. Paul, Minnesota – not the obscure St. Paul in Kansas, a good distance away. But he still managed to turn the truck around at the last minute and we made the show in the nick of time.

Now he was preparing for two different tours, and I had to do a bit of design work on the Peter Frampton rig as my younger brother Rodney was tied up and couldn't make it in. Frampton, an old friend from my Humble Pie days, had just started getting extremely popular and had some huge shows lined up. He still wasn't headlining the larger venues, but the crowds were growing, and he was getting better opening slots on some big dates, and he had just dropped his band's name, "Frampton's Camel," preferring to go solo. He was now being billed as "Peter Frampton." It was still the same band, except for Rick Green, the bass player, who had left for greener pastures, or so he thought. None of us suspected the live album would sell forty million copies. In fact, if I had known that, I certainly wouldn't be where I was. I would have stuck with Peter.

I settled in and unpacked my clothes while wondering where everyone was. It was abnormal, no one home, as Holcombe House was party central and ran non-stop.

Time passed quickly. There was a tremendous amount of work to do for both Clearlight and Lynyrd Skynyrd, so I had to isolate myself from friends and family in order to complete it. I withdrew from social life completely.

I thought about our short marriage, how I had disappeared on the road within a month afterwards, and how awful it had become every time I returned, and I was yearning to return to the road, or to New York... anywhere but home. I knew in my heart our time was drawing to an end. I just wanted out.

Skynyrd was soon hitting the road again, and I had agreed to stay on with them a bit longer, but I had a few misgivings about the travel arrangements. Traveling by commercial airline? With this group? Selma and I had worked it every which way, and it just wasn't economical to put a bus out for the band. Our group was so large, would need two, or even three, if you included the crew bus. The airlines were the most economical, but it was hard enough getting the group into a bus on time. Now we had to deal with airports and airline schedules, and they aren't too flexible.

I rejoined the band in Jacksonville the day before the tour, this time staying at Ronnie Van Zant's house. He and his wife Judy had taken extra steps to making me feel at home, fixing up a spare bedroom and making sure I knew I could help myself to anything I found.

Ronnie and I went fishing when the sun started its way down, out on the little pier he had built behind his house next to his bass boat, Bad Company. We spent a couple of hours tossing out the lures, then reeling them back in, doing our best to make the bait "dance" in the water, hoping to hook that trophy bass.

"Ron" Ronnie started, "this is what I'd be doin' every day if I had a choice. Fishin'. Fishin's just plain good for ya."

"Yeah, I know. I grew up fishing with my father."

He gazed at me from beneath his "Bass Fishin' is Livin" hat, his long blond hair falling limply to his shoulders from underneath it, soaked through from the humidity.

"I wouldda never known that, the way you been handlin' that rod."

"I'm not doing too good, am I? It's been years since I've been fishing. I'm out of practice," I said, as I took a few steps closer to the edge of the pier.

"Be careful now," Ronnie warned, "you don't wanna get too close to the water. You might fall in."

"You don't swim here?" I asked, peering into the grey-green water. It didn't look too appetizing, neither for drinking nor swimming, but it was a hell of a lot better than the water I was used to. I'd spent years surfing in the muddy brown water off Galveston Island.

"Hell no... Jaws!"

"Jaws?"

"Yep, Jaws. He's a mean ole son of a bitch of a gator. Never know when he's around."

I stepped back, my eyes scanning the water. I caught Ronnie grinning at me from my peripheral. "You're kidding me."

"Not kiddin' ya one bit. He's about twelve feet long and mean as hell. He'll chase ya right up the bank, and he's fast."

I stared into the water, squinting. We both scanned the surface for Jaws but didn't see anything. I looked back at Ronnie.

He gave me a nod, then cast his line back out. "Ya know I'm gonna need a lotta help keepin' this outfit together. When I wrote *Sweet Home Alabama* I knew it was gonna piss a lotta people off. That's how I knew it was a hit. But I don't get that feeling with this record. It's good. I know it's good, but it seems stale. I been playin' with these guys so long everything seems stale. Of course we got Dowd in our pocket. The man knows how to make records."

"I've heard the record, Ronnie. You shouldn't be feeling like that. It's good."

I stopped fishing for a minute and just watched him. He was an expert, you could tell by the way he flipped the lure out with precision and ease, and the way he'd pull in the line, let it drift, then pull back on the rod. He was making that lure dance just like he wanted.

"Which song is a hit?" he asked, watching his lure as it streamed back to him, watching it dance as he manipulated it.

"I don't know, the title track?" I asked.

"That's what's gonna be released as the single, but doesn't mean it's a hit. It just won't piss enough people off. You gottta get a rise outta people. The songs have to have an effect on 'em."

"You don't think *Gimme Back My Bullets* will do it?"

"Naw. Maybe *Searchin'*... or *Cry For the Badman*, but not *Bullets*. They got it all wrong."

"So you do think there's some hits out there."

"Naw... I'm just sayin' we might get lucky. The trouble is, I been with these guys a long time and there's just no spark. I need somethin' new... somebody new. We used to get into these great grooves and just jam our asses off when we rehearsed. Now it's the same ole songs... done in the same ole way... it's fuckin' work. The spark is gone. When that spark is gone it's hard to keep people from gettin' restless. I guess I just been doin' this too long."

"It's never too long," I told him. "Look at The Stones, and The Who. They feel that way. I know. I've heard them."

"Yeah, but they have enough money to disappear for a while and get away from each other. We're in a rut. We have to keep on workin' to make our bills. We can't afford to take any time off."

"Surely you're making enough money." It was more of a statement than a question. I had just seen an uncashed royalty check sitting on his coffee table for $38,000.

"I'm makin' money, but it's just enough to pay all the bills. Damn expensive. We've got all our crew, we can't just let them go, and we got all kinds of other expenses. You have no idea."

"I do know. I have the same thing, Ronnie. I've got a business, too, you know."

He looked at me, pulled in his rod, clipping the lure to the cork handle, and we walked back to the house empty handed. The fish weren't biting that day.

"Next time you come out we'll take you out in the Bad Company, then I'll show you some fish."

That was the last time he mentioned the band that night. We had fried chicken for dinner, Judy made it while Ronnie and I were fishing, then we all went to sleep early, knowing we'd have a long day ahead of us.

We were up and off early the next morning. Everyone was providing their own transportation to the airport. Judy drove Ronnie and me at about 1:00.

It was February 1976, but it seemed like spring in Jacksonville. The album had been released a couple of weeks before, and was holding up fairly well. *Gimme Back My Bullets* was getting decent airplay, but it wasn't exactly screaming up the charts. I picked up a music magazine at the gift shop and read it during the long flight from Jacksonville to Denver.

After checking in, always an exhausting practice, everyone hit the bar to toast the new album and tour. That was just the start.

By the end of the night there were quite a few casualties - the hangovers would be horrendous. Luckily I retired early, ordering dinner from room service. I had flown from Houston to Jacksonville the day before and really was exhausted. The rest had evidently caught their second wind.

March 1976

The guys completed an explosive performance in Denver, and it was the first time we got a taste of the audience participation bit of *Gimme Back My Bullets*. First it was a handful of maybe six shells, but as soon as it started it began in earnest - .22, .38, even .45 caliber bullets were being tossed on stage. The crew was kept busy the whole song scampering around, trying to keep the bullets clear of the stage so they wouldn't hurt Ronnie's bare feet.

The other audience participation that night was entirely different. During *Free Bird* the audience dug their lighters out of their pockets and lit them, waving them in the air in time to the music. I'd never seen an audience do that. It was magic. They were very innovative, that audience in Denver.

It was hot there, literally, as the heaters were on all night due to the freezing weather outside. Add a few thousand people shaking their butts off and the mercury really gets to rising. I watched the entire show that night. I wanted to see what all the fuss was about the night before, and after watching, I understood it even less. These guys were anything but stale. By the time they got off the stage they had heated the building up another ten degrees. By the time we left, it had dropped another twenty degrees outside, and when we climbed into the limos our clothes froze – they were sweat-soaked.

Later that evening a small party erupted in my room. I'm not sure how that happened. I never initiated it, it just happened. My best guess – I was getting a free suite due to the large amount of rooms I booked. It was natural for the party to aim for the largest room: mine.

We were all enjoying ourselves, having cleaned up after the show, the warm showers having revived everyone. As the evening began winding down, I found myself face to face with Allen Collins and he was giving me shit, so I informed him I had been trained extensively in karate. It wasn't a bold-faced lie. After all, I did take karate for a half year -

hardly a master. No black belts here except the one with the big belt buckle. Allen was taking it all in, somewhat bemused, and then I informed him that I could kick him in the face before he knew what was happening – much faster than he could react. Of course he challenged me and I was just intoxicated enough to give him a demo.

I really don't know how or why I came up with that bull, and now I had talked my way into a demonstration that I had no hope of completing successfully. But luck and alcohol were with me, and I pulled it off, placing my foot within an inch of his nose before pulling the punch. It should have resulted in either me falling down or Allen ending up with a smashed nose. I couldn't have repeated it again in a million years, but I had very little trouble with Allen after that. Well… less trouble anyway.

The next morning everyone woke up sick – coughing, sneezing, the works. I had to call the Albuquerque promoter and cancel the show due to illness, and Mother Nature was kind enough to grant an assist. Our truck drivers had called and reported that there was no way they could get through New Mexico because the roads were all closed due to heavy snow. It was a battle they'd lose if they tried.

The promoter went ballistic when I told him, screaming that we had to do the show. When I told him there was no way to get the trucks in, he first volunteered to fly out and drive the trucks in himself, then backtracked and told me he'd rent all the equipment locally. I just had to get the band there. After quite a bit of arguing, he finally gave in. In anger I jerked the phone out of the wall and slung it across the room, where it hit the dresser and broke into a few pieces. I went down to the desk and told them I needed another one so I could complete the calls for the day. I had cancelled Albuquerque, squeezing it into our schedule a few weeks later, so we were flying directly to San Francisco. It took so many calls to get us back on track, I thought I almost wore out the second phone.

San Francisco: Bill Graham, Winterland, and old and

dear friends. We were excited. Just being there made everyone feel better. That and the fact I had contacted Dr. Whitehead, who actually came to the hotel and treated everyone in the group.

It now appeared we'd be able to do the performance in San Jose on March 4th before the Winterland shows, which began the following day. San Jose was still Bill Graham's show, but it wasn't Winterland. The San Francisco shows were the ones we were looking so forward to. My old friend Mick Brigden would be in San Jose and it had been a good while since I'd seen him. Mick had been working for Bill for a while, mostly in the management arm of the company but, like all of Bill Graham's staff, he crossed over into other operations as needed.

Bill definitely had the "dream team." He had recruited as many of the top pros in the business as he could get his hands on, and they were all extremely dedicated to him. My old friend Mick, that cocky little Brit, a hell of a guy, would be at all the shows. "Little Hitler" we used to call him. He was short, he couldn't have been over 5'3" and thin, so he had that classic British rocker appearance. I met him when I worked for Humble Pie. Mick was the production manager and I was the lighting designer, so we worked quite closely for a number of years. We toured the world together, Mick and I. The U.S., Britain, Europe, Japan – all of the good stops.

San Jose was incredible, much better than I expected. I guess it was the hippy vibe. Artimus introduced me to his friends, Lee and Jan, and Lee surprised me that evening when he appeared onstage with them playing the harmonica, and playing it well. Jan stood with me at the side of the stage beaming at her man. After the show, I found out he used to be in Strawberry Alarm Clock with their previous guitarist Ed King, so he was really friends with the whole band, not just Artimus.

The Outlaws were on the bill, too - the same group that had opened the last run of shows we had done, so it was a bit of a reunion. The only reason we were saved from an evening of debauchery were the cars. We had driven down in cars and were staying in San Francisco, so we had to return there that night. Thank God. San Francisco was important. We couldn't afford to screw it up.

Bill Graham, a close friend and huge supporter of the band, was promoting the San Francisco shows at Winterland, a beautiful facility he had taken over after the Fillmores were shut down. Bill had done the old dance hall up right for the band.

We walked straight into the South when we showed up for sound check. I was especially appreciative, being the only one actually from Texas, but I guess it was the "country rock" that he was appealing to. Sawdust covered the floor, bales of hay covered everything else. There was even a mule roped off in a corner of the back stage area. Most of his staff were dressed in western garb. It was all good, a real treat for a road weary mob, and when Leon started messing with the mule, it only got better. For some reason, Leon decided that the mule must be there for riding and proceeded to climb aboard. The mule had other ideas. Mules are mean, and this one had apparently heard in advance about Leon. So Leon's about to climb into the pen with the mule, hailing anyone around, "Watch this! I'll show you how to ride a mule."

Sure you will, Leon. Leon crossed the line, the thin rope that defined the mule's space, and that mule was surprisingly protective of that space, spinning around so Leon got a good view of the ass's ass. Leon took this as an indication that the mule was ready to be mounted. The mule was simply adjusting his aim for a well-placed kick. A moment later, Leon was cursing; the mule's aim was true. Leon literally limped through the performance, having been the recipient of hoof to thigh. I believe Leon's cowboy ambitions were completely and permanently extinguished that night.

Rudge was there, he had arranged an interview with

Rolling Stone magazine, and was right in the middle of it all. He had brought a new girlfriend with him, a Playboy playmate, and made the mistake of including her in a photo of the band that appeared in Rolling Stone magazine a few weeks later. Needless to say, his wife was not pleased. I was omitted from the photo, and was just beginning to catch on to that – I was always going to be pushed into the background at important moments in the band's career, at least if Peter was around. I didn't mind. Bruised egos heal. And Peter was the manager.

That Winterland crowd was phenomenal. The band could do absolutely no wrong here. The place exploded with energy as soon as the lights dimmed. The Outlaws had opened the show for us, and Hughie, one of their guitarists, a large and fairly rough looking character, joined the band onstage for *Sweet Home Alabama*, filling out the guitar army. He fit right in.

We partied for three days at Winterland. Three sell-outs, and we all became very close, at least for the week. We got to know Bill Graham's people fairly well, and became especially close to Clayton Johnson, the stage manager, who had bent over backwards to make sure we had everything we needed. Of course it wasn't without its moments. Partying for three days has consequences. On the second night, Hughie got a bit drunk and wasn't allowed onstage with the band, resulting in him drinking more, getting further upset, and finally going pretty ballistic backstage. He was quickly contained by his own crew, and the next night we were one big happy family again.

We enjoyed it so much that we extended our time there, arranging a softball game against Bill Graham's outfit the next day. Since we were flying to the next gig and we had no cars there, I stashed my briefcase in The Outlaws' bus, ensuring that the driver would guard it with his life. Bill Graham Presents vs Lynyrd Skynyrd. A crowd even assembled to see the game. Bill Graham had an experienced, athletic team, for the most part, we had the band and crew, who all claimed to be good ball players, and Rudge, the Englishman. Everyone wanted to play, so I didn't, giving up my position to Rudge. I was elected coach/manager, and even tried to do my job, but from the start it was hopeless. No one listened to a word I said.

It was a gorgeous day in San Francisco, and we enjoyed the somewhat raucous ride to the ball field. Ronnie had a baseball jersey on, and the rest of the crew had outfitted themselves with caps. When we finally got to the baseball park, we discovered the field itself was brown from lack of care, but the turf hadn't been completely worn away so you could still see the baselines. Graham's bunch were all well-equipped, and a few of them were even on the field warming up by the time we arrived. We warmed up for a while, until everyone had arrived and felt they were ready, and then it was time for the coin toss. We won. Bill Graham's team took the field.

I'm not going to say Bill Graham is a cheater, but HE CHEATED. The pitcher's mound had actually become a sunken pit at the little league baseball diamond that had been selected. Bill argued that he couldn't pitch from a pit and needed a proper mound, or at least a level surface, and ended up pitching just to the side of the pit, gaining a distinct advantage over us as the ball came at the batter from a strange angle. Ronnie refused to pitch from the side, preferring to be square in front of the home plate, which put him in the pit... not that it would have made much of a difference.

I found hardly anyone in the Skynyrd group could play softball. Ronnie was good, and Gary, and even Rudge showed potential, but the rest of the guys...

At one point, someone from Graham's team hit a high fly ball to left field. Leon was right there - he didn't have to move more than ten feet, and he was calling for the ball. Artimus had raced over in case he missed it, but remained to one side of him rather than behind him. It was that easy a catch, Leon had plenty of time, and it looked like he had planted himself properly, his arms up and ready to catch the ball. Then the ball dropped three feet to one side of him and continued to roll off the field. Leon just stood there watching the ball roll, looking baffled. Artimus, on the other hand, was chasing the ball off the field. It was ruled an infield home run, but that's questionable. I think it should have been ruled out-of-field due to stupidity and incompetence.

Our batting? Allen had been very vocal about his baseball skills. He struck out three times in a row, standing at the plate in the most awkward batter's stance I had ever seen, his ass sticking way out, his shoulders squeezing the plate as he narrowed the strike zone. I suppose it could get him a lot of walks, but I couldn't see how he could get a good hit, because he was too far off balance. I guess he thought he was onstage, or had the bat confused with his guitar. Ronnie, on the other hand, actually got a hit the first time at bat, and made it to second. Then Rudge was up, and he looked like he was playing cricket, his elbow sticking out at an odd angle. We gave him a little coaching and he did hit the ball, but was thrown out at first. Then Billy struck out, and so it went for three innings. At that point I quit, accompanying Mick Brigden to his little Karmann Ghia to smoke a joint.

By the time Mick and I returned to the field, I saw The Outlaws' tour bus pulling away. It was across the field from us and there was no way I could stop them. They had my briefcase which contained our money and all my books and schedules. I immediately broke into a sweat and reached for my wallet to see how much cash I had. I found my pocket empty. My wallet was also in the briefcase. To make matters worse, I learned that Ronnie had a bet with Bill Graham, and the loser had to take the winner to dinner. I was screwed. It was only halfway through the game, but we were the obvious losers. I was on the hook for dinner.

Dale Furano, one of Graham's crew, who ran Winterland, had chosen a beautiful high-end Chinese restaurant for us that evening for the dinner. It was a gorgeous place, gold and red everywhere, statues, waiters by the dozen – the works. Dale had arranged for the restaurant to be shut down to the public that evening to make sure we had the place to ourselves.

When we piled in, we discovered the tables had all been rearranged. It looked like a board room, with Ronnie and the band, Peter, Bill, Dale, Mick, and me at the head of the table. To top it all off, it was Rudge's birthday, so Dale had the restaurant prepare a cake large enough to feed all thirty-five of us. We ate, drank, and partied until we could take no more, at which time the waiters rolled out the birthday cake. That's when all hell broke loose.

Ronnie stood, swaggered around the table, and grabbed a large handful of birthday cake. I gazed around the room and recognized the anticipation in everyone's eyes. Ronnie was targeting Peter Rudge, and Rudge was cowering a bit, but with a smile. Ronnie took his time before he let the cake fly, enjoying himself, spinning around, making sure everyone had a good look at the handful of cake, and enjoying the amused terror on Peter's face. Ronnie was grinning widely, and I noticed he had removed his hat, which seldom happened. Then he fired a dead accurate shot, hitting Rudge square in the face, in spite of some very fancy footwork.

Moments later, we were engaged in an epic battle. Food was flying and everyone was fully engaged. I slipped out of my chair and slid under the table, where I made myself comfortable, sitting with crossed legs, and prepared for a long wait and determined not to get involved. I saw little from my position, just shoes if anyone came close enough, but I could hear everything, mostly laughter, but there was some cursing going on, and I could hear the projectiles. They sounded very, very sloppy.

I peered out at one point, careful not to disturb the tablecloth too much, because I didn't want my position revealed. This time, I saw up to the knees: shoes and pants, all soaked with food. As I lowered the tablecloth, I realized the room had quieted down. It made me suspicious. It didn't appear they were finished, at least not from my view. What I failed to realize was that it was an orchestrated ceasefire. Orchestrated to flush victims from their hiding places – me.

Suddenly, the table I was under disappeared. When I looked up I saw a huge metal soup tureen just tipping, then I experienced the warm viscous gush of sweet and sour soup being dumped all over my head. I don't recommend it – it wasn't pleasant.

My strategy ruined, my cover blown, I entered the fray, finding that most of the good ammo was depleted. I found that I wasn't any better at food fights than Leon and Allen were at softball. I slung everything I could get my hands on, but the fracas had evolved into a wrestling match – no one could stand up in the slop. The scene was definitely going slapstick: people looked like they were ice skating, carefully scooting to a table to grab a handful of muck, slinging it at their target, then falling to the floor as they were thrown off balance. Once they lost their footing a time or two, they'd resign themselves to it and stay there, waiting for a new victim to wander within range. Then they'd strike and wrestle the unlucky mark to the floor, and that victim would stay put until our entire party was groveling in the slime.

I managed to skate/slide to the kitchen where I found the entire staff huddled. They had a look-out who would peek through the swinging door once in a while, spew out a few lines of Chinese, while the rest of the staff was quiet and wide-eyed. It was obvious they'd never experienced a good ole American food fight.

It was there that I met the restaurant manager, and he was relieved I had wandered into the kitchen – he didn't want to try to find me. We jumped right into negotiations, both knowing that the bill was going to be substantial. We argued for a while, but I was at a bit of a disadvantage, so he got what he asked for. The total came to $15,000. $9,000 for food and $6,000 for damages and clean up. I had little doubt that there was a tidy profit built into it, and I certainly didn't include any tip at that point. I had to trust that he would share his somewhat questionable good fortune with the staff.

Now, all I had to do was find the money, because The Outlaws had mine. I talked Dale into putting the tab on his credit card, but struck out when I asked for additional cash to keep us on the road. I guess I pushed him as far as I could, and arranged to get an advance from the next show before we left. It was awkward at best.

The next day, we all jumped on a bus Mick had arranged and prepared for the ninety mile trip to Sacramento. By the time I finished securing some cash and dealing with the hotel, the band had already loaded and were sitting in the bus like angels.

Even though we limped through the show in Sacramento where I recovered my briefcase, we cancelled the next gig in Fresno. I had to reschedule it. That made two so far and we'd only been out ten days. I didn't have to tell anyone that this wasn't good. But Ronnie's throat was bad – he had no volume and his ears were getting clogged, so his pitch was suffering.

Our travel plans were shot due to the cancellation and I couldn't find any flights to L.A. unless I split the group up, so I chartered a bus. The crew had already departed for L.A. in their tour bus and were well on the way but had no accommodations. Unfortunately, the hotel in Los Angeles couldn't accept us until the next day, so I had to book a one night affair by the airport. Now our rhythm was totally shattered. I was finding our new travel arrangements a bit tedious. It squeezed us for time and curtailed our freedom. We were at the mercy of the airlines.

After a hectic day of arrangements and the hotel shuffle, we finally settled into the Sunset Marquis. We had one day off followed by a couple of performances: one in San Bernardino, one in Los Angeles. We loved L.A. Good friends, hot chicks, and good drugs. Rock and Roll heaven.

The Sunset Marquis, a small hotel off the beaten path,

had become very popular with musicians. It had everything you needed to be self-sufficient: a fully equipped kitchen, a living room, etc.

Soon after we were settled, various members of the group were banging on my door – Money! It was a day off. Gary and Allen were off to look at guitars, the crew were restocking supplies and, of course, there were drugs to be purchased. And everyone had an in room refrigerator to stock. I shelled out what was required and was bothered little for the rest of the day.

Ronnie called saying he wasn't feeling too well, still suffering from the singer's nightmare, a sore throat. When he said he was feeling "flu-ish" I looked up our Los Angeles doctor the promoters had suggested. Then I settled in with Ronnie in his room and waited. He crawled into bed as soon as we were checked in and pulled every cover and blanket he could find up to his chin. He looked bad... sounded worse. I made myself comfortable in one of the chairs, using the other as a foot rest, and settled in for the wait.

Ronnie stayed asleep for the most part, only waking to say he felt like death. One time he woke up for a moment and blurted out "it doesn't matter anyway." I didn't know what he was talking about. It came out of the blue. When I pried, he took a moment, then explained,

"None of the cancellations matter in the long run, Ron. I'll be dead before I'm thirty."

I tried to question him about what he meant, but he quickly faded back to sleep. I wrote it off to delirium.

It wasn't that long before Dr. Schwartz was knocking on the door. Ronnie stayed in bed while I answered it, or tried to. It wouldn't open. It was totally jammed. I couldn't open it from the inside, and the doc couldn't open it from the outside. I fussed with the knob and pulled and hammered on it until it came off in my hand. Normally we would have been howling, but with Ronnie's illness it wasn't funny... at all.

After a call to the front desk, a maintenance man

appeared and after he banged around on the door for a while, he left and said he'd be back in an hour. Ronnie needed the doctor, so we talked the good Doc, into walking around to the back of Ronnie's room and gaining entrance from there. What I failed to tell him was there was no entrance in the back, just a six foot fence. I slid the glass door open and walked out to the small courtyard and waited. Soon I heard Dr. Schwartz on the other side of the fence.

"Ron!" he called. "How am I supposed to get in?"

"Throw me your bag and climb on over." I told him.

"I'm not doing that."

"You have to. What about your oath? I've got a sick performer in here and he's getting worse. We have a show tomorrow."

We went back and forth for a few moments before he slung me his bag. Now, if it had been Allen, he would have grabbed the bag and pilfered it before the doctor could scale the fence. But it was Ronnie, and he was far too ill, and wouldn't have done it even if he felt great.

Dr. Schwartz asked Ronnie a few questions, gave him a short exam, looking at his eyes, his throat and ears, but mainly focusing on his lungs and vital signs, then he broke out the syringes. He had a boatload of drugs in that bag. I saw a variety of uppers, downers, in-betweeners, and who knows what. Schwartz rummaged through the bag until he found what he was looking for – several vials of injectable medications. As he drew a syringe full of a clear liquid he explained,

"This is a mega dose of B12 and antibiotics. Should get him up and running by tomorrow."

Ronnie took the shot right in the butt cheek.

"Motherfucker!" he exclaimed, rubbing his ass.

I thanked and paid the doctor and fortunately, the maintenance man showed up at that same moment. Five minutes later the handle was removed and the door swung open. The doctor left with a bit of dignity.

I stayed with Ronnie through the whole afternoon, making sure he stayed in bed and took it easy. We watched a baseball game between the Orioles and the Yankees where Al Bumbry hit an inside-the-park home run.

Ronnie and I had a long talk after the game. It seems like we covered everything from our families to world events. We talked about how we are both the first born sons in our families, and how both of our Dads were boxers. Ronnie seemed a little shocked to learn that I was younger than he was. He had thought that I was several years older, when I was actually almost 4 years younger. "Aww you're just a kid!" he said, laughing. During this time, I can honestly say we became brothers. Our own views and philosophies were extremely well aligned, if not identical, with a few exceptions. I found that our views on God, religion, and destiny were very similar. We both agreed that things that happen, even unfortunate things that happen, are things we have no control over. What's meant to be is meant to be, and can only be controlled by a power much greater than we are.

Another thing he spoke quite a while about was his daughter, Tammy, and that he had gotten divorced when he was quite young. I had no idea he had been married prior to Judy. His eyes brightened up when he talked about his little girl, Tammy Michelle. He told me he had written and recorded a song entitled "Michelle" about her close to ten years before. Although he didn't get into detail about why the marriage ended, and I didn't pry, it seemed to break his heart to talk about the little girl that he didn't get to see very often.

Another surprising thing I learned – Ronnie's favorite singers were Merle Haggard and Waylon Jennings, and Ronnie really wanted to be a country and western star more than a rock star. Well I'll be damned. Another thing that surprised me to hear was that he wasn't that happy with Peter Rudge. "He's a Limey," he told me, "but he's the best manager we've had so far."

After I went back to my room and collapsed on my bed, there was a knock at my door. It was really loud, so I thought it must have been Allen. He usually was the only one who banged the door like that. It was Peter Rudge. There was a very attractive woman with him. I recognized her, Laura, the same woman from San Francisco.

"Hey Peter," I greeted. "When did you get in?"

"I just did. How are the boys?"

"Ronnie's sick – has a sore throat and a chill. I've had a doctor see him already."

"What room is that? I'll pop by and have a chat."

"Can't. He's knocked out for the night."

"Oh, okay then. What about Gary... and Allen?"

"They're looking at guitars somewhere."

"Really bad timing on my part."

"Looks like it. Do you have a few minutes? I've got a few things to go over."

"Oh, would love to, but I've got a thousand things to do. I'll see you in a bit... maybe have dinner."

"Sounds great. We have a lot to talk about."

They left and it struck me: he had time to spend with the band, but he didn't have time for me to review business.

Members of the band and crew started returning from their assorted ventures in the early evening. Chuck came by to get more money, because the supplies were more than he expected. Leon Tsillis, the MCA rep, had called and a field trip had been arranged, so I needed to get everyone together for that.

And then there was Leon (Wilkeson), who had returned and either found or recruited a few friends - he was flying. True to form, he me hit again for cash. But he was honest about it:

"Roneckerman, I'm gettin' some blow. I need five hundred bucks."

"Man, I don't have five hundred bucks."

"Aw come on..." he started, then he remembered his friends, "This is Carol, and Charlie, he's an actor, and Phil."

"Good to meet y'all." I shook all their hands. Carol gave me a surprising peck on the cheek. She was kind of cute and very friendly. I recognized Charlie. I had seen him on a few TV shows – the guy with the squashed nose - he guest starred in a lot of westerns and detective shows.

I realized it would be very embarrassing to Leon, the bass player of this famous band, to have to beg for money... and I also knew he would if he had to. I spared him the humiliation.

"Just give me a minute – I'll get your cash."

And so the evening went, with visits from most everyone. I just wasn't cut out to be a banker. That evening I ended up going out with Leon Tsillis, Gary, Artimus, Billy, Allen, and Jo-Jo to The Roxy on Sunset where we managed to get a private room. Immediately the room was filled to capacity with people we met at the club and we ended up having an outrageous time... I think. Honestly, I don't remember much.

I had a bit of a hangover the next morning, so I tried to sleep in while the phone went off every five minutes. I finally gave up, dug the phone out from under all the pillows and answered it.

"Ron, I've been trying to get ahold of you." It was Toby Mamus, our publicist.

"Yeah, sorry...recovering," I said. "It was a late evening."

"I've got interviews lined up for some of the guys and Cameron Crowe's coming over to see Ronnie."

"Okay, okay. I'll make sure he'll be ready. Just give me a call when you get here."

Cameron was writing for Rolling Stone, and had been trying to sit down with Ronnie for days. I had no idea how I'd pull this off. I called Ronnie, no answer, so I pulled on some clothes and headed to his room. He had just gotten out of the shower.

"How you feeling?" I asked.

"I feel great, at least compared to yesterday. Thirsty, though."

"That's good to hear. Your throat?"

"Gonna rest it some more."

"Good. The Doctor gave you some shit, didn't he? I wouldn't mind getting some of that myself. Listen, we have an interview in an hour, and we're leaving for the gig in about three hours." I was hoping I sneaked that last part in and it wouldn't hit him right away.

"Damn! This early?" Ronnie was bristling a bit, making a face. I was getting fairly close to him and I could read those expressions and know what he was thinking most of the time. He was not happy.

"It's in your itinerary. I couldn't tell you yesterday. You were too sick. I'll order some coffee and food. It's Cameron."

"Cameron? Okay."

Ronnie disappeared into the bathroom and I ordered food.

Once the reporter arrived, Ronnie relaxed. The guy was cool. Ronnie and I had both known him for years. I told Cameron we could only give him forty-five minutes and disappeared. I came back in forty-five minutes and Ronnie told me they weren't done. They had already eaten Ronnie's food and ordered more. This went on for a while. If you could get Ronnie going, he sure didn't mind talking.

I returned when Cameron had already packed his gear and was heading out the door. Ronnie looked tired even though he claimed to be feeling great. Most likely it was perception: he had been feeling so bad the day before that any improvement would make him feel great, but he was still ailing.

We crawled into the limos a short time later and made the trip to San Bernardino, where we spent the rest of the evening. We ate lunch and dinner at the gig, provided by the promoter, and remained there right up to show time.

Ronnie managed to power through the performance, looking fully recovered, but he was very quiet when we drove back to L.A. Evidently the outing had taken its toll. Since we didn't make it back until after three in the morning, I didn't have to worry about extracurricular activities that night. Everything was closed and everyone was too exhausted to do anything but collapse into their beds.

The next day Peter showed up at sound check and quickly took the reins for the evening, sequestering the group in the dressing room but politely asking me to stay out. It was annoying, but I had no say in the matter and really didn't care all that much, because I was still planning on leaving after the tour. I had been here longer than expected already, although I was experiencing a little subconscious nagging. Should I stay or should I go? It had been bothering me more and more with each passing day. I recognized that this band was one of the hottest groups I had ever worked with, and if I were to stay with them, there could be some great opportunities. But I also had an ongoing production business in Houston and a couple of other groups I had been nurturing. I certainly didn't want to give up all the time I had put into them. And there was this problem with my wife... I had some fence mending to do if I was going to save my marriage. The never ending series of daily fights our marriage had become was out of control. The only time we got along was when we were both either drunk or stoned, or some combination of the two. During those times, I never knew when the situation would turn, and if we started fighting while inebriated, things really spiraled out of control. Alcohol was the most extreme amplifier, but toss in a little cocaine and you have such an explosive situation it reached nitro levels – one shake and you're done.

We made it through sound check and headed back to the hotel, the girls, Artimus, Billy, and I in one car and Peter, Ronnie, Gary, Allen, and Leon in the other. I recognized the distance Peter was keeping from me, and also the distance Peter kept me from the band's founding members. This was a bit curious as I would have thought that Peter would be keeping a close relationship with me, since we had a lot of business to review.

I figured things out fairly quickly. This wasn't so much a business trip for Peter as much as one of protectionism. He was solidifying his relationship with the band, and I seemed to fit into the "dime a dozen" category at the moment. Not that it made much difference, since I only had about a week to go.

A few hours later we piled into the limos again and it was on to the show. Once more Peter rode with the band's founders and I brought up the rear with the rest of the group.

The band's performance that night was absolutely on fire, and I got my first taste of Peter in cheerleader mode. It was a riot.

Most managers I had worked with simply stood in the wings watching the performance, making mental notes. Not Peter - he was working. Talk about Mad Dogs and Englishmen, this was the very definition of it. I was watching a Southern Rock Band and their British manager, and both were working at full steam. As the three man guitar army lined up, their guitars aimed at the audience, with Ronnie Van Zant egging them on from his position by the drum stand, Peter was crouched down, arms flailing wildly, rooting them on. He'd jump from his crouch on occasion, pointing at who knows what. He'd run around the back of the stage to the opposite wing and crouch down again, wave his arms about some more. And then he'd point at something, God knows what, as I couldn't figure it out no matter how well I followed the direction. He was a man possessed, fighting demons, or possibly talking to God. An excitable boy, and there was no holding him back, or, possibly, he was acting out a dream of being on that stage with them, part of the act.

I didn't know quite what to make of it. I watched the stage carefully to see if the band responded to his gestures, and couldn't make out any correlation, so I stood back and watched in amusement.

The band performed every night without a cheerleader, so I doubted if they paid any attention. I watched a portion of their performance from the side of the stage every night, and I'd give them a nod or two and even throw out a "thumbs up" on occasion, or throw in a broad smile to which Ronnie always responded, but I never went full cheerleader on them. They had plenty of that from the fans who went absolutely berserk every night.

No, I was much more reserved, but I did break into a little dance when they played my favorite tunes, and bobbed along every time when they did T for Texas but still, I never thought it necessary to do any sideline directing. After all, these guys had their performance down pat. The only thing interrupting it was pranks on each other, and those always ended up with furor in the dressing room. So I generally kept silent about their performance, it was set and well done, and I figured you don't try fixing something unless it was broken, although, from time to time, they would change their set list to prevent boredom. This was an interesting process, as someone would throw out a suggestion and soon everyone would have something to say. They always asked my opinion, and on occasion I'd give it to them, only to find it was always ignored. I soon simply quit sharing my opinion and resigned myself to writing and distributing the set lists they produced. I became the messenger in that course of the group's business, nothing more, which was fine by me, as everything the band did that included any democratic process usually ended in a fight. And I never had the energy to fight with them. It was everything I could do to keep up with the ungodly hours, never-ending accounting chores, and relentless barrage of daily phone calls.

After the show we returned to the hotel where the band huddled with Peter for a while, and afterwards he made it over to my room, because we had to review the last couple of weeks' receipts and he wanted me to look at the dates that had been added.

I was sitting at the little round desk scrambling over the books when I was interrupted by a rapid knock at my door. It was Peter, dressed in his ironed jeans and white shirt, a black sports jacket - his most common attire.

"I hear you're leaving after the gig tonight," he said, extending his hand. I welcomed him in.

"Yeah, there are way too many friends here. We need to escape before it turns into a party."

He laughed, "I know what you mean, but I have a lot of stuff left to review with the band."

"We'll be here for a couple of hours. Can you squeeze everything in?" I could tell from his reaction he wasn't pleased.

"I don't know. I need to go over business with you, and update the band, and we're going back on the road in March."

"What?" I asked.

"After the band gets through with Europe, we're starting up in the States again."

"Why didn't you tell us?"

"The band needs the money. If we stop now, we won't be able to pay the bills."

"We're making good money. We've been selling out most shows."

"Exactly. That's why we need to stay on the road. We should take advantage of this. They're hot, so we need to do as many shows as we can."

"Peter, I only signed up for a few weeks," I said.

"So what will it take to keep you on the road with them? The guys really like you, they tell me you're the best tour manager they've ever had."

This sounded like a repeat performance of Allen Arrow's speech – the one that hoodwinked me into this operation in the first place. I had learned my lesson and wasn't going to get sucked in by his flattery.

"Look, this band is red hot. I'm not denying it. But I have other business to deal with."

"How can I help?"

I was tasked with some fast thinking. He had caught me completely off-guard.

"Well, you know I own a production company?"

"Yes, what's the name of it?"

"Clearlight Enterprises."

"Yes, yes. I've heard of it," he said, nodding.

"Well, if you really want me to stay, I want them to hire my company for lighting."

"We've already got contracts. And the band is happy with their lighting company."

"I thought you asked how you could help."

"I did."

"Well, that would do it."

"Okay, but don't you think it's a conflict of interest?"

"Not at all – it's a package deal, and I guarantee I'll give them better lighting at a lower cost."

"Well, alright, but we can't just up and change things now. We've got contracts."

"I'll be patient."

"Then you're signing on permanently?"

"We'll see how things go. If you'll get my company on board, my interests would be in one place."

"I'll see what I can do. It won't happen fast."

"Will it happen?"

"Yes, yes, I can make it happen."

"Then it's done. I'll stay on, you help me get Clearlight into the deal, and I'll give them a great deal and lower their production costs. If they pay less for lighting it's in the band's best interest anyway."

And so the deal was done. I had signed on with the group on a somewhat permanent basis and my production company picked up a new client. We started reviewing the books and talking about future business. And to my surprise, Peter turned out to be okay. Most managers I had met were somewhat fixated on themselves. Peter was too, but not to the extent others were. His soul had not yet been eaten away by power. Not yet. And by the end of our meeting I found myself actually liking the guy, which was an unusual and unexpected turn of events, resulting in a win-win situation for all, or so it seemed. But I still had a nagging feeling. I wasn't sure what it was, but something didn't sit right. It had just been too easy.

Ronnie was up and going strong the next day, and our "secluded" hotel was abuzz with fans and friends. Word traveled fast, especially with three days off and the band and crew out on the streets.

They had made it through the show, but afterwards they told me it was one of the hardest events they had played due to recent illness and exhaustion, at a facility that couldn't accommodate the production. Now the crew was as worn as the band after stripping the production to elements that would fit. It had been extremely difficult, and the guys had to do a tremendous amount of work to get the show up.

I was railed, of course, as it all came back to me. Somehow, it was my fault the band had been up for days, my fault the crew had to work so hard, my fault the facility wasn't right... I had no idea any of this was problematic, I hadn't booked the gig, and I didn't do the advance work for the crew.

Rudge conveniently reappeared after my railing, having completely faded the heat. My take on the whole matter? Screw it. I was babysitting a bunch of spoiled kids that confused work with vacation.

We limped into San Diego the next day for one show. The band pulled it off with a solid performance, but it was somewhat disappointing, because we had broken our streak of sell-outs.

It was a large venue in San Diego, the Sports Arena, and even though it had been curtained off so a half-house still looked good, there were quite a few empty seats. It was fairly typical with that venue, though. It was extremely rare anyone sold it out. Ronnie wasn't too happy when he grilled me before the show. He had been doing that a lot lately, wanting to know how full the house was, and how the audience looked. And Gary was soon interested also, having overheard Ronnie and me talking. Normally Gary was somewhat shy and reserved, and never spoke much about business, so it took me by surprise. I told them both that we had a poor crowd, and that was the last time Gary asked.

The next day, a Monday, we boarded a flight to Seattle, leaving at 4:30 in the afternoon. Everyone looked well for a change, and we were certainly ready to vacate California. It had been rough. Not the gigs, necessarily... we had just worn ourselves out from parties.

We had all read our itineraries, and we had all been to The Edgewater in the past, but the note in our tour book that had everyone excited read: "Fish from your room!" We weren't aware of that perk. We arrived at the hotel at 8:30. By 10:00 I got the call.

"Ron, you ain't gonna believe what Leon caught." It was Gary, and I could hear quite a few excited voices in the background. He continued, "It's some kind of weird fish. I've never seen anything like it."

I told him I'd be there in a few minutes. He had piqued my curiosity.

It was ugly and mutated when I viewed it as a fish. When I looked at it as a jellyfish, it all made sense. Leon had hooked a jellyfish... a man-of-war, actually. Colorful, and since it was deflated, now just a shapeless membrane. I couldn't believe they thought it was a fish. After all, they lived in Jacksonville, and a lot of them, Gary and Ronnie, at least, were real fishermen. I left praying that no one would want to eat the damn thing.

The next day I found out that they were all in on it and were pulling my leg. They wanted to see if I had ever seen a man-of-war. They didn't know that I'd spent most of my teen years surfing in the Gulf and we used to throw the damn things at each other.

We finished this leg of the tour a few days later, ending up in Portland where the promoter, John Bauer, threw a party for us, The Outlaws, and Montrose, the opening act. Funny how the party John threw was in my room. Then again, all parties migrate to my room eventually, yet I was the one in the group that had the least interest in partying. Once again, I wished I had known about it. Once again, the advantage of booking a suite backfired.

I was kept up all night… not that I didn't join in, but I really could have used some rest. I'd soon have it – I was homeward bound that evening.

The party was tame, attended by the bands, the various record company reps, and the promoter's staff and their friends. No one was too inebriated at its conclusion – we were all going home the next day, and cross country flights were hard enough without a hangover.

CHAPTER 5

It was a bit quieter than normal when we boarded the plane. I suspect it was the passenger's trepidation. We all got seated when John, our copilot, opened the cabin door and confirmed everyone was strapped in. We were supposed to do the full cabin safety lecture and used to, but after running through it a few dozen times we got bored and dropped the ritual. Now we just piled in, claimed a seat, buckled up, and crossed our fingers. The crossing the fingers part was a very recent addition. And besides, Dean and Allen performing the steward duties caused everyone to fall out of their seats and roll on the floor with laughter. So much for the safety lecture. We felt the shudder as the pilots cranked the right engine. There was a low pitched grinding sound as the engine started turning over, coming to life a moment later with the normal outpouring of black smoke. This was somewhat alarming when it was witnessed for the first time a few months ago. Now it was routine, or at least it used to be. This afternoon everyone was a bit wide-eyed as the engines sputtered to life.

March – April 1976

We regrouped five days later, on March 24th, and hit the road, with the rescheduled Albuquerque show first in a long run of performances. Montrose opened for us. They were on quite a few shows as we continued our monster tour, and The Outlaws were on quite a few of the bills as well. We were becoming good friends with the two bands as the events on the road drew us all closer. It was beneficial, this rhythm we had, especially for the crews, as known opening acts created camaraderie for most of the tour. As far as the bands were concerned, they also developed relationships, but they could go bad at the drop of a hat. The Outlaws were particularly bad about this, as they saw themselves as the "new" Skynyrd, so there was heated competition between the bands. They even had this theme song, *Green Grass and High Tides*, which was structured very similarly to *Free Bird* and like Skynyrd, they closed every show with it. Montrose was a bit different, as they weren't a Southern Rock band. They were more in the hard rock genre, an American clone of the British invasion. Sammy Hagar and Ronnie Montrose had a powerhouse act, with a couple of songs receiving fantastic airplay, and Mick Brigden was on the road with them. Mick and I knew Ronnie Montrose from his stint with the Edgar Winters Band when we were touring with Humble Pie, and I also knew him from his work with Gary Wright, so there was some history.

John Butler was no longer traveling with us. He had been made our "advance" man. Not that we needed one, but it had gotten to the point where he was upsetting so many members of the entourage that it was best to cut him loose. Since cutting him loose was not that easy due to old friendships, he now traveled to the various cities one day ahead of us. Theory was he could visit the venues, or at least engage the promoter, and have our hotel check in and anything else needed ready for our arrival. This outstanding plan didn't last long, though. As the venues were never ready for us until the day we arrived, the promoters usually had another show somewhere, and to have an advance man fly around to check us into hotels was just plain ridiculous. At least we were having far less trouble amongst the entourage.

From Albuquerque we hit Houston, my hometown, and the troops turned out in force. The show was being promoted by Terry Bassett and my good friend Carl Dooley was stage manager. I had also done so many shows at the venue over the years that it was truly old home week. Virtually everyone in the facility, from the manager to the maintenance man, knew me. I was in my element and overjoyed with it, so much so that my joy was contagious, lifting the whole band. The moment we hit The Whitehall, the same hotel I had met Allen Arrow at a few months ago when I signed on to this adventure, I called Alice.

She was ready and arrived at the hotel with Linda in tow. I was quite lucky when the band decided they could do without me that day so I could go home while they did sound check. I was to meet up with them at the hotel when it was time to depart for the concert. At least that was the plan, but Alice preferred to stay at the hotel; she never got to stay in hotels, or so she said. I suspected she had ulterior motives. So by the time Alice and Linda arrived they kind of took over... roaming the halls looking for fun, or trouble... probably both. The rest of the gang, the Clearlight staff, showed up at the performance that night, and the band and crew had a ton of guests of their own.

I had my usual duties to deal with and issued a ton of backstage passes against my better judgment, but the band insisted all of my people get backstage and theirs, too. So we certainly had a packed house that night, at least backstage, although it was sold out in front as well. And what a performance it was. The band was absolutely fired up, much more so than usual. They made me proud.

Following the show, in spite of the large amount of guests... or rather, due to the large amount of guests, we left early, moving the whole party to the hotel to my suite. I certainly didn't mind though, as much of the crowd consisted of my own guests.

Dean had picked up everything of any value from the dressing room and brought it for the party. We had plenty of soft drinks, beer, and two bottles of Jack Daniels... enough for at least a half hour. As the evening wore on, the crowd thinned out, some merely migrating to other rooms. By the time it was completely clear I was more than ready for some sleep. Linda had disappeared with Leon, and Alice had already passed out, so I slipped into bed gently, not wanting to wake her.

The next morning I was foggy, to say the least. The taste in my mouth was absolutely revolting. I was completely dehydrated, and my head was pounding. I glanced over at

Alice before entering the bathroom. She must have felt the same... there was a pillow over her head and I detected no movement. I glanced at my watch - 9:00 am. We had a flight at 11:00. After ordering some coffee and breakfast, I shook Alice awake and called Dean, waking him. I quickly told him what time it was and had him call everyone and make sure they were all up. Then I jumped in the shower, enjoying the bit of relief the pounding hot water offered.

Alice handed me a cup of coffee before she took her shower, informing me she wanted to go to Oklahoma with us, because that we hadn't had any time alone. I agreed and made the arrangements, only to find out later that Linda had made the same arrangement with Leon, so she had also joined the tour.

The limos taking us to the airport were packed. We had three additional passengers, and all of us were so hungover. Then I had to purchase the extra tickets at the airport, so I had Kevin and Dean take care of the band. It all worked out. Luckily there were open seats, but we were damn near late for the flight, just reaching the plane as they were closing the doors.

When we arrived in Oklahoma, I was faced with the same dilemma: I had forgotten to add a car, so we were once again packed into the cars like sardines. We checked into the hotel, the Oklahoma City Hilton, then drove to Norman, home of the University of Oklahoma. We were going to play at the Lloyd Noble Center, the basketball arena.

When we got to Norman, I encountered yet another problem. I had failed to get enough day rooms for the group. I had two rooms for everyone to occupy in between sound check and the performance. It was totally inadequate, since there were seven in the band, plus the Honkettes, Kevin, Dean, Alice, Linda, and me. It equated to seven and a half people per room. The hotel was sold out, so it took a bit of arm twisting (and free tickets), to get two more rooms.

We returned to the hotel in Oklahoma City after the show, and by the time we arrived everyone was too tired to do anything but sleep.

We were up and at it again in the morning: same scene, crowded limos, three extra passengers, three extra tickets at the airport, but at least we had just been through it so it went a lot smoother this time. We arrived in Dallas forty minutes after taking off and were greeted by four limos - I finally got that right.

We checked into the Ramada near the gig and actually had a couple of hours before sound check, and the hotel was within walking distance. That convenience had its cons. Whenever we had a hotel booked that close to the gig, two things happened: 1) people would disappear, making their own way to the gig on their own time, and 2) there were always a ton of guests at the hotel as word always spread. I wisely declined the suite that day, giving it to Ronnie instead, and Alice and I finally had some time alone as the next day was off.

Everyone slept in – it was glorious. As usual on a day off a large portion of our group simply disappeared: some doing their laundry, some out exploring, and others merely catching up on sleep. That allowed a bit of peace, and it was Sunday, so I didn't have to make too many phone calls. Alice and I just lounged around, ordered room service, and watched TV. It was good having a bit of rare time together, and it seemed to repair our marriage, at least for the time being.

The next morning, with everyone well rested, was spent tidying up a few chores. We had a few radio interviews to do. I had grouped them all on our day off to avoid additional work on show days. Most of them were by phone so I had to ensure that each band member was available at the designated time, and either Dean or I would visit the musician's room plenty early to tie them down and make the call. The band hated doing interviews, so it was a bit of a chore.

We enjoyed most of the morning, but our flight came far too early to really enjoy the whole day, and by that afternoon we were in a Braniff plane heading to Minneapolis. Alice and Linda had made their own reservations and made it as far as the airport before the farewells began.

We blew through St. Paul, playing the Civic Center, followed by Des Moines, Iowa, finally ending up in Chicago on April Fool's day. We were staying at the Ambassador East Hotel in Chicago, a grand old establishment that had become one of the premier hotels in Chicago. The rooms had high ceilings with beautiful furniture, a step up from most hotels we booked. Selma and I had tried to upgrade our hotels where we could, finding out it was easier said than done as most of the better hotels refused the band. Our reputation, no doubt, was preceding us.

We had an especially hard time with the Boston hotel, my favorite, when we tried to book it. I even had to put in a call to the manager personally, as I was well known to the hotel having stayed there many times over the years. Once I promised that I personally guaranteed good behavior we were in.

We all got together with Greg Dodd, the Chicago MCA rep, for dinner that evening. There were no food fights, just a relatively quiet evening and a wonderful dinner at one of Chicago's famous pizzerias. Several members of the group were not walking too straight when we finished - they served excellent cocktails. It was a quiet evening at the hotel, too, which was a nice break from the normal chaos we traveled in.

The next morning I visited Ronnie's room to see how he was feeling. I had begun keeping close tabs on him since the cancellations the month before. I was determined to keep him healthy. Once we got to talking, I started thinking that I should keep even closer tabs on him.

"Ron, you aint gonna believe what happened to me last night."

"Try me." I replied, nothing surprised me anymore.

Ronnie told me about his evening. "I got to sweatin' at

about two in the morning, cuz my room was s'damn stuffy. So I decide to go out on the balcony, right? On the fire escape down the hall from my room. I couldn't open the damn windows in my room. They were locked shut. So here I am in my shorts and a t-shirt and I'm barefoot."

"Yeah?" I prompted.

"Yeah, so I get out on the fire escape. Man, it was cold out there. But I needed some air so I walked on out, and before I knew it, the door had slammed shut on me. And when I tried to get back in, that damn thing was locked."

I couldn't help but laugh. He didn't seem to think it was as funny as I did.

"You think that's funny, huh? I'm locked out, fourteen stories up, and I hardly have any clothes on. I'm barefoot! Do you know what it's like bein' barefoot? On one of those steel staircases? It had all of those little spikes on it, you know what I mean? Two in the fuckin' mornin', freezing out, and I'm stuck on a fire escape fourteen stories high."

"What did you do?"

"What could I do? I had to climb down fourteen flights o' spiky steel stairs barefoot. In shorts. And a t-shirt. In freezin' ass weather."

He finally started laughing right along with me.

"You shouldda seen it when I made it all the way down. I had to walk back into the lobby, shakin' my ass off from the cold. And when I asked for my key, guess what they said. They asked me for my ID. So I had to have a security guard escort my freezin' barefoot ass back up here show him my ID."

As funny as it was, I was a bit worried. It didn't sound conducive to his health. Thank God he didn't get even sicker.

St. Louis, Missouri was up next. We had a sold-out show in Keil Auditorium, and the guys even went to judge a t-shirt contest with no complaints... at least not beforehand. It was staged by a local radio station, and they conducted a few interviews with the band while they were there. On the way back, though, they claimed they were hoodwinked. They had expected a <u>wet</u> t-shirt contest. There was no wet to it. I felt a bit hoodwinked myself. A T-shirt contest? With no water? How ridiculous.

From there we hit Kansas City, Missouri, only a forty minute flight, so we had a bit less of a grind. Everything was fine: a sold-out show, a stellar performance – it was smooth sailing.

Then we got back to the hotel and everyone headed to the bar to get in a few drinks before closing. They only missed it by a day. It was Sunday, so bars weren't open, and there were no open liquor stores, so the band gathered in Dean's room for the evening. He had a half full bottle of Jack Daniels. It was empty in minutes. Since the next day was a travel day and they could sleep in, they were extremely disappointed, and the party migrated from room to room for several hours. They'd hit a room at random, consume whatever drinks, pot, or cocaine that was available, and then wander to the next. By the end of the evening, everyone was pretty much cleaned out.

The album was starting to heat up a bit and our publicist was on a roll, so we were looking at interviews in almost every city for a while. The guys weren't too happy about it. As I said, they hated interviews, but it was a necessary evil - a chore they had to do regardless of their wishes. Personally I looked forward to these days with heavy activity. It kept the band occupied and out of trouble… or at least minimized.

We flew to Boston the next day, one of my favorite cities, and checked into that favorite hotel of mine that I had taken so much pain to reserve, The Lenox. The front desk welcomed me and the manager grilled me again, wanting my promise that there would be no incidents. Since I had already been harping to the band about the situation, telling them they had to be on their best behavior, to which they agreed, I felt confident in making the promise. It was, of course, a mistake.

At 3:00 in the morning, the fire alarm went off. I was used to this and pulled the covers over my head, as they usually went off after two or three minutes. Five minutes later someone was pounding at my door, so I jumped out of bed and pulled on my jeans. It was a fireman, telling me to clear out. Now! I pulled on some shoes, grabbed my briefcase and a shirt, and fled. The halls were smoky and the smell intense, but you could still see fairly well. I was disoriented but went along with the flow. Evidently the masses knew what they were doing. We ended up huddled on the grounds and parking lots a few minutes later and I began searching for members of my entourage. I managed to find a few of them huddled together, arms folded, talking, while keeping an eye on the building. I glanced over myself as I approached them. I didn't see anything unusual except for the activity. There was no smoke billowing out of the windows. In fact, I couldn't detect any smoke anywhere. I asked Artimus what had happened. Allen, Billy, and Leon looked at him like he had all the answers.

"I don't know. The smoke was pretty heavy in the hall, though." he answered.

Now everyone was looking back at me like I had all the answers. I could tell from the look on everyone's faces they had no idea what was going on, so I began looking for someone who did. A few moments later I ran into Cassie, Leslie, and Ronnie.

"I don't know what's going on, but Gary looks pretty shook up," Ronnie told me. "He's over by that fire truck. They wouldn't let me talk to him."

"You guys okay?" I asked.

They were, so I searched for Gary. I found him right where they said I would, at the rear of the fire truck, leaning against the bumper, a large blanket draped around him. Ronnie was right, he did look shook up. I walked right up to him, no one stopped me.

"Gary, you all right?"

Gary peered at me from under the blanket, he was

wearing it like a hoodie, and he was shaking like a leaf on a tree.

"Yeah, yeah… I'm alright".

"What the hell happened?"

He dropped his eyes, stared at the ground, and began.

"Well there was this fireplace in my room, you know? So I was laying there watching a movie and smoking a joint and I got to thinking I needed some atmosphere. So I got this candle and I put it in the fireplace. I just sat it on top of the fake logs, ya know?. I guess I went to sleep and it caught fire. The next thing I know this fireman breaks my door down."

"Damn, Gary."

"I know… it was an accident. I'm sorry, man."

"You're sure you're all right?"

"Yeah, I'm fine, I think… just shook up."

The next morning, I ended up putting a $15,000 charge on my credit card for that one, and spent the morning calling hotels and the office.

I wasn't having much luck finding a hotel on my own, but Selma called me back in no time and had secured rooms at a Sheraton, and the move was on. I was lucky it was a day off, but what a way to spend it. I had hoped I would spend it visiting my favorite Boston hotspots, of which there were plenty.

They opened the show at the Orpheum in Boston with the song *Double Trouble*, and we had no idea how appropriate that was. During *Free Bird* smack dab in the middle of one of the hottest sequences, Leon's bass malfunctioned, a fuse or something, so he got pissed and started slinging it around, tossing it in the air, and then Allen pulls the whammy bar off his Firebird. By then Leon was in a full Who rage, banging his instrument on stage and Allen saw this and joined in, although he was a bit more careful with the Firebird, he didn't seem to be going at it like Leon. Then Leon tossed the remnants of the instrument into the audience. Allen did too, in the heat of the moment, but as soon as he did, he ran over to Chuck and pleaded with him to go rescue it. Seconds later, both Chuck and Craig were diving into the audience, then I saw them arguing with the proud possessor of the classic Gibson Firebird. It didn't take long, and the fan obviously wasn't happy, but he relinquished the instrument. Craig removed the strap and let him keep it, and Chuck handed him a handful of guitar picks.

Ticket sales for the second night there weren't that good, and we were hoping we'd make up for it with walk-ups at the door. Now it looked like the prospects for a good walk-up didn't look so hot, so we simply canceled the show, cut our losses, and flew to New York for a couple of days off, which I spent working in the office.

We checked into the City Squire Motor Inn in Manhattan, which was certainly not my first choice, but it fit the budget. We arrived in the late afternoon and there was plenty of time for people to disappear. They were quite good at that - regular Houdinis. There were so many places to go and so many things to do that I didn't even try to track anyone during the stay. I had an enormous amount of work to do as the band was really breaking out in spite of the mediocre record. This summer we were doing a few stadiums, the largest shows for the band yet, so I stayed at the office, knowing everyone would drop by eventually. They knew where to find me, and I knew what they would want – money. There was a lot of shopping to do. After all, we were in New York City.

We had booked a few interviews at radio stations, but no one wanted to do them, especially Allen. We sent Dean instead and he would pretend to be Allen. Often he had filled in for Allen if Allen didn't want to interview. Ronnie, of course, was always there, and he had no problem convincing anyone that Dean was Allen. I couldn't believe they got by with it most of the time. When they didn't, we had some explaining to do.

Since the next day was a show day, everyone was on their

best behavior. No one wanted to cause trouble in New York. It was Rudge's town and home to our management office. We were damned tired anyway.

The crowd was huge at The Beacon, a beautiful old vaudeville theater that had gone Rock and Roll. And, of course, as in any other major music city, we had damn near as many people backstage as we did in front of the stage. And in a traditional theater we didn't have the enormous backstage area that arenas offered. It was a security nightmare. John Butler, our advance man now back as security, helped at the show, but it was a bit hopeless.

I watched the performance from the wings and was forced in front of the onstage monitors due to the crowd. This massive speaker system could make your ears bleed, and the guys were always turned up to eleven so they had to really pump up the volume to have any chance at all of hearing the vocals. I was a bit unprepared since I rarely watched that much of the show from the wings, preferring to go into the audience so I could get the feel of the crowd. Tonight, though, I was onstage, and I was right in front of the side fill monitors, directly exposed to one of Ronnie's favorite "tricks", the kill whistle. When the band performed the intro to Call Me the Breeze, Ronnie would let out an ear shattering whistle. The band and crew knew very well when he'd do it, but I didn't. He cut loose. Most avoided the pain by turning their head and making sure they were off axis from the monitors, but I got the full blast. I couldn't hear a thing for a few minutes and my ears rang for a good twenty-four hours afterwards. I spent the whole evening watching people's lips, smiling like I understood and moving on, avoiding any conversations.

It was at the end of the second show in New York that Leon did his Who thing again. Although he had tossed his bass in the air the night before, he managed to catch it, although it was way north of awkward. He had a lot of practicing to do if he was going to catch up with the Who. So his second bass in a week fell to the floor. I don't know if it was damaged at that point, but it didn't matter. Leon started slinging it around, finally grabbing it by the neck and going full Hendrix, whacking sway at the stage until the neck snaps. He tossed the remnants into the audience and walked off the stage with the rest of the band.

Well, we found out after the show that the bass had struck a girl in the audience, and it had slashed her face and she had to be rushed to the hospital. The next day it was in the papers, so we spent most of it trying to locate the girl so we could apologize and make amends. We found the girl, and she thanked us for caring, and was very gracious about all the gifts we brought her. We felt confident that we avoided a lawsuit and had re-secured a fan's love. Her lawsuit arrived days later.

Following the two powerful performances, both sold out, I agreed to go out with the guys before departing New York. We went searching for clubs the night before and managed to close one down at around two in the morning. Not quite satisfied, at about 3:00 in the morning we demanded the limo driver take us to a club of his choice as we didn't know what would be open.

"This is New York. There must be a club open somewhere. Isn't this the city that never sleeps?" we asked.

He didn't hesitate, and we were gaining admission to The Crisco Disco ten minutes later.

Hardly the place for the Skynyrd mob, we walked in prepared to party. The band split into two groups and started roaming the club. I hung with Ronnie, still on my mission of keeping him healthy. Ronnie and I ordered a drink at the bar, taking no notice of the place and its clientele. We were focused on the bartender, but couldn't help notice some of the strange clothing worn in the room, and the gender of those wearing them. We didn't see a woman in the place. There were some dudes that certainly looked close to being female, but they definitely weren't. When we took a good look at the DJ booth, a giant Crisco can, we put it all together. This place was a gay bar... no, it was a flaming gay bar! There were more piercings in the room than holes in a sieve and surprisingly, everyone in our group had made a couple of friends and were actually enjoying themselves. No dancing, of course, but plenty of interesting conversation, at least what we could hear over the music. I still couldn't hear a damn thing. My ears were still ringing.

Before long the inevitable happened and someone made a pass at Allen. He went berserk, screaming and yelling at the poor dude-in-a-dress, until some of the leather crowd started surrounding them. Ronnie and I noticed what was going on right away and pulled Allen back to the bar, while Gary and Billy drank at a table not far away, oblivious to it all. As soon as we had Allen calmed down, we gathered everyone and called it a night, laughing our asses off in the limo on the way home.

The Crisco Disco, even though it wasn't quite what we had in mind, had been a blast.

We finished this leg of the tour in Cleveland, following shows in Detroit, Philadelphia, and Pittsburgh. Ronnie had been looking around for a new guitarist to fill out his army, and was anxious to audition some players. At the party in Detroit he told me he'd been looking around but hadn't auditioned anyone yet. Then he added that there was only one way to audition for Skynyrd: trial by fire. They had one shot, one song, and it had to be played on stage in front of an audience.

"That'll cull 'em out real fast" Ronnie told me.

I got to witness it myself in Philly. Leslie West would be on stage. He had just dissolved his old band Mountain and was looking around. Ronnie knew the man's history, and he came out of Al Kooper's camp and had enjoyed several hits over the years, so it seemed like a natural. He had also visited us in Manhattan, and even joined the band on stage a few minutes jamming on a couple of songs.

Halfway through the set, Ronnie introduced West and the crowd responded, evidently very familiar with the man.

They had warmed up in the dressing room that evening with *T for Texas*, the band's "jam" number, and reviewed the song structure with West so he'd know when to take his solo. The whole audition centered around the fifteen second solo. He'd either cut it, or say goodbye afterwards.

The band sailed through the number until the solo, at which time Leslie cut loose. The only problem was every note sounded like the solo from his biggest hit, Mississippi Queen. We said goodbye to him after the show and never saw him again.

Pittsburgh was tough. It was a dome, and we couldn't "fly" our sound and lighting systems. Both had to be supported from the ground. This had been problematic as we didn't travel with floor lifts, only chain motors to hang the systems from the venue ceilings. Bob, Joe, and Craig were on top of it though, and had arranged some floor lifts for the lighting. The sound system could be stacked on the wings, but it was still a major hassle for the crew. Once again they had to deconstruct the system, figure out what would work and what wouldn't, and repackage the system on the spot for the evening's performance. Then there was the reassembly that night after the show so everything would be back to normal for the next one. I bonused the crew each $300 for their troubles.

Leon called me from his room in Pittsburgh, damn near hysterical, wanting me to come to his room immediately. Prepared for the worst, I threw on a shirt and grabbed the cash, and ran down to his room barefoot.

When I got there, I was relieved since he appeared fine, in a good mood, and sober. He hurriedly ushered me in and had me sit on the bed while he adjusted his cassette player. He always had this little boom-box that he carried. I had no idea why he didn't just carry it to my room instead of making such a frantic phone call.

"Alright, Roneckerman. You wanna hear some real rock and roll?" he asked.

"Of course."

"Wait 'til ya hear this," he said. "This is what rock n roll's all about. Listen to this. Shhh. Listen. Listen."

He punched the button and I got my first taste of AC/DC. We listened to the whole cassette, and I had to admit, they were the definition of hard rock. That was one thing Leon was always really good at: he kept his ear to the streets, our conduit to what was happening in the music world and he never let us down.

Following Pittsburgh we rolled into Cleveland, and it was a riot, and an appropriate place to end this leg of the tour. We were staying at Swingo's Celebrity Hotel, an aptly named hotel that had hosted everyone from Yul Bryner to Elvis Presley. The Outlaws and Steve Marriot's All Stars, the opening act, were also staying there, so the stage was set for a blowout party. I had toured with Marriot for years with Mick Brigden, so it was really good seeing him for the first time in a while. And what a blowout it was. We had about eighteen musicians, their crews, plenty of booze, a load of groupies, and nice spread the hotel had provided.

During the party Ronnie, Cassie, and I had a short talk. Cassie wanted the band to audition her brother Steve, who lived in Oklahoma. Ronnie didn't seem too keen on the idea, but Cassie made a good case, so we decided to fly him in for his own "trial by fire." After Cassie left, Ronnie told me Steve would be a quick in-and-out, but at least it would make Cassie happy.

As far as the party, this time I had enough sense to book an extra room as I was determined to get some sleep. I wasn't all that successful, because Ronnie followed me to my room. It was one of many sit-downs we'd have. I never knew what condition he'd be in, either, but it didn't matter. Either way, I'd learn something new. When he was straight, I took notes. When he was drunk, I simply listened for something that had a ring of truth to it.

"That fuckin' Leon" he said, "cuttin' that girl's face… and destroyin' all those guitars. And look at Allen. You'd think he'd have enough sense to keep his guitar."

"Shit happens, Ronnie."

"That's what I been sayin'. Shit happens… and it's time for it to stop."

"Um… how much have you had to drink tonight?"

Ronnie looked at me… one of his looks. His face was scrunched up, evil in his eyes.

"I'm telling ya Ron, ya better watch out for those boys. Someone's gonna get hurt."

"Goddamn it, Ronnie. You can't keep going at those guys. One of these days you're going to say this shit to the wrong person. Look, you need those guys. It's a band." I was keeping my fingers crossed, because he could easily turn on me, too.

"They keep on like this, and someone's gonna die."

"What? Are you making threats now?

"No, I'm not makin' no threats. Are ya crazy?"

"Well…it sounded like a threat."

"I'm just sayin'… you can see it for yourself. Someone's gonna… an accident's gonna happen, and they won't pull through.

"Okay, okay. I understand. I'll do what I can," I said, trying to assure him.

"It probably won't make a difference. I ain't gonna be around that long anyway."

"Go to bed Ronnie, you're talking nonsense."

He finally wound down as he continued to unload. I ended up with about one hour of sleep.

CHAPTER 6

I don't know how long we fell before impact. It seems like it was an hour, but I was told later it was only ten or fifteen minutes. We were square in the middle of the Twilight Zone as I remember it. It was a bit foggy, and the sun was just setting, so everything appeared to have the color sucked out of it... only shades of gray remained. I remember the pilot's warning, first over the cabin's P.A., "Prepare for an emergency landing". A few moments later, the door to the flight deck flew open and the co-pilot, John, obviously panicked, wrenched his body in an impossible contortion so he could face the cabin squarely, then stuck his head through the door opening and yelled "Prepare for a crash landing!"

May 1976

We departed in much the same way as my initial meeting with the band: in three station wagons. We were to meet up with the crew at the first gig. This time there were no wild antics on the drive up - that little show had been reserved for my first meeting. We were beginning to gear up for the live album, to be recorded in the first week of May.

Ronnie's talk soon fell into a dusty back corner of my brain, where it stayed present but unheeded, ready to dust itself off and make its presence known when the time was right.

We shot down to Lakeland for a performance at the Civic Center, opened by Pure Prairie League. I'm not sure what the promoters and agents were thinking, but Pure Prairie League was not the act to book with Skynyrd. It was pure suicide for them. Our hard core southern rockers were just not prepared for a "lite" country rock act. We didn't play that bill again, and I'm sure word got back to the agents so they probably wouldn't be on any future shows.

Pure Prairie League didn't get booed off the stage,

mainly because few people arrived early enough to see them, which was a bit worrisome. When we arrived for shows I always checked out the audience. It was half full until the set change, so when I reported that to Ronnie he took it to heart and cracked open a bottle of Jack, his best friend for the evening. The rest of the band happened to join him, of course, as they also knew Jack quite well and before long none of them were feeling any pain. In fact, they drank so much they weren't feeling much of anything. Then this wave of people filled the building and by the time Skynyrd hit the stage, it was a packed house.

The band went on, but halfway through the set they were shouting at each other while on stage, and Ronnie had even shoved Leon when Leon crept up behind him and damn near tripped him. The band quit for a few minutes at that point and left the stage while the audience went completely mad. They didn't care how fucked up the band was - it was all the same to them.

Ronnie reappeared a few minutes later, a bottle of Jack in his hand, and he raised it to the audience, making a toast to them. Then the band rejoined him, and they blazed their way through the rest of the set.

The fireworks continued back at the hotel, and I spent the evening chasing Ronnie from room to room performing damage control. I was careful, I didn't want to get in front of him, else I might be the one damaged. At some point things calmed down, Ronnie passed out, and I got another hour of sleep - my second in two days.

I was warned several weeks prior about Jacksonville. Gary told me that Ronnie hated doing shows in his hometown and the group had a history of cancellations there. I suspected Ronnie had a case of stage fright when it came to his hometown. He appeared quite nervous on the drive back from Lakeland and even mentioned how much he hated performing in Jacksonville.

When I asked him why, he couldn't explain it. I understood to a certain extent. I hated certain things I had to deal with when doing shows in Houston. For me it was all the people. All the denials of tickets and passes for my friends and family... it was a hassle. For Ronnie, it was performing in front of them. He could screw up anywhere in the world and not worry about it. Fans never noticed. But he couldn't stand the thought of screwing up in front of his hometown. Little could scare Ronnie, but this seemed to terrify him.

Most of the group chose to stay at home while in Jacksonville, but Leon and Gary decided to stay at the hotel. The girls, too, chose the hotel. It made sense. Those who stayed at home were all married... some even happily.

The moment I woke up that day my phone started ringing and it didn't stop the whole day. The band and crew had enormous guest lists and I got a lot of calls from friends, fans claiming to be friends, and even people claiming to be family. One guy called claiming to be Allen Collin's brother. Allen had no brothers.

The wives crowded the wings that evening. Judy Van Zant, Kathy Collins, and Stella Powell were dancing around on the left wing; Gary's, Leon's, and Artimus' friends on the right. Everyone else was on the floor.

Atlanta Rhythm Section opened the show, a welcome change from The Outlaws, and miles better than Pure Prairie League, as far as fitting with the band. They were flying on their hit, *So Into You*, and the Skynyrds knew them well from sessions in Atlanta where they shared engineer/producer Rodney Mills. The band was in fine form tonight and Ronnie seemed very comfortable in spite of his earlier trepidations, joking around with the fans, and from their history of car and boating accidents, most of which the fans were well aware. It was their most successful show in Jacksonville in years, and Ronnie was beaming afterwards.

We were on a flight to Miami the next morning, May 2nd, playing the Jai Alai Fronton, after which everyone was flying home for a few days. As usual, I flew to Houston first to see my wife and check on my business, and then to New

York for a day or two in the office. We were well into gearing up for the live recording at our next gig – a three day run in Atlanta.

In Houston my home life had changed for the better. Of course I would never have known it since all my time was on the road. Still, I no longer longed for the road; I didn't feel that urgency to escape to the road, and I had some regrets when I had to leave for the office in New York. I was also enjoying Alice's company for a change, she was showing me a lot of love, and of course it was always a pleasure to see Linda and her little daughter Mona - I was really falling for her. No doubt it was because I had known her since birth and had taken her under my wing.

I was already packed for New York when the call came in. It was Rudge. Ronnie had just called him. Gary had broken a finger the day before and we were going to have to cancel the live recording. This started the ripples that would continue throughout the day. Everyone was phoning each other, all pissed at Gary. My phone was going off late into the night. I still had no details about what had happened, but from what I was hearing, it had to be something pretty stupid. Ronnie was pissed. Tom Dowd was pissed. Everybody was pissed.

After cancelling my New York trip, I spent a few more days in Houston and then flew back to Jacksonville before beginning the delayed tour, spending some time in Bad Company, Ronnie's bass boat. Ronnie and Gary were determined to make a bass fisherman out of me. Gary still had a splint on his finger, but tempers had calmed a good bit. The only thing to do at this point was fish.

We spent a good part of the day drifting around the St. John's River, or at least the swampy bayou called Doctor's Inlet where we were fishing, and failed to catch a single fish. Gary and Ronnie both had bites, and Gary actually hooked one for a few minutes, but we went home empty handed.

Most of the time was spent talking, the rest was spent cursing, as every once in a while we'd have to change course, head into the trees, and unhook my line from a tree.

"You fishin' for squirrel?" Gary asked at one point. I shot him the look and kept my mouth shut. You don't want to get a couple of fishermen going at it – they don't make waders that deep. We talked about all the big ones that got away, and there were some mighty big fish involved. Gary and Ronnie kept telling me about Gramps, that one hundred and twenty five year old bass that everyone had hooked at one time or another, and that everyone just got to the surface, and the one that always got away right before they could get it in the boat. The fish was legendary.

Ronnie, Judy, and I talked for hours about business. We sat at the kitchen table after Judy cleared the dishes – Ronnie and I both helped. Judy had a few questions, and Ronnie had a few complaints. It was most illuminating, and Judy was an incredibly smart woman.

Judy looked me right in the eye.

"Ron, I don't understand how they can work so hard for so long on the road, and they don't make any money."

I stared back at Judy, noticing how pretty she was. She was naturally pretty: no makeup, with those big eyes of hers... she was the girl next door.

"I don't know Judy, I've never looked into it."

"Well... why not?" she asked.

"It's not my place. I do the books and send them to New York. I don't keep a running record of everything."

"Could you?" she asked.

I glanced at Ronnie. He was just sitting there, kind of kicked back, letting Judy take the floor, but he was listening, there was no doubt about that.

"Yeah, I could. I suppose I could tell you exactly how they're doing."

"Please, Ron. This has been going on for a long time. They're huge, but none of us are making any money, really."

"It's Rudge," Ronnie said.

We went to bed a short time later, and I found out she had more insight into what was going on while we were on the road than I did. Evidently there were plenty of calls home and the wives talked, therefore they kept pretty good tabs on us. They also kept that fact well-hidden.

I doubt if the guys knew that their wives knew what they knew. I made a mental note to keep in better touch with the wives. It broke with the unwritten law we had: the band's antics on the road were not shared with wives, and there would be no wives on the road. It made things easy. But Judy was interested in the business, and Ronnie was fine with it. It was her money as much as his as far as he was concerned, so after talking with Judy I decided to keep a copy of everything and to audit the tour books. Ronnie just wanted an easier schedule and easier travel. He didn't want to wreck his throat.

We all returned from the short vacation rested and energized, and were excited about Cassie's brother Steve. Cassie had been talking him up now that Ronnie had granted an audition.

We flew into Kansas City on May 11 from our various home towns. Most of the group was coming from Jacksonville, Cassie from Joplin, Missouri, Steve from Miami, Oklahoma, and Artimus from Greenville. The band went onstage at about 9:30, and midway through the set Ronnie introduced Steve, and then they launched into *T for Texas*. Steve burned through the solo and kept on rocking, running through a red hot version of *Call Me the Breeze*. We had the third guitarist. Kevin and I knew it immediately but it took Allen two more weeks to convince Ronnie.

Then it was back to Indianapolis, this time playing Indy proper, in the Convention Center, one of the oddest venues in the country. It's an L shaped building, consisting of two large halls that meet, so the stage is always built in the "elbow" of the structure. This results in a very odd configuration whereas the performers face a very small crowd that fit into the V where the two halls meet and where the front of the stage is. When the entertainer looks to the side in either direction, however, the crowd extends for a good distance, almost the length of a football field.

The band didn't know which way to play, preferring to hug the sides of the stage so they're aimed at one of the two main halls where the main portion of the audience was.

Evidently this disoriented the boys a bit, and they consumed a good bit more alcohol than usual during the show, ending up a bit sloppy, although I didn't notice much difference in their performance. I was standing on the side of the stage watching, having finished settling the box office, when Ronnie made the announcement:

"We're sorry this was such a lousy show. I don't really know what to tell ya, but we'll give you your money back. Every penny of it. Just go to the box office and I'll make sure everyone of ya gets your money back."

Within seconds, Joe, the promoter, found me backstage.

"Did you hear what he just said?" he asked me.

"Yeah, I heard."

"Is he fucking crazy? I'm not giving any money back."

I thought for a moment before I replied. I'd never run across this particular situation.

"They did a good show, Joe. No one's going to want their money back, but open the box office just in case. When Ronnie says something he means it, at least until the next morning."

"You're paying me back for every ticket." he said angrily as he turned to walk away. He called me later, letting me know he only had to give about half a dozen refunds and I didn't have to worry about it.

Ronnie was as drunk as I had ever seen him that night, and was terrorizing both band and crew. I tried my best to avoid him and succeeded for the most part, directing John Butler to watch over him. I went to my room, hoping to avoid the whole mess.

About an hour later I was relaxing in bed, watching a movie. That's when the expected knock on the door occurred. I crept up silently and peered through the spy glass to see an eyeball peering back at me.

"Open up!" It was Gary. "You've got to do something," he stated as I opened the door and let him in. He stood there, anxious, his hands clenching into fists every couple of seconds.

"What's wrong?" I asked.

"Ronnie's drunk" he explained, "and he's gonna beat the shit out of Billy. They just started arguing, then it got louder, and louder, and louder. Right now they're at a standoff."

I grabbed the microphone pouch I used to stash the cash and stuffed it down the front of my pants. It typically contained about $10,000. I never left money in my room; it was always down the front of my pants where it was impossible to access without my knowledge.

Gary led me back down to the bar. I could hear the commotion well before we entered. The bar itself was relatively quiet aside from my associates. There were a few suited salesmen still nursing their drinks at the bar, a couple in a dark corner - all of them turned around in their seats watching the action in the corner. Evidently there was a fairly good floor show going on. Billy and Ronnie were both standing there opposite a table, glaring at each other.

"Goddamn it, Ronnie. I'm a member of this band too. I should have some say in what goes on." Billy's face was crimson.

"You'll do whatever I say," Ronnie stammered, not quite sloppy drunk, but drunk just the same.

"Whoa! Whoa! What the hell's going on with you two?" I asked, performing my first intervention.

Both of them eased their hostility at each other, turning it against me instead.

"Mind your own business," Ronnie ordered.

"He's all fucked up," Billy added, "and he wants me out of the band. He's always wanted me out of the band."

"No he doesn't, Billy," Gary said calmly.

"Shut the fuck up, Gary, this ain't none of your business," advised Ronnie. Sounded like good advice at the time.

"Okay, what the hell is it, then?" I asked.

"Billy was too drunk to play tonight. He ruined the whole damn show," Ronnie stuttered, weaving a bit as he tried to maintain balance, "and I ain't gonna have it!"

I had seen enough. I already knew Ronnie had punched Billy in the face one time and broken out several of his teeth. I wondered what he was going to break next.

As Ronnie braced himself to start swinging, Gary swooped in, threw his arm over Billy's shoulders, and aimed him out of the bar. Ronnie and I watched them go, then Ronnie started scowling at me. I just sat down at the table.

"Ron, you just don't know what it's like," he told me as he walked toward me and sat down. "I've got to get out there every night in front of thousands of people. Their eyes are on me every second. And I don't need a bunch of fucked up players on my stage. It's hard. You don't know what it's like. Every night I go out there. It's hard, man. And Billy, you ever seen him without a Bud in his hand?"

I wanted to ask Ronnie when was the last time I saw him get onstage stage without having downed a half bottle of Jack Daniels, but since I had no desire to leave the bar with a broken face.

"Ronnie, these guys are your team mates. What are you gonna do? Stand there onstage, singing by yourself? Billy's a great player. You know that. I know it. Everyone fucks up, man. Give him a break."

Ronnie stared at me until his eyes lost some of the blaze. Then he unwound... just relaxed, instantly. The fight was out of him.

"Yeah, but you're gonna have to keep these guys in line. I've had enough."

"I'll do what I can... but don't expect any miracles."

He started laughing and I joined in.

"Miracles," he said. "It's a fuckin' miracle that you and Gary got Billy out of here alive."

We sat there for quite a while, and he filled me in on some of the band's history. "We had a drummer before

Artimus... his name was Bob Burns."

"Yep, I remember Bob."

He peered at me, not quite sure how to respond. "You know Bob?"

"I didn't say I know him. I promoted a show for you guys a year or two ago. Bob was with you then."

"I don't remember that."

"I didn't meet any of you. I was kind of shell-shocked. You guys looked mean and I guess you were having some trouble that night. There was a lot of yelling going on. It just didn't seem like the right time to introduce myself."

Ronnie scrunched up his face – a habit he had when he was drunk. It made him look meaner.

"Well," he continued, "the last time I saw Bob was after a gig. We got back to the hotel – this was a fancy hotel. We were on the third floor. Anyway, Bob went crazy. The last time I saw him he had jumped out the window and climbed down the vines... then he hit the ground runnin'. Just runnin' off, just took off runnin' in the middle of the night. I figured I'd see him on the bus in the mornin' but he never came back."

"Fuck." I couldn't think of anything else to say. Fuck seemed appropriate.

"He ended up in some kind of institution. Now I hear he's a Jesus freak."

We continued the conversation until the bar closed, then went to our rooms. Ronnie tried his best to continue the party. He asked me to join him in his room – he had some Jack Daniels stashed - but I had to get some sleep. They had worn me out.

The next day we were up bright and early. We caught a 10:00 am flight to Evansville, just outside Chicago, for the first stadium show of the season, and we were headlining. It was a four act show, with Earl Slick, Point Blank, The Outlaws, and Lynyrd Skynyrd. It would be the first of many stadiums that summer, each one larger, each one fuller.

The boys were on their way to achieving "superstar"

status. There was no doubt in my mind. That night Ronnie and I sat in his room talking again – a habit we would continue throughout the coming year. The delayed live album recording had to be rescheduled and he was thinking about the location. This wasn't the first time I'd heard about it; Peter had briefed me a few weeks ago.

The first thing out of my mouth was "The Fox. You've got to do it at the Fox." He already knew that, of course. I was out of the loop on recording schedules. The Fox Theater was a landmark in Atlanta, and the city had been threatening to tear it down. I gave Alex Cooley, the best promoter in the area and an Atlanta resident, a call the next day and he was all over it. There were some booking problems with other dates on the theater's calendar, but we managed to get four days in a row there, with a pick up day a few weeks later in the event it was needed.

Ronnie had been making a few phone calls of his own, and had been able to hook up with Cassie's brother Steve, whom he had asked to join the band. Steve didn't hesitate and signed on for an upcoming show in Myrtle Beach, and then he'd join the band in Jacksonville for rehearsals. Long rehearsals… we had a live album to record in a few weeks.

We regrouped and carried on, performing another run of shows on the "Chitlin" circuit – those redneck cities in the deep South, with everyone behaving and my job getting easier, then we hit obstacles. It started with Ronnie. He got extremely drunk one night during a performance and he went way past the fun drunk and straight into mean. It was a short road, that one that led from Dr. Jekyll to Mr. Hyde, and Ronnie hit it full speed. We were at the venue for an unusually long time that night after the show. Ronnie was laying into everyone, letting the band and crew both know who was boss.

Allen was the first one to speak out, "Who the fuck do you think you are?" he asked.

Well, Ronnie, in spite of his drunkenness, knew exactly who the fuck he was, and he let it rip. Allen was out in seconds, having contracted a right cross to his forehead. Ronnie looked around threateningly, looking around for someone else to deck, and when there were no takers, he headed out to the stage where the crew was diligently tearing down the set. Ronnie sneaked up on them just in time to see them lower the huge Confederate flag from the lighting rig. They dropped it to the ground just as they did every night, but every other night they didn't have Ronnie around to witness it.

"Burn it!" Ronnie yelled from the floor of the coliseum. "I said burn it!" he repeated, screaming at the top of his lungs.

The crew looked around in confusion. Few of them had any idea of what he was talking about. Then Craig appeared, followed by little Chuck, and I saw fear in both of their eyes. They ran over to the lighting crew and grabbed that flag, quickly rolling it into a ball, and headed down the stairway leading to the old concrete floor.

"I got it, Ronnie!" Craig yelled out as he raced past us. Chuck was on his tail and it was evident neither of them was going to slow down and face Ronnie.

"We're takin' it out back," Chuck yelled as they ran past Ronnie. "We're gonna burn it."

Ronnie looked pleased, and his whole demeanor changed in an instant. It was magical, the simple act of burning that flag, which had touched the ground in his presence, had placated him. He returned to the dressing room as meek as a lamb.

"Let's get out of here," he told me, and I didn't waste a second.

When we got back to the hotel that night, Ronnie went back on his rampage and everyone quickly vanished, hiding out in their rooms. The few that weren't wise enough to pull off the disappearing act managed to hit the bar as it was closing, Ronnie included. He didn't care much for the bar closing and he let the bartender know it, perhaps a little too well, as within a few moments a couple of cops strolled in, hands on their pistol grips. They popped in, took a look around, and left. That's all it took, and they made the night much easier for me.

Ronnie and everyone else in our troupe went straight to their rooms and stayed there. No one wanted to go to jail that night. I began wondering where I could get some uniforms and badges.

Once back in my room I figured everything had calmed down enough to dive back into my books, and I was right in the middle of counting the cash when there was a thunderous knock on my door. I sat still, careful not to make a sound. I had a pretty good idea of who it was. The knock came again, this time harder, more insistent. I ignored it.

"Ron, open up! I've been shot!"

I jumped from the chair and rushed to the door, flinging it open. I expected to see Ronnie crumpled in pain. Instead I got Ronnie standing straight up, a smile on his face, with his finger outstretched in the form of a pistol.

"Pow!" he said. "Gotcha."

I had to laugh. He knew how to get the quickest response from me. He swaggered in, walking in his drunken style, careful not to lurch or stagger.

"Whew," he said, "it's been a tough night."

"I hear it's been tougher on others."

He glared at me threateningly, his face all scrunched up, then he relaxed, and returned to fun drunk.

"Yeah," he said, chuckling a bit. "I guess so. Sometimes I just get fed up. I can't help it."

"Now I know why you worry about keeping the band together."

"Ya got any pot?" Ronnie looked at me seriously for a moment, then broke into a grin and started out the door, "Ah, nevermind. I better get some sleep." Then he carefully made his way out, never glancing back, and without a stumble.

I found out the next day he wasn't finished, and had been up for a few more hours messing with the crew. He hadn't boxed anyone else, just generally made them miserable. He woke Chuck and Craig up, demanding proof they had burned the flag, and they couldn't produce any, so the night was a long one for them. At some point he finally went to bed, but only after the crew bus pulled out and no one else would answer their door.

A few days later, as we closed out May, we performed our second stadium show, this time at Groves Stadium in Winston-Salem.

We were opening for ZZ Top, one of my favorite bands, and fellow Houstonians. I had known their manager for years and had been a fan of Billy Gibbons since he created The Moving Sidewalks. It was a monster show, and the first of ZZ's Worldwide Texas Tour, the one with the stage shaped like the state. When we pulled in, at about 11:00, we could barely navigate through all the trucks and buses. They had a dozen trucks on the road and half a dozen buses, along with cattle trailers and all the trailers brought in for dressing rooms.

Elvin Bishop and Point Blank were also on the show. Most of the 35,000 people were already in and the field was shoulder to shoulder, the grandstand packed.

We had just rested for a couple of days, if you want to call it that... better said, we had a couple of days off: one in Little Rock, one in Winston-Salem, and neither was all that restful.

It was already warming up on the east coast after a ferocious and late breaking winter and the sun was baking everyone for most of the day by the time the band came on. The audience had mellowed appreciatively after the heat, the all-day drinking, and the Elvin Bishop set. *Fooled Around and Fell in Love* didn't exactly rock people out. When I checked the crowd during set change it appeared a third of the audience had left. I was disappointed when I returned to the dressing room, but decided not to tell the band, and it's a good thing I didn't. As soon as they got thirty seconds into *Saturday Night Special* people started pouring back in, and by the time the song was over, the stadium was once again full.

It was like time-lapse photography.

In order to get to the next gig, RFK Stadium in Washington, I had to rent a private plane, an eighteen seat twin engine Otter.

I can't say it was a pleasant flight. We were all scared to death. The plane was doing some serious rockin' and rollin' on its own, and it was tiny, so we were white-knuckling it. We didn't trust any plane that you couldn't stand up in. That was the rule.

Here we were at another stadium, this one twice the size of the last. It seated something like 90,000 in the stands, so if you add the audience on the field there had to be a 100,000 in attendance.

We were playing in front of Aerosmith, and Ted Nugent was opening. Nazareth was following him (opening for us) so we were in the company of some rock and roll heavyweights. Ted Nugent got the crowd rocking sometime in the early afternoon, but I didn't witness it. We only got there in time to see Nazareth.

The dressing rooms were in the parking lot as the stage and sound wings took an enormous amount of room and there was a long ramp from the parking lot down to the field. It was such a walk and the weather was so threatening that acts were taking limos down to the stage area and dropping them off in full view of the audience. I told the band about this arrangement as soon as I returned to the dressing room. I also told them it really looked like we could get dumped on - the clouds were dark and angry looking and I'd seen some lightning on the horizon. The band didn't care - they were too excited about the gig, but they did start digging through the wardrobe case to find jackets.

By the time I gave them the fifteen minute warning everyone had a wrap of some type except Artimus. He wore the same thing no matter what the conditions: shorts, usually blue jean cut-offs, tube socks and sneakers, and a T-shirt, which he usually removed after a number or two. Today he had donned a sweat shirt over his t-shirt, but I was pretty sure they'd come off during the set.

When John and I returned to the dressing room to collect the band, I found out Artimus' friends had pulled in with their Volkswagen mini-bus. It was canary yellow and had a couple of "hippy" flowers painted on one side. The band had decided they'd forego the limos and wanted to ride in the mini-bus to the stage. Who was I to argue? So, a few minutes later, we rode down the ramp and parked on the side of the stage in our yellow mini-bus. The audience was silent. Then the door slid open, the band exited, and the crowd went nuts. They jumped out of the car, waving at the audience, and then ran up the stairs to the stage where they were fitted with guitars by the crew. It was cool the way the stage was set-up - the audience saw the whole process.

As soon as the band hit the stage, and I'm talking precisely the moment they started waving at the audience as they plugged in, the clouds parted, and this beam of sunlight seemed to focus in on them. As the band played on, the clouds continued to part, and by the third number the whole stadium was basking in sunlight.

The band burned through their set, setting the place on fire, and one of the fans took it too literally. As the band worked its way through *Gimme Back My Bullets*, only about a third of the way through the set, someone launched an M80, and it landed on the canvas roof directly above Ronnie's head. Bam! It exploded loudly, those things were equal to a quarter stick of dynamite, and Ronnie flinched, thinking someone was shooting. John and I figured it out quickly and when Ronnie glanced over at us we pointed to the roof. He looked up and realized what had happened, but from that time on he raced through the set. I was looking into the audience in an attempt to find the culprit, but from the stage the audience was this massive sea of motion that continued until the last crash of *Free Bird*, so it was rather hopeless. As the band walked off the stage that afternoon the clouds rolled back in, quickly enveloping the stadium. We were blessed with the best lighting designer in the universe.

Steve Gaines joined the band at the next gig, Myrtle Beach, and the band blazed through the show, obviously inspired by the new blood. He fit right in, and challenged Allen right off the bat, so the two of them were trading shots throughout the show. Gary would weave in and out seemingly at will, but it was all fairly well planned. Ronnie was loving it, and ordered Steve around like the rest of his army. He was the new recruit stepping up to the plate and knocking it out of the park. There was definitely a new fire burning in the group. It was obvious from the start, and the real genius of the man had yet to rear its head.

With four days off, the crew flew home and the band and I flew to Hilton Head, where we were meeting with Peter Rudge and Mary Beth. It was their annual meeting, where we would review immediate and long range plans, the finances, the tours, etc. It was strictly business, so Rudge had put it together on neutral territory, in a comfortable resort in South Carolina. None of the wives were there, and no one from the office except Peter and Mary Beth. I broke the rule.

Alice was complaining so much about me not coming home for the break, I had to make an exception and warned her she'd have to behave and that I wouldn't have much time to spend with her. She was insistent, so I flew her out, and since she was by herself most of the time, she complained even more than on the phone. By the second day, she finally pushed me over the edge. I was already irritated that she was there in the first place, and we got into a real screamer. The whole thing was ridiculous, and Alice followed me a short while later. We ended up sitting at the hotel bar for the evening. After a few drinks we had forgotten what we were fighting about, made up, and returned to the room.

Hilton Head renewed my own involvement with the group and with SIR Productions. For me to be included in an important meeting meant a lot, and once again I had the hopes that Rudge was taking me under his wing.

One of the biggest problems was the band's overhead,

which was growing immensely each year. The band insisted all of their people stay on payroll year round, whether the band was on tour or not, and it was very admirable of the group. Once we dug into the books, though, and they were shown the figures, they realized the only way to accomplish this was for the band to stay on tour continuously. By the conclusion of the meeting I was appointed the task of keeping tours on budget and doing tour estimates and was made a signatory on the band's production company account. Gary was made President of the company. The meeting was both eye-opening and rewarding, and each band member left informed of the group's operations and status.

It was an important occasion for me, as I was clearly being involved in the group's business. Not that I wasn't happy with my production company and with tour managing, but it was time to move on. It was the most likely way for me to continue. I started in the biz as a tour electrician, then became a stage manager, then lighting director, and now tour manager. Artist management was the next logical step.

We all relaxed the last day, business having been completed, and had a great dinner and a few drinks. We then headed home for the rest of the month - a quick visit with the girlfriends, wives, and families. I didn't need it, but Alice knew where everyone else was going, so I flew back to Houston with her. I would have preferred New York.

CHAPTER 7

Shortly after the second warning, Craig Reed, who was sitting across from me, grabbed our make-shift poker table and ripped it from the cabin wall, scattering chips and money everywhere. I don't know if I just thought this, or if I actually said it, but all I could think of for a moment was "How in the hell are we going to straighten out that pot?" I must have been winning - I don't really remember. Then a bit of panic – Artimus was running up and down the aisle trying to find a seat. Gene Odom, security chief, was also running around a bit, trying to secure something - anything, a terrified look of sheer panic frozen on his face. Having nothing to secure, he began checking the occupants, making sure everyone was buckled in, and generally scaring the shit out of all of us. Somewhat peeved at his activities, I just sat and watched. I was mistakenly wrapped up in my own belief that we were in a plane that couldn't crash. Everything can crash. Later...years later, I learned that Artimus never was secured, literally, to anything. Not even a seat, much less a seat belt. He just sat down on the cabin floor in the tail section of the plane across from the toilet and waited.

June 1976

We had all been extremely busy during our "vacation." I was jumping back and forth from the office and my home, where I conducted Skynyrd business. Every time I went to the office I became entangled in Clearlight business even though Albert was well on top of it.

The band was busy in their rehearsal studio in Jacksonville. Steve Gaines flew in for rehearsals during the last few weeks and according to my phone conversations with Ronnie, he was a perfect fit. A natural. He had been working with Allen constantly, learning all of the parts to the songs, and tossing out a few new ideas of his own. With him came a renewed vigor, a rebirth, for the whole group.

Steve brought this whole new world with him, and even though he was the perfect fit, he introduced a new element to the music... a touch of class, and new songs. The man was a great songwriter and could sing his ass off. Finally, Ronnie had that third guitarist to fill out his army... and a bit more that came with the package.

There was a lot in the cards for the band on this outing. We were first doing a few stadiums, followed by a week in Atlanta where we would finally be recording the group's first live album, and a double album at that. They were really up for the tour and excited about headlining the Gator Bowl in Jacksonville. They had never headlined a stadium in their home town, so it was huge. After the Gator Bowl they'd be flying to Muscle Shoals Studios to complete and mix the live album. It was definitely game on for all of us.

On June 29th I flew into the Detroit airport early to allow enough time to make a few phone calls. I settled in at a phone booth, grabbing a small table from one of the waiting areas. My temporary office was quite the enterprise. I had commandeered the end phone in a long line of them and had my stolen table pulled up under it.

Everyone arrived on one flight this trip, direct from rehearsals in Jacksonville, so we didn't have the normal wait for various flights from all over the country. They exited the gate a bit mixed, with Ronnie, Gary, Leon, Steve, and the girls bright- eyed and ready to go, and Billy, Leon, and Allen dragging from the early morning flight... and, most likely, a late night.

We poured into the waiting limos and settled into the drive to the Hilton in Troy, Michigan. We were performing ten minutes from there at Pine Knob Pavilion, one of the first of the "shed" type venues – an outdoor amphitheater with a stage and tin roof. It was the tin roofs that caused venues of this type to be known as "sheds." Pine Knob wasn't that large as far as the sheds go, with only 15,000 seats on the grassy knoll, and maybe a couple of thousand more under the roof.

We checked into the hotel without incident and spent the evening in the hotel bar, warming up, adjusting into the boozed-up routine that was the road. As was my habit, I left the bar as early as possible so I could get the sleep I knew I'd be craving in a few days. It was amusing, the fact that I drank and partied at home yet stayed relatively clean on the road, and they did the opposite... at least some of them. Others stayed in "tour mode" throughout, drunk and drugged up even at home – it was a lifestyle.

Sound check went great. Steve was absolutely amazing. He didn't miss a lick and fit in so well it seemed he'd been in the band from the beginning. I could tell how proud Ronnie was - he now had his full band back, and I saw it in Gary and Allen as well, as they accepted the new gunner with open arms.

The cars were abuzz on our return to the hotel; Steve had fired them up and was quite excited himself. He was usually kind of shy, and ultra-nice, but hadn't yet warmed up to me, appearing to be a bit intimidated instead, which made no sense at all to me. Perhaps it was just the whole experience. He had just come from a band that drew a couple of hundred people on a good night, and now he was in 15,000 to 20,000 seat gigs. That would intimidate anyone. I assumed he would come around, we'd just have to get to know each other, as I loved his sister Cassie dearly. It was just a matter of time... Steve and Cassie were cut from the same mold.

The group was in fine form that night, with the guitarists slinging solos back and forth, firing notes with machine gun precision, and Ronnie sauntering around the stage as both proud father and commander–in–chief. His troops didn't let him down.

What really amazed me was the way Steve found his place on the stage. There was absolutely no awkwardness at all. I'd been through personnel changes before with bands, and when it came to the stage performance, there were always mid-stage collisions, or at least near-misses, but these guys were fluid. Steve knew instinctively where to go. For most of the band it was no big deal, they'd been playing these stages for hundreds of shows a year for three years now and had it down. But for a new guitarist, who had only appeared on stage with them one time, and who had never performed in front of this many people in his life... to be perfectly choreographed in his stage movements? Unheard of.

The band had rehearsed, of course, but that was a totally different situation. The rehearsal hall was just a little warehouse that had been treated for acoustics. It wasn't that large and barely comfortable, so they certainly couldn't rehearse a full stage performance. It was built for music, for learning and perfecting parts, for inventing and developing songs, but not for live rehearsal. They always skipped that part – live rehearsals – as was common with rock bands. Rehearsals in their small studio were good enough.

That was always troubling for me, but par for the industry, that lack of stage rehearsals. How does a band of that stature just hit the road with no stage rehearsals? I was trained in theater, technical theater, and was used to technical rehearsals, where the sound engineer would learn the intricacies of the music, the lighting designer would learn the show structure and write all the lighting cues, and the performers would block out their stage movement.

In rock and roll, though, every act I'd ever worked with would wing it. No stage rehearsals at all, unless you wanted to call a sound check a rehearsal. They just hit the stage cold when they started a tour and it worked surprisingly well for most of them.

Lynyrd Skynyrd wasn't exactly a production band anyway. We talked about it a lot and they liked the idea of having a larger production but when it got down to it they had all they needed. After all, how could you beat a mirror ball and a confederate flag? That was all the production they carried other than traditional lights and a massive sound system. They were a rock band geared for the trailer park crowd, production wise. It always amused me how the audience reacted to the mirror ball. They went nuts... for a mirror ball! Same when they dropped the confederate flag for *Sweet Home Alabama*. It was like we had set off pyrotechnics – the crowds cheered their asses off... even the Yankees.

When I walked into the box office to settle receipts that night, I was shocked. The facility had about 15,000 seats and I was looking at stacks of deadwood. It looked like 30,000 tickets sitting there. When I questioned the promoters, they looked at me blankly, informing me that those were tonight's deadwood, so I rolled up my sleeves and started the count.

A few minutes into it I ran across tickets from other shows. Things were not right. This was the first show - I didn't need this. The promoters and I argued, sometimes heatedly, but it was apparent from my visuals on the crowd we were a long way from a sell-out, so causing a scene wouldn't do much good and wouldn't get us any more money. But the promoters had shown their hand and I'd never trust them again and I made sure they knew it. And that they'd know I'd be warning other bands and their agents. It didn't solve anything, it just caused friction between the promoters and me, but at least I was a bit defused before I confronted the band backstage. They didn't need to know, and knowing them they'd probably want to go confront the promoter themselves if they did. Then it would spin out of control. I doubt if I could get them out of jail for beating up a promoter in the promoter's town, so I kept my lips sealed.

We had a day off the next day with a late flight so the party broke out immediately after the show. Artimus' friends were there, and they had brought some good pot, so everyone stayed relatively mellow that night, at least until I had gone to bed. I had wised up enough to give Ronnie the suite so everyone drifted to his room and I could get some rest.

The party, of course, ended about the same as usual, with a fight, this time between Chuck and Billy, but Ronnie wasn't drunk, so instead of calling on me to deal with it, Ronnie dealt with it himself. I slept soundly.

After hearing what had happened the night before, I began thinking that I have this group figured out. It was simple – Ronnie Van Zant. He ruled and no one would question him. If I could keep him in line, he'd keep everyone else in line.

I was sitting in my room up to my neck in paperwork when this came to me. I hadn't yet worked out how to implement the plan, especially after he asked me to help him keep the band in line. Keeping him in line should be easy, at least some of the time, but he did have a habit of drinking too much, and then there was the cocaine. He never actually bought any himself but he wouldn't hesitate to do all that was in front of him, and it was usually everywhere. In fact, it was damn near impossible to avoid.

I dismissed my thoughts on group discipline and gazed around the room. I had the box office settlement, daily expense reports, and cash receipts from everyone in and around the group, interview requests, and a barrage of other papers spread out across my bed; overflow from the small circular table typically found in these rooms, and a notebook full of notes on conversations and phone calls I had made in the last week. I guessed it was a good five hours of work just to get caught up, and we had only been on the road one day. This was not a good sign.

July 1976

Following a performance in Dayton and another day off spent actually relaxing, we flew to Memphis for a show with ZZ Top at the Liberty Bowl for the 4th of July.

Our old friends The Outlaws were on the bill, as well as Blue Oyster Cult, whom I was really hoping to introduce. It was another massive affair, with a capacity of 62,000, and it should be a near sell-out, as advance ticket sales were around 40,000. However many there were, the guys got every single member of that audience on their feet. They weren't just on their feet, they were dancing that odd Southern shuffle that Skynyrd fans did – all 60,000 of them. And if you've ever seen 60,000 people out of their minds, in a feeding frenzy for southern rock, then you've seen humans at their best, and happiest.

Problems soon surfaced on these big shows. It seems the ZZ Top bunch weren't too keen on following such a performance. They just didn't have it in them. After about an hour… a rather lengthy set change (most likely to let the audience cool down) ZZ Top took to the stage and received the welcome they deserved. The crowd was ready, and they rocked them well, but they couldn't achieve the same response Skynyrd enjoyed. I hadn't seen a band that could. ZZ Top ended their show with fireworks. Skynyrd did, too, but their fireworks were of the musical variety.

The next morning the entire entourage, band and crew, flew to Atlanta, where we boarded limos and rode to the hotel in Buford at the Pine Isles Resort. We had chosen it because it seemed like a nice, relaxing break from the norm, and so the band wouldn't be bothered by fans and friends. They could concentrate on the recording and on their performance.

We spent that first night in comfort, Tom Dowd and the band huddled together in one of the rooms discussing the set list. Kevin was in the middle of it, and made a few great comments, and they happily adjusted the set. They were doing a great job and I had nothing to add so I remained quiet, mentally keeping track of the discussion, trying to remember as much as possible for later.

The crew was up early the next day, loading the show in as quickly as possible, but taking special care that everything was perfect, or at least as perfect as they could get. They were fresh and rested and had the luxury of staying near the gig. Kevin was up fairly early too, driving a rental car into Atlanta. The band, Dean, John, and I made it in early and waited while Tom Dowd, Kevin, and both the Skynyrd and the remote truck crews fiddled around with the gear to ensure it was working optimally and then positioning and repositioning microphones. Once satisfied, Craig beckoned the group from the dressing rooms where they had been warming up for sound check. It had to be the most professional I'd ever seen the crew and the band.

It was a tiring day. Poor Tom was constantly running back and forth from the stage to the remote truck, trying to get an exact duplication of the stage sound on tape. I don't know how he could stand it on stage - it was too painful for me – ear shattering. The band was of course used to it, and it appeared Tom didn't mind too much. He'd run out to the truck and have a listen, and then return to the stage and talk to the band, making minor adjustments in both the arrangements and the microphones. This was repeated all day, with minute adjustments to everything until he was satisfied. We ran fairly late so the drive back to the sticks was a bit of a nuisance.

Peter Rudge was down from the office and Terry Rhodes, our agent, was there as well, so we had a crowd, but it was under control. The trick was keeping it that way. Accompanying Peter from the office was Mary Beth and Sally Arnold, who handled the British tours and all things Sir in Britain. Sally was a doll, and I fell in lust the moment I saw her. I liked cute rather than beautiful, and this woman was as cute as they get.

We had sold out all three nights, so there wasn't too much to do in the way of promotion, but because we were recording there were a host of other details to attend to. We'd have to lock down the dressing rooms and stage, which would be problematic, as there were a lot of friends in Atlanta. Alex Cooley and I had put together an excellent green room for guests, Alex doing most of the work, or at least his staff. It would accommodate a fairly large crowd, and we ran a closed circuit feed from the stage. We weren't filming or taping but we used a full stage camera to transmit video to the remote recording truck so they could see the stage. From there it was easy to run a signal back to the green room so any guests that wanted to stay backstage would be out of the way yet still see the show.

It's a shame we cancelled the filming, because it would have been a great performance, but Ronnie felt they didn't need that extra pressure. He wanted to ensure the sound recording was the focus. The band seemed a bit nervous as they worked their way through sound check, with Tom stopping them every once in a while and asking for someone to play a part a bit differently, or adjust their tone. They would have gotten pissed off if most people would have asked that, but this was the legendary Tom Dowd, and no one questioned his suggestions. Nine times out of ten, he was right.

It was a thrill to pull up to the theater that night and see the band's name on the marquee and the long line out front. You could feel it was special - that there was an energy surrounding that beautiful landmark opera house. The Fox Theater was one of those grand old theaters built in the 1920s, and its Arabic and Egyptian architecture is somewhat unique, reminding me of the famous Mann's Theater in Hollywood. Not that the architecture is the same, but the grandeur of the architecture certainly is. It was described by a local newspaper as having "a picturesque and almost disturbing grandeur beyond imagination."

We had a few reasons to be excited about this recording, one of which was directly related to the theater – we were doing our part to save it. It had been threatened with demolition for years and every once in a while the pressure heated up. It was at one of those times now. Not only did they need publicity, they needed funds. So we provided both, donating a sizeable sum of the concert proceeds to save the theater.

We had also witnessed the success of Peter Frampton's live album, and everyone knew that when it came to live performance, no one beat Skynyrd. That was the strength of the project. A lot of people thought we were nuts to do a live album with only three years on the map, but we all knew the live album could break the band out and far surpass their previous success. And to top things off there was Steve, our ace in the hole.

In the dressing room the band was nervous and excited, but Dowd was doing his magic, roaming the room, talking to the guys, easing the tension and slowly calming them down. By the time they went on they were a bit looser and they probably played the best show of their lives technically, but they lacked that magic that drove most shows.

It was a great show, the fans didn't miss a thing, but it didn't have the spark the band was after and they knew it. We sat in the dressing room later, talking about what went wrong and what didn't, and Tom had them out to the truck to review the show, and point out any changes he thought they should make. It was a fascinating process as they worked through the recordings. When I left, Tom and the boys were still deep into it, Tom advising them which songs to do, the band sometimes agreeing, sometimes not. Tom had learned a while back that they would do what they wanted regardless of what anyone said, but he did have their ear and respect, so some of his suggestions were put into play without question.

It was late by the time we returned to the resort, almost 2:00 in the morning, just enough time to grab a drink in the bar.

Allen was flying, I think he might have been on speed but it could have just been adrenaline from the show. I didn't really know, but he was on a tear. Most of the rest of the band sat around and talked for a while over some weed in Gary's room, then retired for the evening. Allen, on the other hand, seemed hell bent on finding trouble.

The next day I found out he punched Dean, and that it had all been a misunderstanding. It seems Dean had yelled at Chuck over something at the gig. Chuck went crying to

Allen, so Allen took off searching for Dean and soon found him. Once we got the full story, it was I who had yelled at Chuck. Somehow Allen got the story confused and thought it was Dean, thus the punch.

The complaints were lodged as soon as everyone was roused the following day. The resort was nice, but nobody wanted to spend all that time driving to the gig. Almost everyone felt the same way, so it was decided we'd move into town... to the same hotel where the crew was, only a few blocks from the gig. I began the move.

Now that we were living within a few blocks of the theater, things were getting easier... or harder, depending on how you looked at it. The group was wandering around randomly, which was their habit when there was time off. The guitarists were furiously looking for guitars, not that any of them needed one except perhaps Leon, who seemed hell bent on competing with The Who's John Entwhistle, and had ruined more than one bass recently. The crew was in on the act also, jumping at the chance to add to their stockpile of strings, sticks, picks, and the like. And of course, there were other supplies required – we were here for a week. No doubt someone would soon sort that out.

The following day we broke with tradition and went for sound check for the full day, as everything was now in Tom's hands. We ate dinner at the theater, where Alex had some outrageous soul food brought in, and then the guys just hung out at the gig. Gary, Allen, and Billy even watched some of The Outlaws set. They probably did that out of courtesy, as we'd been pushing them around pretty hard the last couple of days. We denied them proper time to set up and sound check, not through any rivalry, but because we needed every second to get the recording set. You could tell that the Outlaws appreciated it, though, as they beamed smiles to the wings every couple of minutes. Later in the evening, the whole thing backfired and I got into another fight with them. They wanted to be onstage during Skynyrd's performance and I wasn't about to allow it. Both

Henry and Monty (the singer) wanted to kick my ass. I just ignored them, letting security handle things.

The boys were at their peak of performance for the next two shows. From the second they hit the stage, everything (and everyone in the building) just went off. That's all there is to it. They went off! Ronnie was commanding the troops and the troops were firing true, blasting the audience out of their seats. Each guitarist took their turn breaking to stage center, firing off a volley, then the next would follow, then the third, and then they'd trade notes back and forth, weaving three melodies, all anchored by Artimus and Leon. Then Allen would flag Billy, and Billy would play so hard you could almost see the keys smoking. He had me thinking we should place a fire extinguisher on his side of the stage. It was two evenings chocked full of magic.

Tom Dowd was everywhere and had taken a suite at the hotel, so every night he gathered the entire band and they listened to the shows and talked into the wee hours. It took a load off of me, having Tom commandeer the band, and it kept them out of trouble, so I had few worries at the time. I gladly accepted the hand-off to Tom.

While they were rehearsing and performing, I had been tasked with writing the band's acknowledgements for the album, and had collected a list of people each band member wanted to thank. It got fairly long, so it took another round to whittle it down to a reasonable size. When I showed the guys, Gary was the one that spoke up first.

"Sounds like it's been done by... some writer or somethin'..." he told me, "it just doesn't sound like us."

I rewrote it in a couple of minutes, really putting the country to it, and they accepted it on the second pass. Now we just had to get the liner notes from Cameron Crowe.

After the last show we decided that we'd all go out and loosen up, since we'd just put in a hard week. Alex Cooley spearheaded the outing, taking the band, Peter, Terry Rhodes, and me to a local club.

We were about halfway through the evening, all of us

sitting around a large table, yelling at each other in attempts to overcome the music and actually communicate, but it was fairly hopeless. Ronnie was the first to break out the blow. Someone had given him some at the show. He completely ignored the crowd, and simply uncapped a small vial and dumped the contents on the glass-topped table. Gary immediately emptied his as well, and soon Allen had a credit card out and was forming long, thick lines out of the shiny white powder. We thought we were inconspicuous in this place as it was dark, and virtually all of the patrons appeared wrapped up in their own world. Allen did a couple of lines, leaning over the table, a small plastic straw fished out of a drink at his nose. About that time, Alex stood up in a huff, yelling at someone. Alex was a big man. He stood about 5'10" and had to weigh close to 300 pounds. He sported a full dark brown beard and short dark hair, and he was all business. He also "owned" Atlanta... at least as far as music goes, but he had neatly inserted himself into local politics as well. As long as Alex was with us, I wasn't too worried about getting into trouble. Alex always took care of us and he had become one of my favorite promoters. In fact, out of all my business associates, Alex was undoubtedly the best. He was easy to talk to. He was understanding, compassionate, and smart, and when it came to business, you wanted him on your side. That's why he got our full attention when he jumped up from the table.

We recognized the problem immediately. It was difficult to miss: a cameraman from one of the local TV stations was leaning right over the table, taping us laying out the blow, and was about to catch Allen in the act of snorting it. Alex pushed him back several feet with one quick shove, grabbing the camera at the same time. Since the camera was secured to the poor guy, he was whipped back and forth in the action. Alex let him go, scolding him severely, threatening him with everything imaginable, and demanding the videotape from the camera. There was no hesitation and Alex was soon pulling videotape out of the cassette. Then he handed the empty cassette box back to the cameraman, warning him to never show his face in the establishment again. Alex in action, you gotta love it. For such a big man he could move quickly and forcefully.

We stuck around for a while longer after the incident, but the mood was broken, so we failed to close the club. We didn't even make it to last call. The incident did curb the drinking and debauchery that would have followed, so I guess someone was looking over us.

Peter and I managed to sit down for a while on the last day in town. We reviewed the remainder of the tour, and the band's recording schedule. Sally popped in while we were meeting and Peter informed me that Sally would be making the arrangements for a short jaunt over to England. We had been booked to open for the Rolling Stones in Knebworth. We'd also be doing a couple of warm-up shows to burn off the jetlag. I had been a bit upset with Rudge since the day before, because we had pictures taken for the album and I hadn't known about it. Evidently everyone else knew, but I had fallen out of the loop. What really pissed me off was that I was dressed in an old Pine Knob t-shirt and jeans and looked my worst. I would have just stayed out of the damn thing but Mary Beth got all huffy with me and insisted I had to be in it – this was the live album and the whole entourage had to be in it.

I also spent a bit of time with Tom Dowd and the band so we could set arrangements for mixing over the next couple of weeks. We wanted this project in the can as soon as possible, it had been delayed once already, and the record company was looking for it by mid-August. It was tight but doable, especially with our touring schedule, which was relatively easy for a change, because we were doing so many stadiums. The next day we were doing a back to back show, and it was a stadium. This was a big one, a benefit for Jimmy Carter's Presidential campaign, and it was in the band's home town. Alex Cooley was promoting it and had thrown together the whole Southern Rock nation for the event.

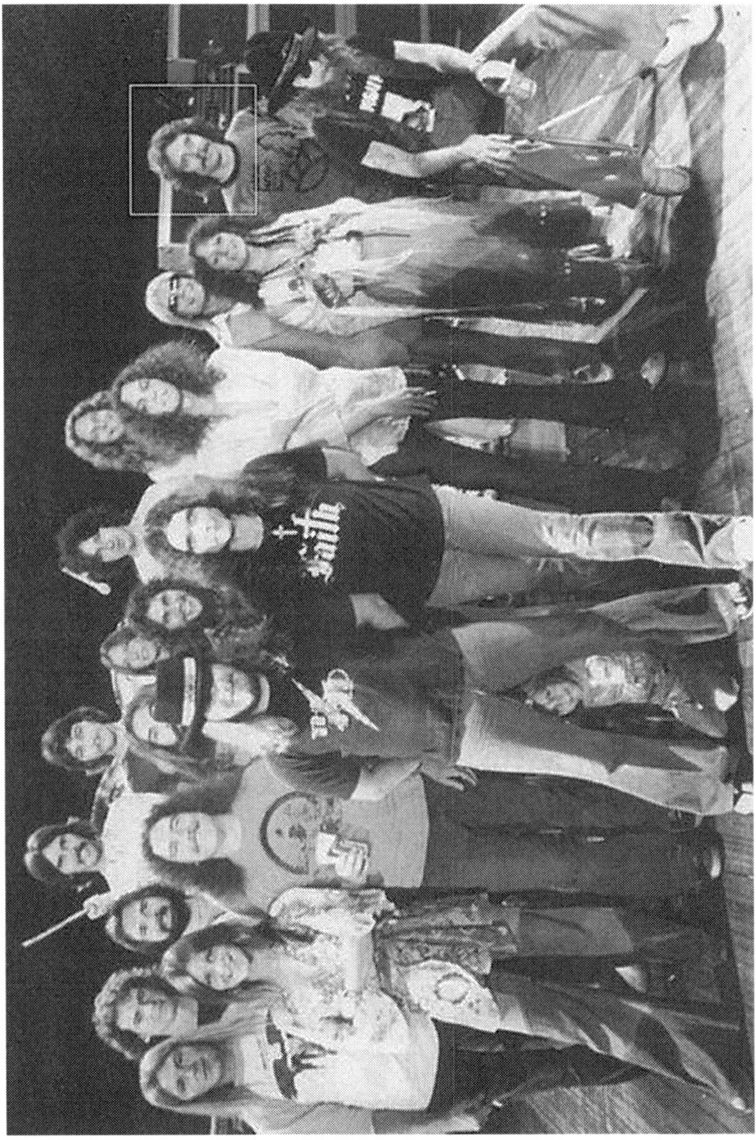

It was an all-day affair with all our friends, including Ronnie's brother's band, .38 Special. The rest of the bill was filled by The Outlaws, Charlie Daniels Band, Marshall Tucker Band, and Grinderswitch. It was a great line-up and no easy feat; all of us had to pass national security clearances to be that close to a presidential candidate. Surprisingly, everyone got through without a hitch, and these were some hot-headed musicians, a number of whom had been in more than a little trouble in the past: almost all had records, a minor incident on a police report somewhere in the country... at the least.

Ronnie was really nervous about the whole thing. He took great pains not to show it, but I had sensed it from the day it was booked. I could see it in his face - he couldn't help it. He hadn't wanted to do the gig in the first place, since he just finished four days straight, and we were heading to Muscle Shoals that evening on a charter plane. Tom Dowd was waiting for them there.

When we made it to the stadium, it was hot and muggy, and we were squeezed into a trailer set up as a dressing room, the norm for stadiums. It was split into a hospitality room and a couple of private rooms, and there was a separate trailer for instruments so they could warm up in private. It wasn't that comfortable to begin with and we had a non-stop parade of friends coming and going, so it became less comfortable as time went by.

Toy and Tommy Caldwell from Marshall Tucker came by, and Charlie Daniels. And then there was Henry and Monty from The Outlaws, and the wives and girlfriends were there, so the dressing room was constantly packed and wouldn't stay cool. Ronnie and I were spending a lot of time outside under the stands where there was some shade.

"Ron," Ronnie started, popping the top of a beer, "I don't think I can do this."

"What?"

"Yeah... I remember a party in Atlanta a year or two ago." Ronnie took a long draw on the beer. I followed his lead. "Jimmy Carter was there," he continued, "and he was just drunk as a skunk."

I had nothing to say. I didn't know where this was leading. I took another sip of my beer.

"Anyway, I been thinkin'. I don't think I can support the man."

"What are you saying? You want us to cancel?" I asked.

"I'm afraid so. But don't tell anybody I'm not supportin' Carter. I wanna get outta here alive."

"What am I supposed to say?"

"Tell 'em I can't sing. I've got a sore throat."

"I can't do that. Are you sure? You know what kind of trouble this is going to cause? This is Jacksonville! Everyone in that crowd came to see YOU." I was pleading a bit. This show was so important.

"Well as far as you know, Ron, I just can't sing. What can anybody say?"

"I can't make you do this, Ronnie, but..."

He cut me off, swelling his chest a bit in threat. It reminded me of one of those male birds on a National Geographic Special.

"I ain't goin' out there. In fact, let's round up everybody and get the hell outta here."

"Go get things going then," I told him. "I've got to go tell the promoter. This really sucks, you know?"

"I know, man. I'm sorry, I just can't do this. I'm not gonna support that man. I shouldn't be gettin' into politics anyway. And remember... I've got laryngitis. I'm not talkin' to anyone. Besides that, I can't risk my throat. It's already overworked, and we have to go finish the album tomorrow."

"Okay, okay. I'm going. You better disappear. And get everyone moving," I said as I headed to the production office. "We're going to have to get out of here fast when I get back."

Needless, to say, Alex Cooley wasn't a bit pleased.

"How can you do this to me, Ron?"

"I'm not doing anything to you, Alex. Ronnie has

laryngitis. He can't sing."

"This crowd is going to go berserk."

"Not if you announce it early enough," I explained. "They'll be okay. He's sick."

"Don't do this to me," he said, looking me square in the eyes.

"Ronnie can't go on. There's nothing we can do, either of us. You know I'd do anything for you, Alex. Anything. But I can't do anything about this."

I was lying my ass off. One thing was true, though – neither of us could do anything about it.

"I guess I don't have any choice," he said. I knew he was pissed, although he tried not to show it.

"I'm sorry, man," I continued my apologies. "Really sorry. I don't know how, but we'll figure out how to make it up to you."

I stopped by the stage to tell the crew, but I told them to wait until Alex made the announcement before they started tearing down. They weren't too thrilled, but at least they were home. Only Kevin and Craig were going to Muscle Shoals, and they were happy about the cancellation, because they'd have time to go home for a couple of hours.

Word traveled fast. On the way to the dressing room, I ran into Charlie Daniels. Charlie's a bear of a man with a short fuse. He lit right into me,

"What do you mean, Ronnie's sick? I saw him just a little bit ago and he was fine."

"Charlie, he can hardly talk. He's got laryngitis."

"Bullshit. I wanna talk to him." Charlie was standing straight. If he'd been a cat his ears would have been laid back.

"You can't. He can't fuckin' talk. He won't see you."

Charlie was a big man, and he was clearly threatening me even though he didn't say anything. I could see it in his eyes. We were head to head. Charlie left in a huff and I raced to the dressing room, finding everyone ready to go. Craig and I talked for a moment, checking on arrangements for the flight, and then Ronnie and I climbed into one of the limos and disappeared. He was hunkered down in his seat, with his head barely clearing the window. I glanced out the rear window to make sure we weren't followed. It was a clean getaway.

The next day it was all over the news. After Ronnie and I left, Charlie had talked the band into playing a few numbers while he sang. It was a good effort but didn't work. The participants in the riot numbered about 15,000, and another torn up stadium was left in our wake.

Next was Birmingham, where I arrived a day early, July 15th, same as the crew. They had a 7:00 am stage call that morning, the doors opened at noon, so if we did a sound check it would have to be done by 10:00. And the sound check had to be done.

We had a few new crew members that kind of came out of nowhere, surprising me. I had been tasked with controlling costs, but in New York I found that the band had added David St. John to the crew to take care of the piano. And another fellow, John De Castell, had been added for merchandising by SIR. The whole damn thing seemed to be moving in the wrong direction, and no one had even bothered mentioning it to me, at least not until after the fact. I was hitting a brick wall on the cost control assignment.

I met the band at the airport and we went straight to sound check. This gig was a good one, at Rickwood Field, the oldest standing baseball field in the country and it looked it. It seated about 10,000 people in the stands, and with the field open the number increased to about 20,000. Point Blank, Journey, The Outlaws, and Johnny and Edgar Winter, all acts I knew well, were on the bill. Point Blank was managed by an old friend, Bill Ham, the same manager for ZZ Top, and he had hoodwinked me into providing support for Point Blank through Clearlight a few years back, staging showcases and small shows in Houston. And Johnny Winter and I had actually played guitar together at some parks in Houston during the '60s. Once again I was surrounded with old friends.

It was a quick sound check. We had little time due to the number of acts on the bill, so we ran through it, ironed out a few technical glitches and headed for the hotel, where we had a good seven hours to kill.

True to form, the band spent a large portion of that time getting primed for the gig. So primed, in fact, that they decided they wanted to go to the show early so they could catch some of the other acts. That was never a good idea, because once the band hit a dressing room, the routine started. It was a habit for the band to start drinking as soon as they arrived.

We reached the venue at about 6:00 and wouldn't be going on until 9:30 that night, which left over three hours for drinking. I certainly wasn't happy. I never wanted the band at a gig more than two hours before stage time. Any more than that was far too dangerous. But today it was getting far too dangerous to leave them at the bar in the hotel. The funny thing: the band claimed they wanted to see some of the other bands. Once we got to the gig they never left the dressing room. Forget all the other acts, there was plenty of booze, pot, and blow.

Artimus, Cassie, and Leslie did accompany me to the stage, though, and we watched Journey perform – that was who we really wanted to see. And Billy managed to squeeze onto the stage during Johnny and Edgar's set. He wanted to watch Edgar play his portable keyboard. Edgar used it like a guitar, slung around his neck, so he could wander the stage instead of being locked down to a piano.

By 9:30 everyone was well into the booze, but had tempered their buzz with cocaine, so they were set to perform. In spite of six hours of non-stop drinking, they went out and slayed the crowd. I'm sure they were well lit from the booze, and I was in awe that they could still perform. It had to be the coke, loose from the booze and pumped from the coke – the current rock and roll recipe. It appeared to be a recipe that worked, at least this time, because they effectively transformed that stadium into one huge party. Everyone in the stadium was rocking, and rocking hard.

The drinking continued after the show and throughout the night at the hotel. The band closed the bar, except for Ronnie, as he was concerned with his throat. I'm not sure where that moment of sanity came from. Once the bar was shut down, the party simply moved and Dean had had the wisdom, or stupidity, depending on how you looked at it, to load up on alcohol from the gig. He had a full bar going in his room. As it was closing in on 4:00 am the party finally thinned out and the guys evidently retired. We had to leave the hotel by 8:30 that day, leaving less than four hours to sleep, which was plenty by our standards.

We were doing Tulane Stadium July 17 and expected a crowd of 50,000. It was us, J. Geils Band, and ZZ Top, and the Top had that crazy Texas World Tour going, complete with a stage shaped like Texas, rattlesnakes, a Buffalo, a Texas Longhorn Steer, a couple of buzzards, and a herd of tarantulas. I'm not sure how well all of that worked. It's kind of hard to see a couple of rattlesnakes and those tarantulas from the stands, and the Buffalo and Steer didn't dance at all, they just stood around chewing their cud and shitting, but it was the idea that was important. If they had put the buffalo, steer, buzzards, and rattlers all in one cage and called it a petting zoo, they might have had something. Or they could have put them all in one big cage with ZZ Top and you'd really have something.

I thought it was all a bit insane, and steered way clear of the snakes. Not that I got close to the rest of the critters, it's just those snakes... and during the day rumor ran rampant – the snakes had escaped. We found out later that it wasn't true and that the ZZ Top boys started it at every stop – it kept things interesting.

I entered the production office as soon as I got to the gig, finding quite a party atmosphere. Evidently things were going well. Don Fox, the promoter, was there, as well as Jim Donnely, J. Geils' road manager, Pete Tickle from Bill Ham's camp, and a few other people. The bill was not clear and we couldn't figure out who should open for ZZ Top. I had arrived thinking J Geils would be opening, they arrived thinking Skynyrd would open. There was quite an argument about the whole thing and the contracts weren't specific. We tossed it back and forth for quite a while but couldn't get anywhere. Both J. Geils and Skynyrd were huge, but I kept insisting Skynyrd was way bigger than Geils. You can imagine what Jim Donnely was telling me. It was a stalemate so at Pete's suggestion, we flipped a coin. Skynyrd lost. I never left the gig, since the band would be there soon.

When they showed up and I sat down with Ronnie, Gary, and Allen and explained to them the situation. By the time I got to the coin toss they were already irritated, which wasn't surprising - they all had fierce hangovers. When I disclosed the results of the coin toss, Ronnie spoke right up.

"Fuck it. I'm sick," he said. "I ain't openin' any shows."

It had been a long time since Lynyrd Skynyrd had been an opening act. Now that I thought about it, it was a terrible billing. Three hot acts, granted, but there was no opening act. I certainly didn't blame Ronnie for not wanting to open a show. He had paid his dues. And to tell the truth, his throat had been bothering him, so it wasn't a flat out lie.

"You know, guys," I told them, "we can't start cancelling shows. It doesn't take long to get a bad reputation, and we've cancelled quite a few this year already."

This caused a bit of a stir as they knew I was right. In the end though, Ronnie won. Once again I returned to a production office with bad news.

"I hate to break this to you, but Ronnie's lost his voice. We have to cancel."

Everyone in the office went ballistic. All of my buddies turned on me. There was nothing I could do but take it. First, Pete Tickle, then Jim, and Don Fox topped it off. I left the trailer, having taken all of their guff, gathered the band,

and split.

When the crew got back they let me know the whole show had turned into a bit of a disaster. Since the schedule had changed, the show was delayed and no one had announced that Skynyrd had cancelled. Since most of the audience treated the show as an all-day affair, they had been drinking in the parking lot for hours, and for a few hours more after the gates opened. By show time most of them were shit-faced, and after the J. Geils set, when the Skynyrd announcement was finally made, they came unglued. It brought back all of my old friend Sarge's advice. The New Orleans police, however, handled things a bit differently, driving their cars right into the crowd with lights a blazing. The cars were followed by a small army of uniforms, batons drawn and shields out. The skirmish was short, and after someone made an announcement from the stage telling the police to get the hell out, which they did, the crowd's attitude reversed, the trouble ended, and ZZ finally took the stage. That's when the crew left, having had enough of the spectacle.

After the New Orleans fiasco we all flew to our respective homes for a few days. Only two days on the road and we needed a break. I had some thinking to do, as this last outing was unacceptable, and we had a whole summer of stadium shows ahead of us. It appeared I also had a lot of work to do verifying our slots on all future shows.

I accompanied Ronnie to the airport later and saw the group off to Muscle Shoals. I would have liked to go there myself but I'd be of little use. I didn't get involved in the recording process. They had a good team, it wasn't my element, and I wasn't invited. I had my hands full anyway, I had only one week off with a wife I hadn't talked to in a while, a load of work in the office, and a run of stadium shows to organize and prepare. But at least I'd be home.

It was strange when I walked in the door. I had spent so much time over the last few years on the road it had become the norm and I was very uneasy being in one place for any length of time. Life changed so dramatically when making the transition, it was completely disorienting. I'd become used to being waited on, as on the road all meals were provided, or were available with a phone call, I traveled in limousines, and I rarely worried about money. Now everything was reversed. I no longer ate out for every meal, I'd cook for myself, I'd drive myself, and money was a constant worry. It was a very schizophrenic lifestyle.

Collapsing into bed as soon as I walked into the door, I cared little to get the last week's tour accounts finished. I was exhausted and feeling quite ill.

I slept for two days, rarely waking except for food or trips to the bathroom. I'd come to occasionally and it always took me a moment or two to orient myself. I was used to a hotel and waking in my own bed just wasn't right - it didn't feel natural. There was also nothing to do, at least nothing urgent, and that fact was tucked into my subconscious, which ensured I rested easily.

The morning of the third day home the girls rousted me. In my absence they had become best friends. Alice and Linda both jumped on the bed right before noon, forcing me to get up and take them to lunch.

Satisfied after a meal at one of my favorite restaurants, my disorientation subsided but when we returned home I still had this nagging feeling something was wrong. I went in to Clearlight knowing I would never be able to finish the tour books today so I reasoned that they could be put off until tomorrow. The shop was bustling. Albert had hired a huge crew to assemble the new lighting rig, and Peter had ordered a set piece, multi-colored chase lights inset into aluminum and Plexiglas steps. We had little time and limited funds to build the units. My brother Rodney had given Frampton a "sweetheart deal" on the project, and it was likely we'd lose money. That, of course, made Albert very nervous, and I shared his concern.

Alice and Linda wanted me to go out to dinner that night but I had gotten home so late it was unthinkable to me.

They took off anyway, promising to bring food back. They returned and woke me up for dinner, which I ate in bed. I hadn't yet recuperated from the road and was still suffering a bit of exhaustion.

I fixed myself breakfast the next morning, and while seated at the dining room table, a room rarely used as it was too formal, that feeling overcame me again. Something was wrong. Then it hit me. There was no tap dancing, no whistling. There was no Walter. I immediately left the table and toured the property, looking for my circus dog. He was nowhere to be found. Later that evening, when Linda got home from St Luke's Texas Heart Institute, where she worked as a nurse on Dr. Cooley's transplant team, she told me that Albert had put him down. Walter had gotten to the point where he could no longer walk due to arthritis and a host of other rather nasty ailments.

When I heard this I wanted to go to bed yet another two days. My poor cow-headed, dachshund-bodied buddy. I'd never see his tap dance again, or hear his whistle. That evening, after a sandwich for dinner, I climbed the stairs to my bedroom and collapsed in sorrow.

By the next evening I had recovered from the shock of Walter's demise and was feeling whole again. I had also slept for three days so I was feeling my oats. It was time to spend some time at the office, get some work done, and party as much as possible at night. That's as close as I could get to the road life. I really did love it, in spite of the fact that I hated life by the end of each and every tour. I had put off doing the tour books yet another day, but I purchased some cocaine from one of the guys at the shop so I could pull an all-nighter and have them finished by morning.

The next morning I went to the office and locked myself in with the leftover cocaine so I could finish reviewing and sign-off on the payroll. Albert stayed where he was the most comfortable, pushing the crew in the shop.

Having completed an exhausting week of catch-up at the office, by Thursday I was ready to rock and roll again, so

Linda dropped her daughter off at her mother's house, and Linda and Alice took me out on the town. We had dinner and then it was back to the Second Office, where they managed to get me drunk enough to dance. Once I got drunk enough to dance, which was rare in itself, I would dance until the place closed. Not that I'm much of a dancer, I was definitely not with it in the disco scene, but I managed to keep from completely embarrassing myself.

After closing the club down and a brief fight with the bartender over whether we had ordered our last round before the bar shut down, we returned home. At that point we all decided it was time for some pot, and Alice volunteered to go get some.

In spite of the late hour, Linda and I joined the other revelers in the house and continued the party. Albert was there, as well as Jim Brace and Mark Howard, both Clearlight employees, and a few other assorted characters. There was plenty of tequila, so we started in on the shots and margaritas. Then we started the games. Christine McVie had taught us a drinking game called Colonel Puff Puff, which was a short term memory test with a certain degree of coordination involved. It involved repeating a rhythmic line of text, which was repeated and added to as each person took their turn, and then you would clap your hands and complete some other gestures. If you got it wrong you had to take a shot. To put it the most simply, there was a huge amount of tequila consumed and we played until we were nearly blind.

The sky was just lightening, turning into that pale grey of early morning as fog rolled in. I watched from the dining room, gazing out the bay window as I sat next to it, chair half turned, my feet resting on the bottom of the window. The coffee couldn't have been better – it was the best I'd ever had at the moment, yet it was the same coffee I drank every morning. I had recovered. Deep in thought, I was pondering the upcoming tour and wondering how my marriage was going to survive... wondering if I wanted it to survive.

The day before my departure, Alice and I managed to sit down and talk, which was rare as we preferred to avoid discussions, as they always led to fights. I had begun feeling that the only way to keep this marriage alive was to go ahead and have it out, one way or another. It wasn't like I could ease into it, and I wasn't used to beating around the bush anyway, so I just asked her,

"Why do you always leave and stay gone all night when I come home? Where do you go?"

"Don't you party all the time when you're on the road?"

"It's hard work on the road," I argued, "and I can't party... I have to make sure everyone else doesn't party too much."

"Oh, you party," she replied. "You party. Don't give me that crap about how you don't have any fun on the road."

"I didn't say that. What I'm saying is that it's hard work on the road. I always have to be the responsible one. I never get any sleep. First one up, last to bed. You have no idea."

That was it, really – it was the same argument we always had, with each of our perceptions of my work 180 degrees off from the other. It was hopeless. Even when she came out on the road where she could see the amount of work required, she was always in the middle of the parties, away from me, so her own perception was always reinforced – the road was nothing but fun... one big party.

Having spent most of my time working and arguing, it was time to hit the road again. I was very disappointed when I left – Alice had gone out the night before I left and didn't return until sometime after two in the morning... again, and with no explanation. We had spent the morning fighting about it, right up until it was time for me to leave, and by that time I was so pissed off that Linda had to give me a ride to the airport. Mona came with us so I calmed down during the ride. At the airport I kissed both of them goodbye, and gave them a big hug. It looked like they were becoming my alternate family.

We were facing a run of stadiums on our next outing, and a quick trip to England, then a return to the U.S. to continue the Tour that Never Ends, all while mixing and finishing the live album. A grueling schedule, no doubt, but one that we were used to.

After my short stay at home I flew to Los Angeles to meet with Steve Wolf to talk about a headlining stadium show in Anaheim for the next year. I figured Skynyrd could fill it by themselves by then. It would be our largest show yet and I was determined to secure the band their largest payday as well. After a couple of days of meetings I squeezed $50,000 out of the gig. We had been receiving a wide range of fees depending on the locale, ranging from $5,000 to $25,000, but we had never received much over that. I was rather pleased with myself. Steve Wolf made me promise nothing would happen this time, one which I was glad to give. I gave them all the time, if they were broken it was never my fault – I could always credit it to the band.

From Los Angeles I flew to New York, where Sally and I huddled for another couple of days to iron out details for the upcoming Knebworth show. It was great working closely with Sally. My crush was still on but I was successful in hiding it from her and everyone else. After all, I was married and intended to stay that way since I still had some faith in the institution.

Ron in 1976 – you can see that he carried the bank bag in the front of his pants.

Heading to the stage:
Billy Powell, Steve Gaines, Ronnie Van Zant, Ron Eckerman

Photo by Ben Upham

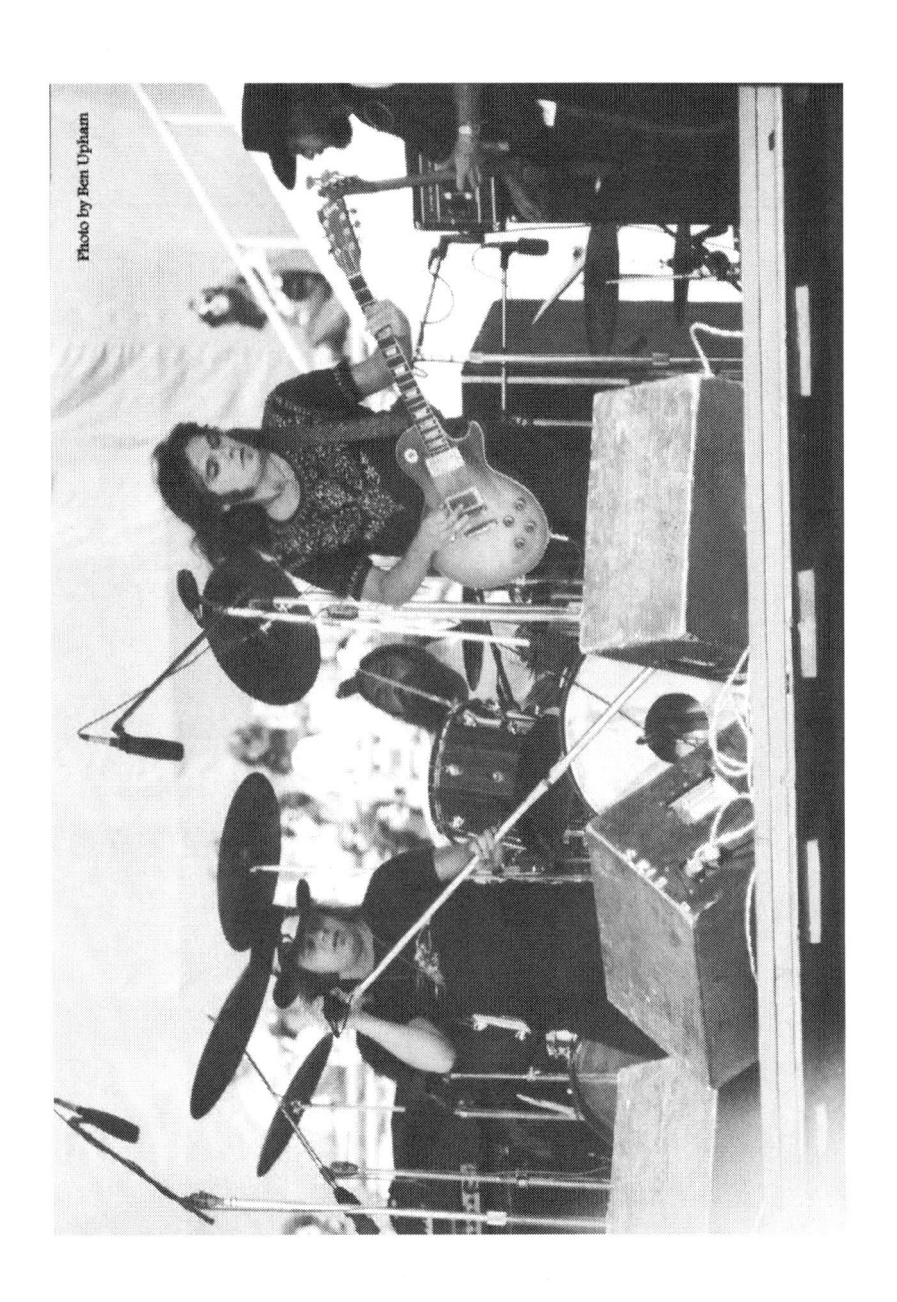

Photo by Ben Upham

Photo by Ben Upham

Ronnie Van Zant
Photo by Neal Preston

Leslie Hawkins, Steve Gaines, Cassie Gaines
JoJo Billingsley

by Neal Preston

Fox Theater 1976 Band and Crew

Ronnie with a fan's child backstage. Photo contributed by Karen Griggs

Leon with a fan's child backstage.

Ron Eckerman in 77

Ron Eckerman in 76

Linda, Mona, and Ron

CHAPTER 8

Gene had ousted Ronnie from his nap. He had been stretched out on the cabin floor, sound asleep. "What the hell's all this ruckus about?" That was the last thing I heard him say. Forever. The tension was building as we glided silently down. Everyone had gone comatose. I was still upset about the poker game but I, too, had gone silent. There was absolutely nothing anyone could do. We were slowly and silently drifting down, but it still didn't seem like we were in danger. I had seen an empty highway in the fading light and was convinced we were going to land on it. We were gliding smoothly, seemingly in complete control.

July - August 1976

When I arrived at the Miami airport on July 24th I had some time to kill before the band's flight landed. Luckily I ran into Steve Gaines, Bob O'Neil, and David St. John. Bob had flown in from Memphis, and David, the new keyboard tech, flew in from Dallas. We steered ourselves towards the bar but Steve, Bob, and I ended up getting coffee instead. David toasted us with his beer from the bar across the corridor. We didn't have long to wait and heard the group ten minutes before we saw them, spread out across the terminal, marching in unison, intense – they looked like they did when they were about to go on stage.

Turns out they had been arguing all morning as well. Not a good start for any of us.

We then proceeded to the Marriott, where everyone isolated themselves in their rooms for the evening. No camaraderie on this trip, at least none in view. We weren't too good at this start/stop style of touring.

By the time we gathered for the show the next day, things were returning to normal. I'm thinking everyone went through something like I did when they left... it was a common problem when you have loved ones at home.

We never got a sound check, and seldom did when on the stadium circuit, which was one of the reasons we used our own monitors. Although our new system wasn't without bugs and we'd yet to have a gig that afforded enough time to work them out, it was better than dealing with unknowns every day. And we had a new monitor mixer, Kenny Peden, so it meant double trouble, but at least we were using the same gear with the same person operating it. We expected it to get better each day.

The show at the Miami Baseball Stadium was initially booked with Poco and Crosby, Stills, Nash, and Young. Unfortunately things fell apart a few weeks before the show, with the CSNY bunch fighting amongst themselves – they should just settle it with fisticuffs like Skynyrd and keep on trucking. But they didn't, so it ended up as the Lynyrd Skynyrd / Marshall Tucker / Grinderswitch bill, which Poco rounded out, claiming title to a spot due to the original booking.

The whole thing just created more tension between us and the Marshall Tucker crew, they had the attitude that they were "saving" our show - we figured they were lucky to get a big gig.

It was hot and humid so tempers were short. That was turning out to be the norm for the summer, the heat, so you drank like a fish and sweated it all out by the end of the day. Maintaining hydration was a challenge, especially with the band who always preferred alcohol to water. After surviving the day, and performing surprisingly well considering all the tension in the air, we boarded a plane and flew to Tampa, where we'd repeat the same show the next day. From there it was home for two whole days!

I walked in expecting the worst, but hoping that things would change. They hadn't. Alice didn't spend too much time around the house while I was home, so I didn't either, just biding time at the office until the tour restarted. Alice came home late both nights long after I had gone to sleep. I guess things had changed after all, as Linda and Mona weren't there; they were at Linda's mom's house, so I had little reason to stay and every reason to leave. My whole perception of marriage was like a yo-yo. Up one day, down the next.

The next airlift took us to Pensacola, where we all flew in from our various homes, but our flights arrived close enough to gather at the airport. I arrived first and waited for Artimus. Then we met the rest of the group, piled into the waiting cars, checked into the beautiful downtown Sheraton, piled back into the cars, and to the Auditorium for sound check. The band finally got to tune in their monitors properly and were back in a coliseum where things were slightly more comfortable. It wasn't that we didn't like the stadiums, it's just the erratic schedule and fragility of the recent shows had burned us out. We needed a shot of normal back-to-back touring to put us in our rhythm. .38 Special opened the show for us, so Ronnie had his younger brother Donnie, who was a founder of .38, sing with him on *Sweet Home Alabama*. That was quite a treat, for the audience as well as the band and crew.

The next day I was awoken by a surprise phone call. I picked it up, slightly irritated that I couldn't sleep in, and heard a gruff voice on the line.

"Is this Ron Eckerman?" the man asked.

"Yes..." I barely replied, rubbing my eyes.

"This is Detective Randall (name changed to protect my ass) with the Pensacola Police Department. We have one of your group with us.... a Mr. Allen Collins."

"What happened?" I asked, exploding out of a sound sleep to trembling awareness.

"Mr. Collins has requested that we call you. Hold on a moment and I'll put him on."

I heard the shuffle of the phone.

"Roneckerman, man, am I glad to hear from you."

"What the hell's going on?"

"I got busted, man. They've got me in jail."

"Well, yes, I gathered that already. What did you do?"

"Uh… I had a few white crosses."

"Fuck, Allen! How'd that happen?"

"I don't know. You've got to get me out of here. They're going to lock me up."

I heard the phone shuffle again.

"Mr. Eckerman?" the voice asked.

"Yes?"

"We've got your boy here, and he's in a lot of trouble."

"What are you charging him with?" I asked, feeling my face heat up and my body pumping adrenaline like crazy.

"We're charging him with possession with intent to sell. He had about 500 amphetamine tablets on him."

"Jesus Christ. How much is bail?"

"$10,000. But he'll have to appear in court in a few days, and he can't leave the county."

"He can't leave the county?"

"No sir. He'll have to see the judge first. And even then he's not going to get out easy. We take this stuff seriously around here."

"Sir, do you know who he is?" I asked, clinging on to the slight hope that maybe the officer was a fan, or at least his kids were.

"No, I don't, and I don't care. As far as I'm concerned he could be the President of the United States. I'm still locking him up."

"Okay, I'll be over shortly," I said, after taking down his name, number, and the address of the police station. I sat in shock for a second or two, considering my options, then I pulled out my master list, the one with all the attorneys on it, and found the one in Pensacola. I dialed the number, praying that he was in. A few moments later the receptionist put me through.

"Andrew Sheppard here," (Another name change to protect the innocent and not-so-innocent).

"Mr. Sheppard," I started, "my name is Ron Eckerman with SIR Productions. I'm afraid I have a small problem with a band that I manage."

"Which band is that?" he asked.

"Lynyrd Skynyrd. We have a performance tonight and I just got a call from one of our musicians. He's in jail."

"What for?"

"He got busted with some speed."

"You need to get over here as soon as you can."

He told me where he was and how to get there, and I got there fast. He took me right in to his office.

"Let's see," he said, "who is the arresting officer?"

"A Detective Randall," I answered.

"Detective Randall... I believe I can help you out here."

"What's it going to cost and what can you do?" I asked, getting straight to the point. I was growing a bit impatient as I had no idea what was happening to Allen, but I had a good idea of what could happen.

"What's the bail?"

"Ten grand," I said.

"$10,000... you have that kind of money?" he asked.

"Not in cash, but I can write a check... a personal check. I have about $5,000 in cash, and I'd have to write a check for the balance." I explained. I sure as hell didn't want this to get screwed up.

"Well, $10,000 is a nice round number. I'll take care of this for that completely. You won't have to worry about the bail. In fact, you shouldn't have to worry about a thing."

"Done." I replied. I didn't hesitate a second, placing $5,000 dollars in cash on his desk and reaching for my checkbook.

"Just listen to this," he said as he picked up his phone and dialed a number from memory.

"Detective Randall? This is Andrew." A pause, then he gave his last name, followed by another pause. "I'm doing fine, thank you." There was another short pause before he continued. "Great, great. Listen, it seems you have a friend of mine locked up in there. He's from a band – the name's Allen Collins."

I couldn't hear the other half of the conversation. I didn't need to.

"Have you made out your paperwork yet?" he continued, and there was another pause. "Okay, good. What you say we get together for dinner and make out that report?"

After a moment or two he hung up the phone, looked up at me and said, "It's over. Your boy's on his way back to the hotel right now. He might even beat you back."

I thanked him repeatedly, to which he replied it wasn't a problem at all, and that I shouldn't hesitate to call if I had any more trouble.

Within a half hour after I arrived I was on my way back to the hotel. Problem solved. I had never had an inside view of our justice system at work, but my eyes had certainly been opened. I knew that we had been extremely lucky and this was more a rarity of justice than the norm.

The band performed that night to another sold out show, but in spite of pledges of good behavior, there was trouble. Leave it to the fans and their attempts to get on the stage. It had become a real craze in the last year or two. John was the one that caught him. He was heading straight for Ronnie, and looked just wild enough to cause some damage. John had him in a headlock in seconds, and was rushing him off the stage via the rear stairs. I didn't see him for a while after that, but in the dressing room I overheard a bit of the conversation between him and Allen.

"Man, that guy skidded across that parking lot."

That was all it took – I let John go, and sent him packing to Jacksonville.

Turns out when John got back to Jacksonville he had some gun charges and was going to be going away for a while. John had been packing a small handgun the whole time we were out. Handguns and this group don't mix, it's in Ronnie's own words, "Handguns are made for killin'...ain't no good for nothin' else..."

It was uncomfortable in the dressing room after that, and we had had the trouble with Allen earlier, so we loaded the cars and raced back to the hotel. I wanted us as far away from the city as possible but we couldn't get a flight out that night. I suspected we were being watched and another bust was imminent with that much money changing hands that fast and the incident with a fan at the show. But the lawyer held up his end, the cops didn't seem to care much about any fucked up fans, and we were left in peace. We soon forgot the whole episode, or at least had tucked it neatly away in the back of our minds.

The next day I called SIR and informed them of the night's circumstances. Then I called Houston to find a replacement for John. Robert Delgado, this large Mexican-American who used to tour with Mick Brigden and me when we were out with Humble Pie, was available. Mick used to call him Beaner, and it had stuck. Mary Beth was well acquainted with him too, and was delighted, so I had a ticket sent for him. He joined us in Nashville, where we had a sold-out show at the state fairgrounds with Point Blank, .38 Special, Ted Nugent, and Johnny and Edgar Winter.

I introduced everyone to Robert, calling him Big Robert, and also told them his alias was Beaner, so they had quite a choice of names. He was perfect for the gig: funny, good natured, patient, and big. Everyone called him either Big Robert or Beaner, depending on who was around. If it was just us he was Beaner. Iff we had guests he was Big Robert. The guys took him right in and he soon became a regular – our Southern gang of Village People was growing.

The guys completed a good show in Nashville, but it wasn't the best they'd done, and they knew it. The gig was kind of strange, as there was no audience allowed at the front of the stage. They were all a short distance away, so the usual mob at the front of the stage was missing. It was odd, and affected the band tremendously - they were playing long distance.

We never got our rhythm on this leg of the tour, and after a day off we ended it on August 1 back in Macon, Georgia, with .38 Special and Montrose. It was good working with Donnie and the guys from .38, and Peter Rudge came down again. He still wasn't taking any chances with his band in Macon. Now he had two of them there, as he also managed .38 Special, at Ronnie's urging of course. But they were as solid as a rock... solid as a rock band, anyway. You never knew what would happen with anyone in the music biz.

Peter commandeered the band after the show, barring me from the meeting, as usual. I was getting used to it. It still pissed me off but I certainly wasn't privy to all their business. I took the time to show Big Robert around and get to know the guys from .38 Special. I knew Donnie fairly well already but had never spent much time with the rest of the band.

I also took a trip a couple of floors down to see Sammy and Ronnie from Montrose, but as soon as I saw them, they acted very strange, very defensive. I drifted from that scene quickly, trying to figure out how that relationship had gone bad. I couldn't even remember the last time I saw them, and certainly hadn't done anything to cross them. I chalked it up to another road mystery and let the incident slip into a recess of my mind.

From Macon, the band flew to the studio to mix the album. This was certainly nothing I'd be involved in, I wasn't doing music production. My responsibility was for live performance. That was what I was hired for and what I did best, so I split my time between Houston and New York, preparing for the next leg of the never-ending but certainly slowing down tour.

CHAPTER 9

My thoughts turned to the inevitable – we were going to look pretty damn foolish trying to hitch a ride. Twenty-six people standing by an airplane in the middle of the highway. Then my brain took off on its own and I started thinking of the publicity. This was going to be huge. If people had never heard of the group before, they were certainly going to know who they were now. Especially since we were up against a wave of disco. Southern rock wasn't the "hot spot" it used to be. We were selling out almost every show, but now we'd have a front page headline in every newspaper in the world. I was certainly spinning this. Couldn't help myself. It's the nature of my thought process, the nature of a manager. And the last thing on my mind was an actual crash. It simply couldn't happen.

August 1976

Peter Frampton, Skynyrd, and Yes – that was the bill at the Hawthorne Racetrack in Chicago. It would be the first of many shows with Frampton, who was flying high off his live album. The first of many shows I would be doing with my younger brother, Rodney, and a Clearlight crew. Jim Brace, Mark Howard, and Steve Lawler were on the tour, old friends of mine whom I hired as the Clearlight client roster swelled. We were still working in a frenzy, trying to keep up with all the tours, and had personnel moving in and out of the company at breakneck speed. A lot of our recruits would join up and hit the road, only to find out that it wasn't quite the glamorous life they expected. I even hired Linda's estranged husband Rocky, who lasted about three weeks. A lot of these guys would simply get chewed up and spat out, such a high turnover was nothing we weren't used to.

The show was an eye opener. Lynyrd Skynyrd was untouchable. It was a mistaken billing, one that worked in our favor. It didn't work out that well for Yes and

Frampton, though, as Skynyrd attacked the stage with a ferocity that neither Yes nor Frampton could compete with. They didn't do badly... the stadium didn't empty, and both of the other acts were great, but there was a steady line for the exits after Skynyrd. This was the first time Beaner had experienced anything like it, and he couldn't stop telling me how amazing these guys are.

"You ain't seen nothing yet," I told him.

I flew from Chicago to New York early so I could get to the office, leaving Big Robert to get the band to the city later in the day. I was meeting with Sally Arnold to finish final tour details, and to try and finish and turn in the books from the Chicago outing. Sally was our go-to girl, which I was very pleased with, so Sally and I worked hand in hand for the next two days.

Then the airlift was on again – this time from Chicago to London via New York. Peter and Mary Beth were already in England as Peter was handling the Stones' tour. We arrived in London toasted – those overseas flights always took their toll, and we weren't the best passengers on the plane. Far from it. Our concept of flying didn't drift too far from our concept of touring: drink as many drinks as you can to pass out so you wouldn't feel the trip.

The plane landed with our entourage intact. No one was thrown off the plane. It would be a bit difficult to throw us off in mid-flight, granted, but that didn't mean they didn't want to.

The stewards were quite pleased when we first boarded. After all, we did have a bit of notoriety and they were rock stars, but our status definitely correlated with time spent on the plane. By the time we crossed the Atlantic we were out of favor with the entire flight crew and most of the passengers. By the time we arrived in London, the boys were jetlagged and hung over big time, walking zombies... with tempers.

We got through customs and immigration easy enough, it appeared they just wanted to get us through and out of the terminal as quickly as possible. It was a good thing Big Robert was with us. He was cracking so many Mexican jokes in a British airport that you couldn't help but snicker.

We flew into Heathrow, so there was quite a drive ahead of us, and we were still on U.S. time, even though it early in the morning, our bodies told us it was evening. We checked into the hotel with ease, and everyone retired to their rooms for a while.

We did a warm-up show at Hemel Hempstead the next day, August 19th, to get a taste of the Brit gigs, which were always challenging.

Then it was on to the Knebworth Fair, where we would be opening for the Rolling Stones. It was quite a venture, just getting into the gig. The quaint British roads were packed and were barely adequate for the traffic. It wasn't often that they had a half million people showing up in Reading, where the Knebworth festival was held.

We managed to get to our trailer early in the day, and after making ourselves comfortable we began roaming, both individually and in groups, as there were a ton of celebrities there. This was the show of the century, with us, 10CC, Todd Rundgren's Utopia, Hot Tuna, and the Don Harrison Band, and it was rumored to be the Rolling Stones' last concert ever. That, of course, proved to be false, as Peter had stated it was the Stones' last concert at the Knebworth Fair, but when the press latched on to it they added the last show *forever* tag.

About midway through the day, Leon grabbed me.

"Roneckerman, come on, come on," dragging me and Gary into a nondescript trailer to one side of dressing room alley. It was dark inside - not pitch black, but your eyes definitely needed to adjust for a while as the sun was blazing outside. Leon, Gary, and I pressed ourselves into the circle, all of us lined up against the walls of the dressing room, strangers for the most part, all with one goal – getting as high as possible while maintaining function.

It was a challenge. I waited patiently and quietly in the

cool, dark comfort of the trailer and I was rewarded within seconds. The joint came from the right, I took a mighty hit off of it, and passed it to my left, my eyes adjusting just enough to recognize individuals.

The individual to whom I was passing the joint was my hero, Jack Nicholson. He saw the surprise in my face, and answered with his classic look – he raised his eyebrows and shot me that sinister smile. Here's Johnny. Once I blew all the smoke out of my lungs I turned to him.

"McMurphy?" I asked.

He just smiled, raised his eyebrows again, and replied, "Yep, Randle McMurphy, at your service."

I gave him my best raised eyebrows, a smile, and the joint. Shortly afterwards Leon, Jack, and I were out of the trailer and walking towards the stage.

We were walking three abreast with Leon on the far right, yapping non-stop to Jack. We were approaching the chain link fence that secured the stage, which had a small gate built into it. I saw it all before it happened. Leon wasn't going to clear the gate. He ran straight into the post, and he was still looking at Jack, so he took a direct shot to the right side of his face and crumpled to the ground. It was just like a Road Runner cartoon, where Wylie Coyote runs into a cliff, hangs for a second, and then slides down the cliff face. So went Leon.

We ran into Paul McCartney on the way to the stage, and stopped for a moment to talk. It was just small talk and neither Jack nor I was very good at it, and Paul was a bit aloof anyway, so it quickly ran its course and Jack and I proceeded to the stage. I found out later that Cassie and Leslie also ran into Paul, and he snubbed them, so later, after the Skynyrd performance, when he wanted to meet them, they snubbed him right back.

The stage at Knebworth was huge, and the opening was staged with these giant blow-up lips, and there was a long ramp, probably forty feet, that curved down into the audience. When you looked at the "big picture" right before the Stones went on, it looked like the Stones' logo, with big lips surrounding the stage, and that long ramp was the tongue. During most of the day it was like any other stage, as the ramp was covered with a black tarp and the lips were deflated. There was plenty of room to run, so the crew had made up some really long guitar cords so our pickers could use the ramp.

We sat through most of the other sets in the dressing room trailer, making short trips to the stage to monitor the event. Things were running late from the start, as the crowd was much larger, and had much more trouble getting in than expected. Since the first act didn't go on until most of the crowd was in, we added that hour delay to the list.

By the time Skynyrd went on it was at the prime part of the day, just as the sun was setting, providing this great orange light beaming onto them. Lighting by God again. He always did a great job.

The concert in full was filmed, and was released more than 20 years later in a documentary entitled *Free Bird the Movie*.

The crowd, all half a million of them, was fairly reserved. This was something I expected – British crowds were different than Americans. It must have been that stiff upper lip thing. The band was hotter than ever and relatively straight for a change and was working their hardest to get some response out of the crowd, who were milling about, fetching beers, and generally treating the show as background music. The band kept it up, playing their fiery tunes, weaving those guitars, building the performance up and up, until finally, when they launched into *Sweet Home Alabama*, the first fifty rows or so started moving to the music. Peter was doing his best as cheerleader, crouching down in front of the side fills, punching the air and flailing his arms about, his eyes shifting from the crowd to the band and back. They didn't leave the stage as they normally did, ending the set with *Sweet Home*, but just walked to the back of the amp line for a smoke and a drink. Then they went back on to the praise of at least some of the crowd and launched directly into *Free Bird*.

Most of the crowd continued to mill about, but there were quite a few who sat back and listened attentively as Billy played that delicate, classic intro, and then Gary laid his guitar on top. It was a tough crowd, to say the least, but then the ballad portion of the song came to an end, and the guitar mania began. That was when the audience transformation also began, and about two minutes into the onslaught the entire audience came to life.

Everyone had been warned throughout the day that the ramp (the tongue) that extended into the audience was off limits. That was for Mick and the boys, but you can count on Ronnie. He could care less about any rules, especially from the Stones. He was out to beat them at their own game so he crept up behind Gary and Allen during their solos and pushed them down the ramp and into the audience. Then he stood there with them, swaying, using subtle moves of his arms to direct his soldiers. Then he went back up the ramp a few steps and, like a quarterback, waved Steve Gaines down, and now had all three of his sharpshooters on the ramp with him and the entire audience was going nuts. This pressure cooker kept heating up, with everything going fine until Leon decided to follow Steve. That's when we found out that Leon had been short-leashed.

Gary, Allen, Steve, and Leon were blasting their way further down the ramp, full speed ahead, planning on getting some upfront and personal time with the audience, with Ronnie about ten paces behind, flagging them on. Then Leon hit the end of his cord, and he looked like he was doing the Limbo. It bent him straight backwards from the waist and almost pulled his bass out of his hands. (This can be seen in the concert footage and you can see me, as well, in the background jumping up and running suddenly when this happened.)

The band finished the last ten minutes of their set split, the guitarists and Ronnie down the ramp, the rhythm section: Artimus, Billy, and Leon at the top, and even the girls were dancing around the stage, goading the audience on, having left their position. Peter was in on the act too, cheerleading from the sidelines, much more active than usual. Seeing half a million folks rocking out, about half of them playing along with the band on air guitar, was astounding... and powerful, and something never to be forgotten.

It was all like a dream once we were back in the dressing room, everyone had experienced it and no one could believe it. The audience, somewhat taxed from a long day of drinking and drugging, had been awakened. They'd been shaken awake by music.

Two hours later the Stones took the stage. I was told they were having technical problems with the lips. I suspected they didn't really want to follow Skynyrd until the crowd had some time to come down from the trip. Evidently I was correct, as the reviews in the music mags and papers the next day claimed that Skynyrd "skinned" the Stones on this one.

We were on our way back to the hotel before the Stones appeared – everyone had wanted to see them but when I pointed out that we wouldn't be granted stage access the band was ready to hit the road. There had been a bit of partying before we packed it in, but it wasn't excessive. Everyone was simply fried from a long day in the sun. We still had jetlag and we only had one day before we were returning to the States. That was to be followed by a quick run of four shows over five days, followed by a couple of days off to catch our breath. There was no sense hanging around Knebworth waiting for the Stones, especially when no one knew when they might take the stage. They finally got on just before midnight.

KNEBWORTH FESTIVAL 1976
WELCOMES AMERICA'S CONFEDERATE ROCKERS
LYNYRD SKYNYRD
ALONG WITH THE BEST ROCK & ROLL BAND IN THE WORLD
BRITAIN'S OWN
ROLLING STONES
ALSO
10 CC
AND
TODD
RUNDGREN
BANK HOLIDAY WEEKEND
AUGUST 1976

The stage at Knebworth

Knebworth Concert
Allen Collis, Ronnie Van Zant,
Gary Rossington, Steve Gaines,
and Ron Eckerman at far right

CHAPTER 10

The atmosphere in the plane was that of a ghost ship. Everyone and everything in it was blank: zombies hurtling to the end, blank faces, and vacant eyes – all pale, the color had washed out of everything. I had never realized how important color is in spite of being a lighting designer for many years. It's human nature - we never appreciate what we have until it's gone, and when something is taken from us, something invaluable to our senses, it tears a hole in our very being. I'm sure everyone in the plane was experiencing the same feelings... one glance through the cabin confirmed it. Now color had vanished, and all normal sounds had vanished, only to be replaced with an eerie silence accompanied by the faint rushing of air from outside, and our ability to think had vanished as well. Minds were occupied with one thing: prayer. Although no one on the plane was overly religious, everyone was deep in prayer. God... help us.

August – November 1976

Springfield, Massachusetts was where we picked up the U.S. tour again on August 24th. We had flown into Boston so we wouldn't have to deal with New York. To tell you the truth, it wasn't much better, but at least we were reasonably close to Springfield, and the connecting flight was only forty minutes.

Johnny and Edgar Winter were on the show, an act we had worked with, so we knew there wouldn't be a hassle on stage, and everyone had managed to get some sleep on the plane - the sedatives we scored before we boarded the flight in Heathrow came in handy.

We finished August with a show in Lewiston, MA, followed by South Yarmouth before finishing up at an outstanding gig in Asbury Park, N.J. It was with Jeff Beck, every musician's hero. We opened for him, and no one minded... it was the least we could do. After all, he is the guitar God.

The entire band stayed at the show that night, and watched Beck's entire performance, something you don't see every day, and something I never saw again.

September 1976

Back in Houston things were in a frenzy. The Peter Frampton set was running late and over budget and it was getting close to impossible to make the deadline. The latest set-back came after I was home for a few days. We had just assembled about ten of the pieces complete with all lamps and wiring in place, and the Plexiglas that served as steps. It got fairly cool that night, after a sweltering day, and the Plexiglas had contracted, fracturing about 90% of the pieces. We were almost back to square one. Each unit now had to be disassembled, new plexi cut, and then reassembled, insuring there was enough room for expansion. Nothing but major headaches on that front.

The band had a few days off but they were chomping at the bit to get going again. They were working on a new album, even before the live one is released, and wanted to get into the studio to lay Steve's tracks down. He had a song that was ready to go, it was from an old project he had done, and he had written a new one since he had been with the band. This had enthused Ronnie, and he was also ready to go with a couple of new ones, so we had hurriedly thrown a session together with Tom Dowd at Criteria Studios in Miami. Everything was set. I had flown to New York and was working on the next tour when the news came in. It happened a couple of days before they were supposed to go to the studio, on Labor Day weekend. I was sitting in the office I now shared with Chris Ehring, who had been hired by Peter to run publicity, both for Skynyrd and a few other groups Peter managed.

Selma buzzed me and told me I needed to take a call. It

was Ronnie.

"Ronnie! How's everything?"

"Not good. That fuckin' Gary… and Allen."

"What happened?"

"Car wrecks. Both of 'em."

"Oh my God. Are they okay?"

"Nothing too serious, but Gary's hand is all messed up."

"Damn. That's going to set us back."

"I've about had it with the whole lot of 'em. Here I have a baby on the way, tryin' to make sure I gotta secure future. I can't put up with this shit much longer."

"What the hell happened?"

"Quaaludes."

"Idiots," I snapped back.

"I don't know what to do about this," Ronnie told me.

"All you can do is write about it," I said, trying to be clever.

"Smart-ass."

We were off the phone a few minutes later, and the staff and I were trying to figure out the next step. We cancelled the studio. Tom wasn't pleased. Then we cancelled the first few dates of the tour as well, including a monster show at Anaheim Stadium with Aerosmith.

Ronnie was calling every few days from Jacksonville, and he was mad as hell. He had been laying down the law, and was none too pleased with his boys.

Gary had tested his new car against an oak tree over Labor Day weekend. The oak tree was damaged but would survive. Gary's car did not.

Allen had his own accident – totaled his car but he was left only with minor injuries. It could have been much worse. Some hefty fines had been levied against Gary and Allen, Ronnie told me, and he had warned them both that he had had about enough, and if they wanted him to stay in the band they had better get their shit together. He went on and on about how this band was not going back out until they were all cleaned up. It was time to get serious, this was business, and so on. It went on for days, and then he called with a change of course.

"We've got a hell of a song. It's called *That Smell.*" He had written a song after the car accidents, about whiskey bottles, brand new cars, and oak trees that get in the way. The chorus was "Can't you smell that smell? The smell of death surrounds you." I'm certain you've heard it!

On September 19th, he called again, much later in the evening than he usually called.

As soon as I heard his voice, I asked, "What have they done now?"

Ronnie started laughing, and continued when he caught his breath.

"No man. It's not that. We had our baby. Melody. She's the sweetest little thing you've ever seen."

I congratulated him and gushed as much as I could. I was really happy for him. He'd been so excited when he told me Judy was pregnant, that that now paled in comparison.

In the meantime I had been working on a show in Houston. I had called Louis Messina, the new promoter in Houston, having moved in from New Orleans, and asked him to put a hold on The Summit for November 24th. He promised me he would and that he'd be glad to co-promote the show with me. I then talked to Ronnie and Peter about promoting our own shows. Ronnie was fairly keen on the idea, but Peter preferred to stay out of the promotion business, saying it was all he could do to stay ahead of the management game. In the end I convinced them to allow me to promote a few shows in the future. It was the perfect opportunity: the band would make much more money, and I would make what I should without adding any expense to the band's operation. It was a win-win situation.

By the time Gary healed enough to play, about three weeks had passed. I had spent the last week in New York with Peter and Mary Beth, and they had graciously included me in future plans not only for Skynyrd, but with the management company.

Peter asked if I would move to New York where I was needed, and offered additional money from SIR if I would. I told him I would seriously consider it and then we sat on his sofa, reviewing demo tapes to decide which groups to take on in the future.

We listened to Cheap Trick, and looked at their pics and promo package, but decided they just didn't have the right look – that was quite a blunder. Then we talked about Fleetwood Mac as Peter had been hot on them for years. If we could sign them, Peter offered Mary Beth and me an equal percentage of the management fee. This was all well and good, but I knew there was no chance of that one happening, and I didn't have the heart to tell Peter that the band despised him. I have no idea where it came from, that animosity between the Mac and Rudge, but they must have had relations sometime in the past. All I knew was that when his name came up in conversation one time, Christine McVie said,

"Oh, please. Peter Rudge is the last poufter we'd have around."

Finally it was time to hit the road again, and we made the airlift to the first gig in Wichita, Kansas on September 21st, still flying by commercial airlines. I was overcome with joy to be back out on the road with what I considered my real family. Alice could hardly be considered family anymore – it had gotten that bad.

We hit the circuit and hit it hard. Moving from Wichita to Omaha, and then a dreary day off before heading back to Lawrence, Kansas, followed by a stint in "the big skies," we finally weaved our way to the West Coast. The whole stint through Wisconsin, North Dakota, and Montana was relatively uneventful, with the guys in the band coming to the conclusion that the area had nothing to offer. Nothing to offer except the endless plains and big sky… and, by unanimous decision, the women with the largest breasts in America.

There were numerous parties as usual, which I successfully

avoided, but no trouble... or at least nothing major enough to note. We escaped relatively unscathed, both physically and financially.

October 1976

We checked back in to the Sunset Marquis, our home away from home, promptly upon our return to Los Angeles. It was good to be back, especially with a healthy band.

It was the usual scene, but we had only one day off and that was the night before the gig, and that day was spent traveling so the flurry of activities we would normally have were heavily curtailed.

The gig was at the Starlight Bowl in Burbank, kind of an out of the way open air amphitheater, so the heavy contingency of L.A. music industry was almost non-existent. It had sold out early and we did very little in promotional activities. It was a simple slide in, do the gig, and slide out, and we did it relatively unnoticed.

That night, Ronnie and Gary arrived at my room and had a young girl with them.

"Ron, I want you to meet someone. Linda... Linda Blair."

I had not recognized her at first.

"Hi, Linda. I'm Ron Eckerman. It's really nice to meet you. I loved The Exorcist – it scared me to death."

They got bored with me pretty quickly, said goodbye, and started touring Linda around the hotel. She was there right up until the time of our departure. That concerned me. She seemed awfully young.

From there, we crept up the coast to Santa Barbara, then on to Concord, finally working our way up to Spokane, Seattle, and Portland. The Santa Barbara gig was memorable. It was a college town, with college girls, and they loved to show their boobs. The band loved it, and none of the rest of us minded it, either.

We made one detour off the West coast in between Concord and Spokane. I assumed Terry Rhodes thought the tour was looking too easy for us, so he threw Salt Lake City into the mix. Actually I knew better, and Salt Lake City made a lot of sense, but as far as the band was concerned it was thrown in just to mess up the schedule.

We had climbed a notch on the West coast, graduating to coliseums rather than the smaller theaters we had appeared at a few months ago. It was a big step, adding about 10,000 seats per venue, and in most instances we either sold out or came damn close. The band had been on good behavior on the tour, and Ronnie stayed reasonably sober. All in all, everyone had calmed down considerably, and John Butler was finally off the tour. I have to credit the absence of John to the better behavior of the band, at least partially. I don't know why, exactly, but there seemed to be a correlation between the band's behavior and the presence of John. Perhaps he created the tension for job security. I'd never know now. Big Robert had fallen into his gig well, and he was glued to Ronnie. He watched him like a hawk, which relieved me of some of my chores, so I was thankful he was with us.

The atmosphere in and around the band had done a sharp 180, which I credited to the new blood, Steve Gaines. He inspired them all, both musically and personally. Leon was even using his time to good purpose. He surprised me in the dressing room several times, showing me new songs he had been working on, which were really difficult to make out on bass, but he got the ideas across.

Steve was always showing the guys a new song or hot lick he had come up with, and Ronnie was scribbling lyrics all over the place. He never needed them as he seemed to memorize everything he wrote, but I still had a bunch of scribbled lyrics I had collected just in case.

Since things had become so much calmer, it gave me the opportunity to actually mix with the band a bit and I began visiting their rooms after the gigs. It was quite an eye-opener, as I had been on the road for years and resigned myself to hotel living. Then I went to Artimus' room and it really knocked me out. He carried various scarves and materials he had picked up over the years and had completely redecorated his room. I expected the normal bed and dresser/TV arrangement with a small round table and a couple of chairs by the window as normal. I walked into a Middle Eastern tent, complete with burning incense and muted lighting. Nothing was as it should be.

He had moved his bed out from the wall and to one side, and had removed the second bed frame completely. It stood in the corner but the mattress and box spring had been stacked on the one he kept, giving him a bed that was about two feet taller than normal. He had also walked the dresser into the corner, where it now sat in the corner. The round table was next to the dresser with the TV on it, and everything in the room had been redone with these Asian and Middle Eastern scarf motifs. It was very exotic, and the scarves he had draped around all the lights set it off perfectly. There was incense in the air, and after letting me in, he climbed back onto his bed and assumed a yoga position. It had such a calming, peaceful effect on me that I wanted to stay, so Artimus and I had a long talk about everything astral. Midway through the talk, he let it slip that he had taken some acid a few hours before, which helped to explain the elaborate redecorating.

By the time I left, he was laughing hysterically at everything, and when I walked out the door he was deep into *The Planets*, that fantastic classical piece by Gustav Holst, and was listening to the *Mars* section over and over.

From the west coast we broke all ties with rationality, traveling east, inserting a gig in Denver on the 12th and New Orleans on the 14th to help provide some funds to get across the country. It didn't make a whole lot of sense, but this was rock and roll. There were a lot of things that didn't make sense. We were following the money, and the money led us back to New England.

Barry Fey showed us a good time in Denver, promoting a sold-out show, and insuring his caterer loaded us up with his famous barbecue ribs. We always remembered Bear's ribs – it had a lot to do with our willingness to repeat Denver so often. Plus, the fact that the fans were so rabid.

New Orleans was also a unique experience. It was the band's first gig in Don Fox's famous concert club, The Warehouse. The Warehouse is true to its name: it's a warehouse. It's dark with no frills, the acoustics left a lot to be desired. There was a mismatch of carpet on the floors, and the smell of stale beer always hung in the air. It's a wonder anyone would come to see a show there, but the place was legendary and had a draw of its own. It was a habit with quite a few residents; every couple of weeks they'd go to The Warehouse – it didn't really matter who was playing, but if you caught someone you really liked, it was a bonus.

The Warehouse was the envy of concert promoters across the nation and quite a few promoters were scurrying to put their own "warehouse" together. Few were successful.

We had ample time to travel from New Orleans to Landover, Maryand on the 20th – five days, so most of the band flew home, although Cassie and Leslie decided to stay in New Orleans for a day or two so they could explore the French Quarter. I would have loved to stay with them, but work called, and I had the Houston show booked, so even though I wasn't too keen on my home life at the time, I flew home.

I walked into a vacant home when I made it back to Houston. It wasn't surprising. In fact, I was getting used to it. I settled in, unpacking my bags, throwing most of the clothes in the washroom, and began working the phone.

I remained on the phone for hours, still wondering why the house was empty. Linda would be working, Jim and Albert were probably at the shop, Rodney was on the road with Frampton, but Alice should be around. Then again, Alice was never around. I don't know why I even kept the house anymore. I didn't use it. Apparently Alice didn't use it much either, but at least Linda and Mona had a safe place to stay.

Alice finally made it home, with Linda and Mona arriving a few minutes later, followed by Albert and Jim. It was a bit awkward, everyone arriving home at the same time, as everyone knew Alice and I weren't exactly the lovebirds we used to be.

While in Houston I ran the figures on the November show, and Alex Cooley came in to meet with us and set up a partnership while Marilyn, my assistant, handled the local promotion. Alex was brought in by Terry Rhodes to assist in promoting the Houston show just in case I got sidetracked, which could happen at any moment when you consider the mob I ran with.

The preliminary arrangements went smoothly, but I was concerned going head to head with the Top, so I came up with this great campaign to get all the local DJs and personalities behind the show.

I stole (borrowed, really) the Jack Daniels logo, and had it redesigned for Lynyrd Skynyrd. It was cool. On the first pass my artists, Jon, misunderstood, and I never met with him to proof it. Once it was published in the Houston Chronicle I saw the errors. Instead of just using the Jack Daniels logo pattern, he had recreated a whole bottle.

On the second pass, however, Jon did a great job and made the necessary changes. The new ad was just what I had in mind, and served multiple uses

Then I had one pint whiskey bottle labels made with the new Lynyrd Skynyrd /Jack Daniel's label. We bought a couple of cases of those one pint bottles, steamed off the labels, and stuck the Skynyrd ones on. I gave them away to all the local DJs, personalities, and radio stations to promote the show. It was for them, for their own consumption, to get them excited, and it worked, at least until the radio stations started giving them away over the air. That's how Jack Daniel's got wind of it.

Now the local Jack Daniel territory manager wanted to see me. I figured he wanted to do an endorsement deal with us. I got it wrong.

I arrived at his office in downtown Houston right on time, and I was only kept waiting a moment in his secretary's office. When I walked in he seemed pleasant enough, offering me a seat in front of his desk. He was a massive man, probably about 6'3", and must have weighed more than 250 pounds. On his desk sat a pint of Jack Daniels, complete with the new Lynyrd Skynyrd label. He got right to the point.

"Do you know how many laws you're breaking when you change a label on a beverage?" he asked gruffly.

"No, I don't think I do," I said. This wasn't what I thought it would be.

"Do you know what we could do to you for changing and using our logo?"

"I don't know that either," I said. "These were meant to be gifts to people for helping us with the concert."

"What about this?" he asked, slinging a newspaper to me. It was folded back to an ad for the concert, with the full blown label in use.

"Yeah, I figured we should continue the image."

"I don't think so," he told me, "what you'll do is discontinue use of these ads, and you will not change any labels on these bottles. In fact, you won't do anything that even resembles a Jack Daniels label."

I apologized. He accepted, and I ran right into his doorway as I was leaving. His secretary laughed a little when I passed her desk.

"He can certainly intimidate people, can't he?"

When I didn't answer she continued, "Don't worry about it... at all. He won't do anything."

With that said I didn't change a thing, but I didn't give any more whiskey away. I never heard from him again and I continued the whole campaign, which the group totally embraced, adopting my design into their t-shirts and merchandising. They made a considerable amount of money off of it and both me and Jack Daniels received nothing, unless you want to count the meeting. The Jack Daniels manager got to ream me and I got reamed.

Lynyrd Skynyrd's Old Time Old Rock n' Roll Brand Florida Sour Mash Whiskey

While in Houston I called my mother, advising her about a Time Magazine article due out in a few days. The reporter had interviewed me so I knew mom would get a thrill out of it. By the time it was released, Mom had told all of her friends and family and half of Houston was looking for it. Then it hit the newsstands and I wanted to call Mom back, but it was far too late for that. Entitled "The Rotgut Life", the reporter described our life on the road, and he nailed it. It was your basic "white crosses" (speed) for breakfast, whiskey for lunch, and anything and everything for dinner" type of piece. My mom never said a word to me about it.

From Time Magazine October 18, 1976:

The Rotgut Life

No American rock group works harder or equals the decibel level of Lynyrd Skynyrd, a band of seven Southerners who seldom see their homes outside Jacksonville. An energetic blend of English heavy metal and funky, rural blues, Skynyrd's music occasionally dominates its lyrics, but their rabid fans like it that way. The group has sold more than 3 million albums. It's 5th LP, ONE MORE FROM THE ROAD, has recorded sales of 350,000 copies since its release 4 weeks ago.

Most pop bands must tour constantly to stay afloat, and Skynyrd's "Torture Tours" are legend. Occasionally the group will give 250 concerts during 300 days on the road. During one 95-day stretch in 1975, they did 88 one-nighters. Last week they traveled through 4 Western states, giving 5 concerts in 7 days. The ceaseless motion soon takes its psychic toll.

"After awhile you turn dingy," says Ronnie VanZant, 27. "Your mind and body won't take it."

Morning-after blues are a particular problem. But a quick Dexamyl, followed by several white crosses puts one right for breakfast. A little scotch on the bus mellows the transition between motel rooms, and a bottle of champagne primes one for the performance.

"This is a rotgut life, but why worry?" smiles VanZant. "We attract mostly drunk people and rowdy kids who come to shake."

The main release for the group is simple violence. Between them the members of the band have chalked up over a dozen arrests on such charges as assaulting a police officer and possession of amphetamines. Last year Skynyrd ruined more than half the exercise machines at Nashville's Spence Motor Hotel. During a recent trip to Bristol, England, VanZant threw an oak table out a fifth-story window.

"We were just having FUN, letting off pressure," he remarked afterward. "It was funny when the cops came in and looked at us like we were mad dogs."

Drummer Artimus Pyle's recent target was the Macon Hilton, which failed to include sugar with his room-service order of iced tea. "I tried to throw the TV out the window, but it wouldn't fit. So I splintered everything else." He sighs: "Whew, it always feels better without that tension."

With a $40,000 line of credit, plus $2,000 pocket cash carried to take care of impromptu pillage, Road Manager Ron Eckerman, 24, promptly pays damage bills averaging $1,000 a month. That does not heal all wounds. In many cities, none of the major hotels will rent rooms to Lynyrd Skynyrd. When the band plays in Atlanta, for example, they stay at a resort an hour's drive from the city. Bassist Leon Wilkeson is not concerned.

"We're hot now," he says. "Let's keep running."

I was more than pleased to get back on the road. The band flew into Landover, which was just Northeast of Washington, DC, so we flew into the Baltimore airport to avoid beltway traffic. The Capital Centre, a relatively new sports arena, sat in the suburbs of Washington, D.C., and held about 20,000 attendees for concerts, and the boys damn near sold it out, riding on the success of the new live album, *One More From the Road*.

It also had these giant video screens hanging off the scoreboard, and it was one of the few times we had a video shot of the concert. The band was restless, all but Ronnie, having a few days off and traveling from New Orleans to Jacksonville and then on to Landover, and were ready to get back into the routine.

Ronnie was a bit distracted from the road life, because he had a new baby. It was really that lifestyle, the road, that beckoned us, and the road life was the life we chose to live, preferring it to our home lives, which were repetitive and boring – gaps which we simply tolerated. That was why the boys always got into so much trouble when they were home. Thank God it was time to hit it again, in the nature we preferred, back to back shows until we were ready to collapse.

From Landover we traveled to Boston where we had The Outlaws back in tow. We didn't stay at my favorite hotel. That one was done with us, but the good old Stouffers took us in. The band had been on good behavior recently and remained so while in Boston... we remembered the last time we were there.

We were up early the next day, catching a puddle jumper to New York, which was a little frightening, as the small plane seemed so insignificant squeezed between all the jets when we taxied out... and when we taxied in once we arrived.

I was back in New York, my home away from home. It always amazed me how much I'd taken to the city. We rolled in fairly early as we had a sound check and some interviews to do, and I needed to get by the office and dump my briefcase. I was carrying tons of paperwork I needed to get rid of. Things were popping in the city, as the new album was in the Top Ten, and the band was on top of their game, having slacked off the partying for a while. That's what those oak trees will do... Gary can tell you that. They have a way of calming you down, those trees, and work very efficiently when you run into them at 45 mph.

Ronnie and I even decided to hit the gym in the hotel before we got too busy. Ronnie and I attacked the machines with gusto but soon it wasn't long before we were done, sweat pouring from us. Ronnie suggested we start out slow and work our way to better health over the course of the tour. I agreed, more than ready to quit. Neither of us was in bad shape, but we both smoked and it showed. Even though we had the best intentions, Ronnie and I never approached a gym on the road again.

We had two days at the Palladium, a scruffy old movie theater/vaudeville house. It was the place for concerts, as it held enough people to be worthwhile yet provided an intimate setting for a show. It was also a full on theatrical house, with a grid system for flying scenery in and out, a beautiful proscenium, and real dressing rooms, and it was a fairly easy gig to play except for the road cases. The stage was rather small, so they ended up tucked into every cranny, creating a small maze which had to be negotiated to get to the stage.

On the first night, at the end of an especially hot performance, during *Free Bird*, Leon broke a string and it really pissed him off. It's almost impossible to play a bass if you break a string so when it came to the final flourish, he went out WHO style again, tossing his bass in the air and letting it fall to the ground, then picking it up by the neck and slamming it to the stage, finally tossing the useless instrument into the audience. Leon was just pissed off, and he ruined a perfectly good bass. This was the third in a short time and they weren't cheap – over a grand each.

The next day it was in the local newspaper. Turns out the instrument struck yet another girl when he threw it, and once again we spent the day trying to apologize. In spite of our good will, a lawsuit was filed. It was the second; Leon had started a collection.

After the show, MCA Records took us out to a great dinner at The Palm where we gorged ourselves on lobster. They had the best, and largest. We had a few drinks, some more than others, until the regulars were quite inebriated.

At the start of the show in New York, I couldn't find Artimus. He had disappeared several times during sound check. Although the band didn't seem concerned, not even when I gave them the five minute warning, I was mystified. Were they going on without a drummer? I followed them to the stage, with Craig leading as usual. It was very strange when they took to the stage without Artimus, and I should have known what was going on.

The band started that rumble of *Workin For MCA*, but with the guitars only... no drums. Then there was a roar from the crowd, and when I looked to the stage, there he was. Artimus was not only being lowered to the stage on a pipe, he was hanging by his knees, upside down, and that pipe was coming in fast. It slowed and finally stopped as he reached the drum riser, and then he made an extremely awkward dismount, managing to land on his drum throne and strike the cymbals perfectly on cue. He was lucky.

I reamed him after the show, and finally got it across just how dangerous this was, and how he put his and everyone's well-being at stake for the stunt. The stunt was never repeated, so I assume I got through.

There was quite a party at the hotel that night. I gave Ronnie the suite and everyone ended up in his room for a while at least. After an evening of drinking and debauchery, with guests often disappearing into the bathroom for a boost, the pairings began, there were a lot of women there.

After my wake-up call I laid in bed for a while watching the news on TV: the usual stuff, the NY marathon had been won, Mao was replaced in China, a cricket match made headlines. Sufficiently bored, I swung my legs over the side of the bed and winced from the pain. My knees weren't bending, or at least not bending as well, and the pain was intense. I pulled them back into bed, panting. It had taken my breath away.

I ordered breakfast, wondering if I had injured myself when Ronnie and I had visited the gym. I didn't remember anything unusual, but Ronnie and I flew through the rotation quickly, and really didn't exercise that much. It was more of an effort for show. Ronnie showed me he could exercise, I did the same, and then we called it quits. No sense breaking into a heavier sweat or waking up sore. At least that was the thought process.

I limped along for another week, finishing this leg of the tour, and suffering the cold as we ran through Rhode Island, Connecticut, and New Jersey.

November 1976

We started off November with Flint, Michigan, then played Kent in Ohio, and all we could do for the day was sing "Four Dead in Ohio" as all of us felt that song strongly, and here we were right in the heart of the event.

From there it was back to NYC for a performance in Long Island. By then I had picked up a cane and my knees were starting to swell, causing a flashback to their old road manager, Gary-on-a-cane. I was becoming Ron-on-a-Cane.

Ronnie was getting very concerned with my health; it was kind of difficult to hide the cane and the limp, and Rudge and Mary Beth were also taking notice. When I arrived at the office after the Long Beach gig, Rudge, Mary Beth, and I sat on the couches in Peter's office. It was decided that Mary Beth would go out with us for a while to give me a hand, and that she would do the upcoming Japan tour.

"You've been to Japan, haven't you Ron?" Peter asked.

I replied that I had, so when Peter suggested that Mary Beth manage that excursion, as she had never been there. I agreed. Then he asked if I could move to New York to help with management again and even offered me a higher salary. Since I loved New York and there were additional funds involved, I accepted. I was turning Yankee.

I spent a week in the office; the band had all gone home for some vacation, and my knees kept on swelling. After seeing a doctor, I called home, letting Alice know that I was probably going to be hospitalized in New York once we returned from Canada, where we had a single gig in Toronto on the 15th. Alice didn't return the call for a couple of days, and when she did, I wished that she hadn't.

"I'm just too busy to come to New York," she told me.

"Why not? What the hell are you doing?"

"I'm busy. I have a life, you know."

I was confused. Alice didn't work, didn't attend school, and didn't do anything that I knew of, but she was too busy to come to New York? It was baffling. I thought I knew her well. Then we got married and the truth reared its ugly head. Ever since our relationship had been on the rocks. It was a true love/hate thing we had going on, but the balance was swinging, with the hate side gaining momentum.

I had to admit it was probably more my own fault than hers, as I spent over nine months of the year on the road. If I wasn't on tour with someone, I was flying around taking care of other business. On the rare occasion I put any thought into it, I realized part of these travels were really attempts at avoiding my home – avoiding confrontations with her.

Mary Beth and I met the band at Kennedy airport and we boarded the flight to Toronto a short while later. She had brought some hash with her, a little sheet of the stuff that was about a half inch thick and four or five inches square, wrapped up in aluminum foil. We had enjoyed some together the night before but I was unaware that she had brought it. When we went through customs, I was made *very* aware of it. The customs agent chose my bags for a random search.

I placed my two bags on the inspection table and he promptly unzipped the larger of the two. He threw the top open, and right there, on the top, sat the aluminum foil. I didn't remember packing it, and I looked over at Mary Beth, who was in the lane across from me. She flew right through customs and was taking care not to look my way. She knew what I had. She had put it there.

The agent grabbed the aluminum foil package, carefully placed it to one side, and proceeded to probe my clothing. He was thorough, patting the clothing as he removed each piece, then patting down the case itself. Once he was satisfied, he neatly folded all my clothes and placed them back in the suitcase and then placed the aluminum foil package right back on top, just the way he found it, and waved me on through. I would have been sweating bullets if I allowed myself, but I kept cool, thanked him, and proceeded into Canada. I had run the gauntlet… and won. But my heart was pounding – this was definitely as close as I ever want to get to smuggling.

I was increasingly hobbled as both knees grew to the size of softballs, and after the show in Toronto, Ronnie pulled me aside.

"You're hurting too bad, Ron," he told me, "so I'm sending you home."

"I can't go home, Ronnie. I hate it in Houston."

Ronnie and I had spent plenty of time discussing our home lives, so he knew I was going through some rough patches.

"I don't care where ya go but ya gotta get better. So go home, Ron. Houston, New York, wherever you're callin' home these days. I'm orderin' you. Understand? Same as I would with Allen or Gary or Steve or any of the guys. Get your ass straightened out so you can come back. If you keep goin' downhill, you won't be doin' us any good, and you won't be doin' yourself any good, either. I need you. You go get yourself well."

It was no use arguing with him once he'd made up his mind, and I knew in my heart he was right. I wasn't doing myself or anyone else any good.

The next morning I called SIR, who wanted to know who was replacing me. I didn't realize that was my responsibility, so I called Jeff Dunham, another of the guys I had toured with. He worked with Brigden and me when we were out with Humble Pie. He could do it, but told me he thought they were out of his league. I told him that was nonsense and that I'd be home the next day to go over things and show him the ropes. I thought Jeff was pleased, or at least he should have been, because he'd just been hooked up with the definitive American band. I called Ronnie and told him what was going on; he was fine with it, then I called SIR and got their blessings.

Jeff picked me up at the airport when I flew home. I briefed him on the band, and tried to cover all the personalities of both band and crew, and could tell it was fairly overwhelming. Jeff told me I'd have to tell him the whole story again – he wanted to take notes. When we arrived at Holcombe House, he helped me in and got me settled on the couch, and then fetched all my luggage. It took several hours, but we finally got through everything. He had a quick primer on box office settlements, his biggest fear, and tour management, which he was accustomed to. He took copious notes, especially on each band and crew member, and, as our meeting came to an end, I gave him the same warning that Allen Arrow had given me:

"Don't let Dean carry your briefcase. Trust no one with it."

CHAPTER 11

I stared blankly at the players sitting across from me. They stared blankly back at me. Our card table was in shambles, having been ripped from its mooring, now hanging lopsided against the wall of the cabin where it normally hung square. Cards and money were scattered about... a few dollars here, a few dollars there – most had fallen to the floor, and I noticed face cards everywhere, all landing face up, all that royalty staring back at me. And they were all black. We still felt like we were in a controlled flight, we weren't sinking like a brick. Instead, we were gliding comfortably, but now even I was starting to feel a bit panicked. My secure thoughts of the publicity coup had diminished, and my head was slowly filling with a much grimmer reality.

November – December 1976

After explaining everything to Jeff, I limped into the bedroom and collapsed into bed. My knees were now the size of footballs and no longer flexed, so I had to walk stiff-legged. They were like water balloons. If you pressed on one side all the fluid would simply shift to another location, it was a squishy mess with a hard circle of knee cap floating around in there somewhere. The pain was unbearable and had gotten to the point where suicide would spring into my mind, but it would spring out just as quickly. It wasn't even close to an option, just a quick thought of instant relief.

Along with the pain came depression. I was unhappy that I couldn't function normally, concerned about the longevity of the illness, worried about my marriage and my position with the band and SIR, and then there was Clearlight. I was so deeply involved with so many things my dysfunction seemed it would collapse my entire world. I dug around all the medicine cabinets and hiding places, finally locating some Percocet, so I fell asleep and remained that way through the afternoon and into early evening, when Alice came home and stuck her head in the door to check on me. I heard Linda and Mona, as well as a few other houseguests. I grimaced and swung my feet out of bed and made it about ten feet, then returned. Alice was making me dinner, which she brought to my bed. Linda introduced me to her new boyfriend, John. I enjoyed the meal and conversation and pulled the covers back up to my neck, still unable and unwilling to walk despite the painkillers.

Later that night, things were so quiet, I decided to get up and roam the house. I was unsure if Alice had gone out, but she certainly hadn't joined me in the bedroom. I grabbed my cane, pulled myself out of bed, and hobbled down the stairs. The pain bordered on intolerable. Since I was stiff-legged, I had to kind of hop down the stairs, and every time my foot impacted the next step the pain would shoot up my leg from the knee to the point things would go grey. Then I'd rest until my head cleared and take the next step. It took a while. When I turned the corner and passed into the living room, I found Alice lying on the sofa with Linda's boyfriend John.

Neither Alice nor John saw me. I raised my cane over my head, coming down on the glass coffee table in front of them, destroying it with three blows. The first was the best, shattering glass everywhere. The remaining two blows were out of frustration - the damage was done with the first. Then I just continued, not stopping until everything in the room that could be broken was, screaming at the top of my lungs the whole time.

John and Alice were both startled and scared and scrambled to their feet. I'm sure they thought I was going to beat them to a bloody pulp, but I was simply working the rage out of my system. I'd never harm a human unless they threatened me, but I love to destroy inanimate objects. They don't put up much of a fight. My demolition work had woken up Linda and Mona, and Linda made it downstairs in time to see my wife and John run out the door.

Linda settled Mona back to sleep, and came into my room

and climbed into bed with me. She was as pissed off as I was, so she started in, explaining what Alice had been up to.

"She's been screwing around on you for a while now," she started, "and I'm so sorry I haven't told you, but I'm Alice's best friend... or I thought I was. I'm so sorry," she said. I thought it wasn't cool at all of her to keep it a secret what was going behind my back until after it affected *her*. After all, I was providing a roof over her head and trying to be a father figure for her daughter. But, she was sorry, so I let it go. We ended up spending the night together. I found myself wondering why it hadn't happened before.

The next day, after getting Mona up and in school, Linda took me to the hospital where I would spend the next week. They sliced and diced my knees, scraping out dried blood and draining the fluid from beneath the kneecaps. The pain had increased multi-fold, something I didn't even know was possible, so I was begging for the Dilaudid they were pumping through me.

Once released from the hospital, with my knees still the size of footballs, Linda, Mona, and I moved to the Stouffer's Hotel not far from the hospital. I needed some home life so it made perfect sense to move to a hotel... home sweet home. Linda and Mona both loved it.

Holcombe House and my relationship with Alice were now officially finished. That era of my life was over; that chapter of my life was closed.

My knees were definitely not getting better, so Linda took me to see my old doctor, Dr. Porras, who had immigrated to Houston from Columbia. He examined my knees and wasn't sharing any of his usual jokes. After probing around a bit and looking over the x-rays, he looked me square in the face, and his expression wasn't one I wanted to see.

"You know, we have nothing like this where I come from," he started, "I'm not sure there is anything we can do for you here. We could continue with treatments here in the States, but we aren't very successful with this. First, we don't know exactly what's going on. It appears to be a very severe and acute onset of rheumatoid arthritis, but I have not seen it progress so rapidly before. We have ruled out everything else. We really don't know exactly what it is. To tell you the truth, most patients will end up with this on and off for the rest of their lives."

This certainly wasn't sounding good. "So what do I do?"

"Like I said, we don't have anything like this in Columbia. If you can, I think you should get as close to the equator as possible, and stay there for as long as possible, or at least until your knees are back to normal... if they ever are."

His prescription didn't sound too bad, actually. And if it was really my only shot, get me on a flight - I'm ready.

When I got home and explained the situation to Linda she hit the phones, and everything was arranged. Her friend Her friend DeNise was staying in Guadalajara with her boyfriend Tony, who was attending medical school there. They had a big house on the outskirts of town and would be vacating it within the next two weeks. We could have it until the lease expired a month later.

I met with Alice the next day. She was staying with a girlfriend in an apartment not far from Holcombe House. She pleaded for us to stay together. It was really sad, and I did feel bad about the situation, but our marriage was dead.

I talked her into checking into a rehab center for a month. At least she'd have a nice clean start, but I felt a bit like a heel checking her into a rehab facility and running off with her best friend... well, her ex-best friend. Life can get complicated quite easily, and it felt like I had just been sucker-punched and bitch-slapped, but at least I now had a future I could look forward to with Linda and little Mona. I liked the idea of being a father.

During the week, I was promoting the Lynyrd Skynyrd show, a Dickey Betts show, and a couple of dates with Della Reese, all in Houston, so that kept me grounded. I'd be seeing the Skynyrd boys again Wednesday and couldn't wait. I was praying I'd make it through all of it.

The Houston November 24 show was sold out. In fact, it was oversold. Once the building filled, my buddy Sarge found me and told me I had about 300 angry patrons that couldn't get in. He explained that he had to do something, because the crowd was milling around and didn't look like they were going to leave. When I asked him what we should do, he pulled out a roll of generic tickets.

"Let's get them in. We'll sell these tickets as standing room only, and let them know they may have obstructed views. That'll be the easiest way."

As a result of Sarge's advice, Lynyrd Skynyrd held the attendance record for the Houston Coliseum until it was demolished. Sarge went home with an extra $300.00, his commission on those tickets.

I spent some time talking to Ronnie in the dressing room that night and walked him to the stage, my arm draped around his shoulder, both in friendship and for extra support so I could walk.

I couldn't make it up the stairs leading to the stage, so I asked him to do a good show in Houston for me as he marched straight up the stairs. He went out and did my will – it was a breathtaking show. He pulled me aside as soon as he came off stage after the performance, grabbing me by the shoulders and looking me straight in the eye.

"Ron," Ronnie said, "you're still hurtin'. Hurtin' bad. You're finished until you go get yourself well. Ya understand? I ain't gonna tell you this again. Here I thought you were healin' and I get to Houston and find out you're workin' and promotin' a bunch o' shows. Get your ass well."

My first impulse was to argue the point, but I really didn't have a leg to stand on... literally, so I just responded,

"I love you, man, so I'll do what you say. I don't like it, but it is what it is."

"You'll be fine. Rest up, get your health back. We have a hell of a year ahead."

We started back to the dressing room, me limping and holding Ronnie's shoulder for support.

"And hey... I love you too, Ron," he said. "I usually don't tell guys that, you know what I mean? You're my brother, you got nothin' to worry about."

To say I was discouraged would be an understatement. I was severely depressed. Ronnie said don't worry about it, though, so I did have something. My concern was the unknown, if I'd ever heal.

I disobeyed Ronnie and followed the group to Fort Worth, the next night, where they were playing another of my venues, the ones I worked constantly, the Tarrant County Convention Center.

Ronnie knew I was there but also knew I wasn't there in any official capacity, so after a short explanation he let me get away with it. He knew I was going back home the next day, and then going on to Guadalajara for rest.

I soon noticed that Joe Barnes was missing. When I asked Ronnie about it, he kind of dismissed me, he didn't want to get into it, so I asked Craig where he was. Craig told me that Joe and Ronnie got into a fight on the plane, that Ronnie had punched him a couple of times, so Joe quit on the spot and caught a flight back home. Now they needed a good production manager. I suggested Clayton Johnson, from Bill Graham's bunch, but didn't know if he would take the job. At least it was something to think about.

Dickie Betts was on the show that night, and Charlie Daniels, and next door was Frankie Avalon. It turned into a wild evening.

Dickie cornered me right before Skynyrd was going on and wanted to see the band. When I told him he couldn't, he gave me a small vial of cocaine and told me to give Ronnie and the boys a toot before the show. So I accepted it and disappeared into the dressing room. I limped over to Ronnie, handing him the vial, telling him it was from Dickie, and that he wanted to make sure they had a good show. I was going to just give Ronnie the vial – he was just supposed to take a toot, then I was going to return it to Dickie.

It appeared Ronnie still held a grudge in spite of the peace offering, so he wipes a portion of a counter off with his sleeve, takes the vial, and dumps the entire contents. Then he pulls out a bill, rolls it into a tube, and snorts about half of it, then the bill went to Gary, then to Allen, then Steve, and everyone else in the room that wanted any.

I returned to the hallway, empty vial in my pocket. Dickie was still there, patiently waiting for my return and for the rest of his blow. I handed him the empty vial. He looked at it, looked at me, tensed up like he was going to throw a punch, then he just turned and left.

"Ronnie said thanks!" I called out as I watched him storm out.

I still had one more score to settle before I went on hiatus. I went to Charlie Daniels' dressing room, found him, and talked him into coming with me. I had some people I wanted him to meet. He followed me down the hall and into a corridor that linked with the other theaters in the complex. I guided him to the meeting room where Frankie Avalon and company were. Frankie was so heavily made up – and limp wristed. I knew Charlie was going to hate this.

Then the introductions began – Charlie was introduced to Frankie and all the sweet guys surrounding him, and they kept Charlie tied up for about a half hour. They were fans, they loved *Fire on The Mountain*. I left Charlie with them but he caught my eye as I slipped out the door and gave me one of those "I'm-gonna-fuckin-kill-you" looks. It cheered me up so much I forgot about my knees for a while.

Three days later, on November 28, my 25th birthday, Mona, Linda, and I were on a Mexicana Airlines flight to Guadalajara. It was warm and sunny, and we were so excited. I had accepted Ronnie's advice and I didn't have a care in the world at the moment. Although I did however, remember feeling like at age 25, I was getting old. That's hilarious to remember that now.

It was tempting to stay there forever, but after a couple

of weeks, it was a miracle that my knees were almost back to normal. My cane and the new one I had purchased at a market both stood in the corner, unused and unloved.

It was about that time that I started thinking about the band and longing for the road. It wasn't that the family experience had gone bad... far from it. I was loving life, but home was New York, or at least in a hotel somewhere in the world other than Mexico. In ten days it was time to go anyway, the lease would be up.

We left in time to get home for Christmas. We wanted Mona to be home in Houston so we could spend the holidays with family.

Back in Houston, I called Ronnie and the office. I called Rudge and told him I was well and ready to get back to work. He grilled me about my health, but finally told me to get back to New York.

I was on a plane the next day, telling Linda to get packed, as we were moving to the city.

Once I met with Peter and felt secure enough in my job, I flew back to Houston to get the girls, then all three of us returned to New York.

CHAPTER 12

I gazed out the window at the approaching landscape. It was dark but I could still see an open highway with no traffic. I could still see wide open fields on both sides of the plane, but I could also see that we were heading straight for a patch of woods about three times as wide as a football field. The woods appeared to be made up of tall pines. I couldn't really see well enough to discern exactly what the forest was composed of and it really made no difference at this point. All I knew is that it was a thick forest – thick as the east Texas woods I had grown up knowing. And if I was correct it would be comprised of large trees, perhaps a hundred feet high, and the ground cover would be at least chest high and so thick you wouldn't be able to walk in it without a path or a sickle with which to create one. I realized one other thing at the moment: the forest was approaching fast, or rather, we were falling much faster than I cared to acknowledge.

January – February 1977

The band was due to arrive in London from Tokyo on January 25th, so I flew in on the 20th to help Sally finish organizing the short tour. We were doing twelve shows in three weeks, crisscrossing England to ensure we covered the whole country. The band had grown quite popular since the live album had been released, and the well-publicized appearance at Knebworth had spiked popularity. England was catching on, and catching on fast. One of the music mags even reported a healthy market for confederate flags, but that was probably a result of our publicist's work, not actual sales.

The moment I arrived at Heathrow, I saw Sally. She gave me a warm hug and a light kiss before searching for her Mini in the parking lot, and then we were off.

It was a bit unnerving, driving on the wrong side of the

road again, especially with Sally driving. I'm not saying she was reckless, but she was definitely aggressive. She dropped me off in London at the Royal Lancaster and stayed until I was settled in so we could visit a pub and have a quick drink. I was suffering from jetlag, so it did me in quickly. Sally made plans to pick me up in the morning and I retired to my room. This was far more difficult than I expected, as in spite of my jetlag and the drink, I was wired. It was the time difference, but after tossing and turning while, I finally fell asleep.

The band and crew came through customs in small waves. Sally and I were waiting on the other side of the barricade and every few minutes a couple of the entourage would pop through the door.

Ronnie and Cassie were the first ones through and Cassie gave me a warm, lingering, welcome kiss, right there in the waiting area. Ronnie gave me a big hug. Mary Beth and Gary were next through, and Mary Beth also gave me a quick kiss on the cheek as Gary and I punched each other's shoulders. Big Robert and Dean brought up the rear, Big Robert high-fiving me and Dean affording a quick smile. He wasn't in the greatest shape after the long flight.

By the time we loading everyone into cars, we had spent a good four hours at the airport and it was yet another hour's drive to the hotel. It was exhausting, just getting the band in, so Sally and I sneaked off and enjoyed a drink at the local pub. When we returned, we found our sneaking off for drinks, which was to prevent the band from getting started, was futile. The bar was full… and most of the patrons were from Skynyrd.

Ronnie and I soon moved to a private table so we could talk, as it was getting loud in the bar. It was drinking hour, and the Brits took that very seriously. He told me about the tour and how different things were in Japan. When I asked him if he liked it, he skirted the issue and guided the conversation to the big fight. I half expected to hear about an entanglement with some Japanese black belts like the time the entire band got their asses whipped in San Francisco by some Korean martial arts experts, but what I got was a story about German tourists. It seems they had a battle with some Germans in a Japanese disco. Evidently the Germans were drunk, and I could only imagine how drunk the Skynyrd crew was. A fight broke out and soon all of the Lynyrd Skynyrd guys were engaged, as were all of the Germans. Ronnie told me he was drinking champagne and that he was using the bottle as a weapon, and that those Germans have damn hard heads. No matter how many times he hit this guy over the head, the bottle wouldn't break. It pissed him off so much he gave up the fight, gathered the troops, and got the hell out of there just as the police arrived. All of the Germans were arrested.

We talked for a while more, catching up on things, and I told him about Linda and Mona, to which he replied,

"That doesn't surprise me. I figured you guys were gonna get together."

Then he told me about Gene. I didn't know Gene but I had heard about him, he was one of Ronnie's oldest friends in Jacksonville. And he was ready to get back on the road. I was hesitant. Our payroll kept expanding, and I told that to Ronnie, but he told me to do what I had to, and that he needed Gene on the road. I promised I'd put things in motion.

During the three nights of performance at The Rainbow in London we were inundated with music mag reporters, old friends of the band, and a handful of celebrities. The band was up to the show, which always amazed me when I was suffering from jetlag, but the adrenaline always started pumping the moment they hit the stage, so it took more than jetlag to get the boys down.

Leon had developed this habit of tossing his bass into the air at the end of each show, which was really quite humorous since he never knew exactly where it was going to come down, resulting in a lot of near misses and some pretty hairy catches. When you watched him you were never sure if the object was to dodge it or catch it. I'm pretty sure that's what Leon had in his mind as well. Am I going to get beaned, ruin the bass, or catch it? No one ever knew the end result, least of all Leon.

Bobby Pridden showed up on the last night and arranged an outing for us. Bobby mixed monitors for The Who, and had gotten to know the group well when they opened for them in 1973. The next day we were all out visiting a few of the lads over at Stevie Winwood's house, where they had a recording project going. Stevie was there, and a host of other musicians, mostly unknown to me. The Rolling Stones mobile truck was parked half in the driveway and half on the lawn, and there were miles of cables reaching from it and snaking through the house, as they were recording in various rooms to get the right sound. It was a bit bizarre but well worth it when you listened to playback. They had amps down hallways, organs in small bathrooms, and mics everywhere you could imagine, sometimes using three or four mics positioned in various spots in the house to record a single guitar track from the bathroom. It was unique, and the sonics and echoes they were achieving were amazing. The only complaint was that no one felt they were playing together. They were all isolated, so it was like a bunch of guys doing solo projects that would be melded together at the end.

The recording ceased once we arrived, not that it appeared they were in the middle of anything... it was all one big experiment based on individual inspiration. Bobby showed us a good time and we all got thoroughly soused as the night wore on.

Ronnie, Steve, and Gary were on their best behavior, and Ronnie was the coolest Southern Gentleman you've ever seen, acting very reserved and fitting in well with the "proper" Brits.

We were soon back in a bus, a British bus, hardly comparable with an American one, and certainly not a tour bus by any stretch of the imagination, but it rolled and was fairly comfortable, so it would do.

From there we completed a three day run, knocking out shows in Bristol, Portsmouth, and Birmingham. Other than the band's usual fiery performance, the gigs were uneventful until we hit Birmingham. That's a rough city. It was half occupied by rough and tumble blue collar workers. The other half were unemployed youth that migrated towards trouble, since there was nothing else to do.

We were treated to one of the rowdiest head-banging crowds we'd ever witnessed and it gave the impression (not through the music, but through the crowd) that Skynyrd had gone punk. It was a wild scene, all of those skinheads bouncing around, with occasional clashes and flash fights that seemed to worm their way through the audience until dissipating.

After the gig, Bob Davis and Peter Robinson from MCA decided to throw us a party. Bob was from the legal department and lived in the U.S., and Peter was the head of MCA London. In their goal to show us the best time possible, they had selected a Greek restaurant, one that went full Greek, and had dancers who smashed plates on a stage after dinner. They even provided plates for audience participation, so it appeared perfect for Skynyrd.

We jumped the gun a little on the plate smashing. They told us it was okay to smash plates, so as soon as we finished eating, we would dash the plate on the floor, or just crack it on the table. Then Leon had the bright idea of cracking one over Billy's head. Billy cried out, both in pain and anger. The problem was that the plates that they served the food on were not for breaking. They were china, and fairly durable, and when they broke, shards of glass would break off and fly about. They straightened us out on that in a hurry, before anyone or anything was too damaged. Then they hurried the soft clay plates, the ones for breaking, to our table, and within seconds they were distributed and flying. The party ended when we got tired of dashing them against the floor and walls and started breaking them over each other's heads. Evidently that was frowned upon. I don't know if there were damages that night – MCA picked up the tab, which delighted me, because it saved me from arguing with the restaurant management, and I had a headache - some of those plates were harder than others.

From there it was a day off and on to Manchester, which was actually quite nice, an enjoyable city, which got even nicer as the night wore on. We finished the sold out gig and returned to the hotel, where everyone settled in relatively early as the bar closed at midnight. For such a supposedly civilized society, known for their drinking, they had yet to learn how to operate a bar. Closing at midnight is ridiculous.

A couple of days later, we found ourselves in Glasgow. We had been warned about the city. If there was anyplace the band would be getting into trouble, it would be here. The town was rough, there had been high unemployment there for years, and the skinhead crowd was wreaking havoc. Come to find out they were the least of our worries. There was something else in the air in Glasgow... a general uneasiness, and so the band took to drink as they often did in times of stress.

By the evening the group was roaming the bars, then the halls, then back to the bars, generally running amok, while extremely drunk. I had secluded myself in the room for most of the evening but finally boredom overcame me, so I decided to do some roaming myself and see how my cohorts were doing. I left my room, wandered down the hall, and entered one of the two elevators that serviced the building. I was surprised to see two couples in the lift, both decked out to the max. The men, brawny individuals, were in their finest, most likely rented tuxes, complete with cummerbunds or vests, and their dates were decked out in absolutely beautiful formal gowns. I said hello to the couples and was greeted by angry stares, which was rather baffling, but hey – this was England... Glasgow, so I blew it off as a cultural thing – maybe they just took a disliking to my long hair. Theirs was cropped close.

I faced forward and settled in for one of those silent elevator rides... the norm, but as soon as the doors closed everything flashed red for a split second, then went black. The next thing I know, the door slid open and I found myself in a bloody heap on the floor of the lift. Once the door was fully open the fight or flight urge kicked in and I staggered to my feet, clinching my fists, yelling at the rather large crowd of formally attired couples. They had gathered at the door and were waiting for the lift. Now they were watching the show. I must have made quite an appearance, blood pouring from wounds above my eye and mouth, and since I had been out for a while, the blood had accumulated, pooling in the bottom of the lift and covering my face and shirt. I staggered up from the floor, fists clenched, ready to duke it out with my attackers. I was in full fight mode, yelling at the crowd to find my attackers. I was ready for them. Everyone just stared at me blankly.

Someone finally escorted me to my room. I must have blacked out again as I had no idea how I got there, and then a doctor showed up. Evidently Sally or Mary Beth had sprung into action. The doctor took care of me right in my room, using half a dozen stitches to sew my left eyebrow, and treating a cut cornea with some drops. By the next morning I was sore but otherwise no harm done... not counting the stitches and black eye. One thing, though: I certainly fit in better with the group. No one was surprised to see their tour manager with a black eye. I was clueless about the whole scene and remained that way until Billy and Leon dropped by.

"Hey," Leon began, "Billy's got something to tell you, Roneckerman..." yielding the floor to Billy.

Billy hemmed and hawed for a second, then got to the point.

"I'm really sorry, man. They must have thought it was me. You see...."

Leon cut him off, "Billy beat the shit out of one of those

guy's sons."

"Is that right?" I asked. "What the hell did you do that for?'

"Well, we just got into this argument, and he was real drunk, and it kind of escalated until I had to punch him out."

"You were a bit drunk yourself," Leon added.

Now we were getting somewhere. "So you beat some kid up?" I asked.

"He wasn't a kid. He had to be twenty." Billy answered.

"That's a fucking kid, Billy. You can't do that."

"I know. I know. I was drunk."

Leon interrupted again, "He couldn't even fuckin' walk. Don't know how he threw that punch."

"Enough," I said, my split lip hurting every time I talked. "You guys get out of here. I've got to sleep. We can talk about this tomorrow."

I managed to get some sleep before the phone came to life with its annoying British double ring.

"You still up?" It was Ronnie.

"Barely."

"Oh… well, listen. Melody took a step."

"What? What is she, five months old now?" I had done some quick calculations in my head.

"Yeah. Well I just had to tell ya," he said, "she didn't walk really, but Judy said she's standin' up – if you hold her hands, she stands up."

Ronnie was so excited – I had already seen tons of photos he had with him. I stroked his enthusiasm for a while, heard more about Melody and Judy, then I rolled over and engaged the tooth fairy.

With two days off after Glasgow, Sally arranged an outing for us to visit her friend, Lady Anne. Lady Anne was of royal blood, the real thing, and lived in this beautiful and enormous estate, surrounded by about twenty acres of well-manicured grounds, complete with a garden maze. The band was on their best behavior, but it didn't last. We found out that Lady Anne made the band look somewhat tame. She was outrageous. She was refined in the British tradition, but totally berserk, which made us fit in quite well. We were quite at home with nut cases. And don't get me wrong, Lady Anne might have been a nut case, but no more so than anyone in my own family, so it wasn't that bad. She just had more money to fulfill her desires, which led to more insanity. All in all, she fell into the category of awesome with my bunch.

We had been loading up pretty well that night. Lady Anne kept the butlers circulating with a variety of drinks. It was really cool – waiters and butlers stood around watching for a glass to get low, and then they'd shuffle by with a whole tray of fresh drinks.

We all got a taste of how the ultra-wealthy lives – it was just like in the films. We proceeded to drink some of the finest wine I've ever had, accompanied with silver trays of exotic hors d'oeuvres until we were full and well plastered. The evening was great, everyone acted civilized to ensure a good impression, as this was our first bout with royalty.

Then Arti pulled one of his tricks. Unbeknownst to any of us, Artimus had dropped acid and sneaked out the front door and was now roaming around the grounds. This didn't upset any of us, since we knew Artimus dropped acid regularly, but when Lady Anne found out, she freaked out.

"The lions are out!" She kept screaming. "We have to find him! The lions!"

We then realized that Lady Anne had a highly secure estate. Instead of armed guards, she used a trio of African lions, which were extremely effective. About half of us started roaming the grounds in groups of four in our search for Artimus – Lady Anne said we should be safe in those numbers. Artimus was finally found roaming around lost in the garden maze, and the party was abandoned. I apologized for any trouble and thanked her for her hospitality. Lady Anne gave me a big kiss and told me if I ever wanted to come out again, I was welcome, but advised against bringing some of the boys back with me. She also extended the welcome to Ronnie. I suppose at least the two of us made a decent enough impression.

Upon our return to the hotel, Sally and I somehow wound up in my room. We were a little drunk, it was sexually charged; we both knew it; and then she hit me with some words that probably saved me a world of trouble. It was simple.

"I think we should avoid this. People who work as closely as you and I do should never get involved."

She was right. She got her point across, my crush vanished instantly, and I had to agree with her. Linda filled my thoughts instantly, and I felt relieved. Sexual tension: a real trouble-maker sometimes.

We continued on, performing at Leeds University, the same place where The Who recorded their famous album, *Live at Leeds*. The band was at their best, whipping the Brits into the usual frenzy, making them all Southern rebels for the night.

Ronnie dropped by my room later that evening. He had scored a bottle of Jack and needed a drinking partner. He caught me in a moment of weakness, and I agreed to be that partner, and he mixed the drinks. I had ice, so they turned out to be Jack on the rocks. After a while, we were laughing our asses off at each other's imitations of British accents. Neither of us could help it, we'd been around the limeys too long.

We were laughing so hard we almost didn't even notice Allen's familiar loud pounding on the door. He had Gary with him, and they glared at me as they entered my room. You could cut the tension with a knife. Neither of them sat down.

"We know Peter Rudge is paying you, Ron Eckerman." Allen charged. This time, the pause between my first and last name indicated he meant business.

"Yeah, you either work for him or you work for us," Gary added.

"Wait a minute," I said, "I'm working for you guys no

matter what."

"Nope. You're either with us or against us," Allen said, shifting from one foot to another. He was just his usual amped up self.

"That's ridiculous," I said.

Ronnie was just sitting there observing, trying to keep the grin off his face. He was amused by this whole thing. I glanced over, hoping to catch his eye. I needed some help here.

"It's not *ridiculous*," Allen argued, "if you're working for *him* in New York, how can you be on *our* side?"

I tried to argue as Ronnie sat there, watching, drinking, and grinning, and finally, he came to my rescue.

"I asked Peter to hire Ron," Ronnie interrupted.

He caught me off guard. He was lying his ass off for me. It was certainly his turn.

"We needed a spy up there."

That silenced Gary and Allen. Ronnie was a friggin' genius. Everyone relaxed a little bit and we talked for a few more minutes before Allen and Gary left, dragging Ronnie with them.

CHAPTER 13

Darkness was closing in quickly as we silently sliced through the thick humid air hanging over some unknown location. I had no idea where we were. I did know we were no more than ten minutes from our destination of Baton Rouge, so we had to be somewhere in Louisiana. I guessed that the freeway below was I-10, one long piece of elevated highway that bore through some of the swampiest ground in the country, rivaling the Everglades in Florida. I was bent over in my seat, my head between my legs, in the classic crash position the cabin crew illustrated to me on every flight I had ever taken. It was automatic - their lessons had certainly taken root in my brain. My eyes kept being drawn to the Ace of Spades, which had curiously fallen square in the middle of my field of vision. The cabin was now completely silent – there was no sound penetrating from the outside, no engine noise, not a trace of the constant vibration we felt during every flight. Things were quiet... deadly quiet. I straightened up for a moment, alarmed at the Ace filling my vision, and turned my head towards the front of the plane.

March – April 1977

It was good to be back from England, where it seemed like we could never rid ourselves of the chill. It was like that on almost every trip I had made... always cold, always wet, and the chill would settle in to the bone and wouldn't be relieved until you exited the country. True, there were some balmy days, but it would always revert back to the norm.

The band had the whole month of March off and most of April, which they were using for vacation, writing, rehearsing, and recording, but mostly for recording. They'd been popping in and out of studios for a while, grabbing snippets of licks and putting new material on tape as soon as it was written. It was an astonishingly creative period for the band, and one that seemed to be keeping them out of trouble. And I, after a couple of days' rest, would be settling into my new position at SIR.

Peter Frampton, who had just purchased a huge estate about a half hour from our house, gave me a call, so we drove over in the Camaro to check it out. Penny, his girlfriend, was there. I remembered her from the Humble Pie days – she was going with Mick Brigden back then. She and Linda hit it off immediately.

Peter and Penny showed us around. He had a huge L shaped living room which was filled with road cases, amplifiers, drums, and a piano, all piled in one corner. The other side of the L was a normal living area with a huge sofa, but it was still sparse, he hadn't yet started decorating. We made ourselves comfortable in the den with the giant television and then he introduced us to his new discovery, "frothy coffee", which he made by whipping a spoonful of instant coffee with a spoonful of hot milk until it foamed, then filled the cup with hot milk. Mona, at first a bit shy, warmed up to Peter when he showed off his new puppy, Rocky, and sang the song he had written about him, *Rocky's Hot Club*. Then we listened to a bunch of obscure albums he was unpacking while sipping Courvoisier. Mona was sipping hot chocolate and playing with the puppy. His estate was beautiful, with a mansion of a house set back a hundred yards or so from the road and the acreage surrounding the house dense forest. We stayed as long as we could, long enough to get a buzz, which I then had to neutralize with a couple of cups of coffee before driving home. It didn't seem to help much - we still got lost.

Toward the end of March, I started looking around for alternate methods of getting the Lynyrd Skynyrd band and crew around the country. The bus situation was expensive and uncomfortable due to the size of our entourage. It kept on growing in spite of my efforts to cap it, and although I realized we needed the support staff as the band became more popular, I also realized the consequences to our overhead. I had become an essential part of the band's organization and was conducting most of the business for them. Peter, Mary Beth, and I would plan the "big picture", but it was up to me to see everything was implemented. This freed up Peter's time for the new acts he was developing and afforded him more time to work with the Stones, who were going through some serious changes themselves. Since the buses were out and commercial air was ridiculous, I started looking around for a private plane. When Peter and I discussed it, he was okay with it, as long as I could bring it in for the same price as we were currently paying for transportation.

Once I started crunching the numbers, it made even more sense, and I discovered additional reasons to travel by private plane. My thought process was this:

If the crew was traveling with the band, we'd have to travel at the convenience of the crew rather than the band, so in most cases, we'd have to leave after the gigs. This would curtail the parties after the shows, as we'd only have enough time to return to the hotel, clean-up, and board the plane for the next stop. In theory, the band would drink much less, party less, and stay much healthier.

After sharing my findings and thoughts with Peter and getting his blessing, I began searching for a plane in earnest.

My search eventually led to Addison, Texas, to a small aircraft company called A&J Leasing, and I understood that they had both Jerry Lee Lewis' plane and his ex-pilot, so I booked a flight to see it. Since I was traveling I also booked to Jacksonville to see the band and hear the new tunes, and to Atlanta to meet with Ted Turner about doing a show in Atlanta Stadium this summer. Peter had even gone so far as to make up a gold baseball, done like a gold album, to present to Ted from the band.

I walked into the studio building unannounced and unnoticed. The entire band was in the studio in the middle of a discussion, but I found Kevin in the control room, and he played me a take on *Sweet Little Missy* that they had just completed. It was a bluesy little number that reminded me of a Brit rock band, but they had managed to put their Southern edge on it. The song was good but really didn't grab me, which was one of the reasons I kept myself divorced from the recording process. I had a firm belief that anything that wasn't a hit was a waste of time and artists certainly didn't appreciate it. Ronnie and Gary had worked hard on the song and were very enthusiastic, Kevin reported, so I was prepared when I walked into the studio.

"Hey, Ron Eckerman," Allen said. No pause this time. Seemed it was back to normal after the confrontation in England. He had his guitar hanging from his shoulder so we didn't even try to shake hands.

Everyone looked up and turned their attention to me; greeting me, but there were no hugs or handshakes, because they were in the middle of something. I sensed this, excused myself, and went to the control room to talk to Kevin, who was also visiting.

"It's been slow," Kevin said. "They've gone through all kinds of changes on this song. Ronnie really likes it, but they can't seem to get it to pop the way they want."

"What do you think?"

"Oh, I like it. I'm not sure it's their best material, but I like it. Some of their other stuff, though, is killer. *I Know a Little* is going to be huge." He lowered his voice a little and leaned toward me. "I don't know about the project, though. These songs just don't have any pop to 'em. I get better sound out of our eight track at home"

"Yeah. I heard," I said, just as I heard the group start a little jazz number – nothing I'd heard before. Ronnie entered the control room, clapping me on the back.

"You heard it?" he asked.

"*Missy*? Yeah, it's good."

"It'll get better, you wait and see," Ronnie said as he sat down in one of the chairs at the console and punched a button. A moment later I was listening to the song again. After listening to it a couple of times, Ronnie and I joined the band in the studio. They were all milling about, smoking cigarettes, having finished whatever they had been discussing so I picked up one of the guitars and started messing around.

"I love Les Pauls," I told Allen. I had chosen Gary's guitar. I ran a quick riff I had been playing, stolen from Bob Welch. Allen immediately picked it up.

"Damn, I didn't know you could play." It was the first respect Allen had shown me since I showed off my somewhat questionable karate abilities in Denver. Allen took the riff and expanded on it and a couple of minutes later he had a song.

I unstrapped the Les Paul. If I played an instrument too long I would be exposed — I wouldn't dare call myself a musician. I just knew enough to muddle through a couple of songs, but it changed a lot between Allen and me and I got a bit of extra respect from the band as well. They showed me a few more songs they'd been working on before I left, and from what I heard, they were coming up with some killer tracks.

The meeting with Ted Turner was a complete waste of time. I met him in his office after lunch, which was full of "yes" men, all smiling, all milling around his office, surrounding me, all waiting on Ted. I gave him the gold baseball, and made a little speech about how it was from the band in appreciation of what he's done for baseball and the city of Atlanta, and steered the conversation to the stadium. I told him I would love to see that place filled to the brim, and that Skynyrd could do it. He countered by offering to let them play at the seventh inning stretch. We were so far apart, and he was so distant, that I could see this was going nowhere, so I told him I'd think things over and get back to him in the future. I wish I would have brought someone with me, or at least brought some reporters or a photographer. It would have given me some muscle.

The next morning I was on a plane to Addison, Texas. The plane we were considering certainly looked comfortable, and would easily carry our entourage in comfort. It was a roomy cabin, having been cut down to twenty-four executive seats from the normal forty passenger configuration. There were overstuffed swivel seats scattered about the cabin, a sofa in the front, and tables and chairs in the rear. Jerry Lee Lewis had been flying around in it for years and had just acquired a new jet, which is why it was available. It was about thirty years old but appeared to be in excellent shape. The Convair 240 was made as a replacement for the old DC-3, and I'd certainly flown in enough of those over the years.

   The research I'd done reinforced the leasing company's claim, that the Convair was one of the safest planes ever built. I found that of all the Convairs ever built, only a little over twenty had crashed, and only two were due to a mechanical problem. It seemed like the perfect solution. We talked about the price, and I suggested some alternative ways to price the trips to lower the cost, then gathered a copy of the plane's maintenance records and flew back to New York. It was a whirlwind trip.

At the office I was kept busy with recording schedules, as the guys slipped in and out of studios depending on Tom Dowd's availability and their progress with new songs. We were also putting the finishing touches on the tour in support of the live album and beginning to plan the release of the new album with another extensive tour to support it.

Things just kept growing, even as the band was inactive and in the studio, and it was obvious they were likely to be the largest rock band in American history within the next year or two. It was an extraordinarily talented band of misfits that had managed to define Southern Rock. And with the new album they'd be going much more mainstream; it was Steve's influence. He'd broken them out of the mold. I looked at them as "a rock band from the south" now, not a Southern Rock band. It was exactly what was needed.

I flew down to Criteria Studios in Miami to check on progress in mid-April, where the boys were recording with Tom Dowd. While slipping into the lobby of the nondescript office/industrial building I ran into Mack Emerman, the owner, and he beckoned me to his office.

I was expecting to have to pull out my wallet for damages, so I was surprised when he invited me to dinner at his house that evening. Mack and I knew each other from other bands and he wanted to spend some time catching up. Unfortunately, I hadn't yet seen the band so I couldn't make any plans yet. I promised him I'd drop by his office before the day was out and let him know.

I checked with the receptionist and found out which studio the boys were in and wormed my way down the hallway into the control room. Tom and Barry, the engineer, looked up from the console for a second, then dove back in – they were listening to a replay while the band listened in the studio. I gazed around the room, staring at all the weird wooden "sculptures" hanging about the studio. There was quite a hodgepodge of those things, which looked like someone had visited a building site, gathered the scraps, created a montage of them, and then hung them randomly about the room. The room corners were the junkiest, with the wood all vertically aligned, but cut to vastly different lengths and then glued together. As haphazard as it looked, it all had been meticulously engineered and designed, creating the acoustics of the room, which were essential to the recording process. There were mics and stands strewn about the room, as well as amplifiers, all scattered about, and all separated by foam and carpet baffles in an effort to isolate the instruments. Cables were everywhere - you had to be careful moving about in the room or you'd unplug something, knock over a microphone, or simply trip and fall.

When they finished listening to the playback they continued, and Tom pushed a button on the console, opening up the control room mic, telling the band to run the song once more.

They nodded, talked amongst themselves, and launched into *What's Your Name*, a snappy tune I hadn't heard yet – but one of the best I'd ever heard with some of the most clever lyrics ever. Another hit, no doubt in my mind. About fifteen minutes later, after they had made a satisfactory scratch track, the guys took a break and I entered the studio. Steve and Allen were just lighting cigarettes, and Ronnie was sucking down orange juice out of a quart container.

"It's about time you showed up," he said, setting his orange juice on the floor next to him.

I walked over and gave him a handshake and hug as Gary tapped on the window to the control room, then motioned with his hand, tipping it up in indication he wanted something to drink. A moment later Barry could be heard through speakers,

"Craig's not here right now."

It caught me unexpected, coming out of nowhere – it was like the voice of God.

A moment later Tom chimed in, "I'll get you something, Gary. What do you want?" That *was* the voice of God, as far as the recording industry was concerned.

Gary asked for a beer, just speaking into the air, where room microphones picked him up. "I'll have a beer if you don't mind." Tom appeared a moment later, a Budweiser in his hand. I could see Barry in the control room, busy, making notes and studying console settings. They were using a Neve board, a beautiful console and the pride of the industry, but it had an enormous amount of faders and knobs, so he was taking meticulous notes on settings. There was another engineer next to him; it appeared they were sharing the chore.

"So Gary, what do you think of that guitar sound?" Tom asked.

Gary took a sip of beer before responding, "I like it. I don't know what you did but it sounds pretty damn good."

Tom worked his way around the room, talking to each of the musicians, and then approached Ronnie.

"That tempo right for you?"

"You can dance to it, can't you?" I lingered around the studio for a while, listening to a few more songs, until the band finished their break and got back to work. Ronnie wasn't needed at the time, because Tom wanted to spend some time with the musicians, so we moved to the lounge where we could talk.

"Ron," Ronnie began, "I've been thinkin'. Seriously, we've got to get this act cleaned up. I'm tired of shellin' out all our money in damages."

"Yeah, it'd probably be cheaper to just buy our own hotel chain."

"It probably would, huh?"

"So what's the plan, Ronnie? How are we going to get these guys on board?"

"Not sure...that's kinda why I wanna talk to you."

"You're the group's leader. Ever thought about leading by example?"

Ronnie grinned as he removed his headband. "Yeah, I guess that's one way. Another way, though, is to get Gene out here."

"Gene Odom? Have you talked to him about it?"

"Kinda. He hasn't really given me a commitment yet. But I know Gene. He will."

"Okay. Well, then we'll have to get rid of Robert."

"Beaner? Man, I hate t'see him go, but I do need Gene."

"So how's the project moving?" I asked.

"Fuckin' Tom," Ronnie replied.

This was a shock. The band had been in love with Tom ever since the *Bullets* album.

"What's wrong with Tom?"

"You wouldn't believe it, Ron. When we came in here the first day he had all the amps lined up in a row. No isolation or nothin'. It was like we were doin' a concert or somethin'. The man's lost his mind."

"That's odd. Doesn't seem like Tom"

"No, it don't. How do you record an album like that? I think he's stuck on the live album. He wants to do another one."

I had nothing to say. I didn't want to get mixed up in recording wars. Touring wars were as much as I could handle. We sat in silence for a few minutes before Ronnie started up again.

"I know the man likes to capture that live sound, but you can't do a studio recording like that. Anyone can tell ya that."

"I don't know, Ronnie. Maybe he has a new idea. You can't really knock the man. After all, he's the king."

"And royalty's often insane."

We were cut off when Tom walked into the room. He was fetching Ronnie, so I was left sitting at the table a few minutes later, scratching my head. This was totally unexpected. I returned to the studio a short while later and watched and listened. To my ears, which were blown out years before from exposure to concerts, everything seemed fine. But that's why I divorce myself from the music production part – it wasn't my thing.

The next day April 15th, Ronnie, Gary, and I flew to Atlanta. They were presenting a Gold album of *One More From the Road* to the mayor. After the ceremony I saw Ronnie and Gary off to Jacksonville and I flew back to New York.

After I returned to New York, we got back to work on the tour as the band began rehearsing in earnest while still fussing with the album. They had recorded enough tracks at Criteria, but when they really listened to them they were far from satisfied.

They were going to go on the road doing a split set, with about half of it the old music, the other half material off the next album. It was gutsy, but they had been doing a few of the new songs for a while now, ever since last October, and they were well received.

We had also closed the deal on the plane, so our traveling should get a little easier, and we would be able to avoid commercial airports and most of the security. Now we could just pull up to the plane and load.

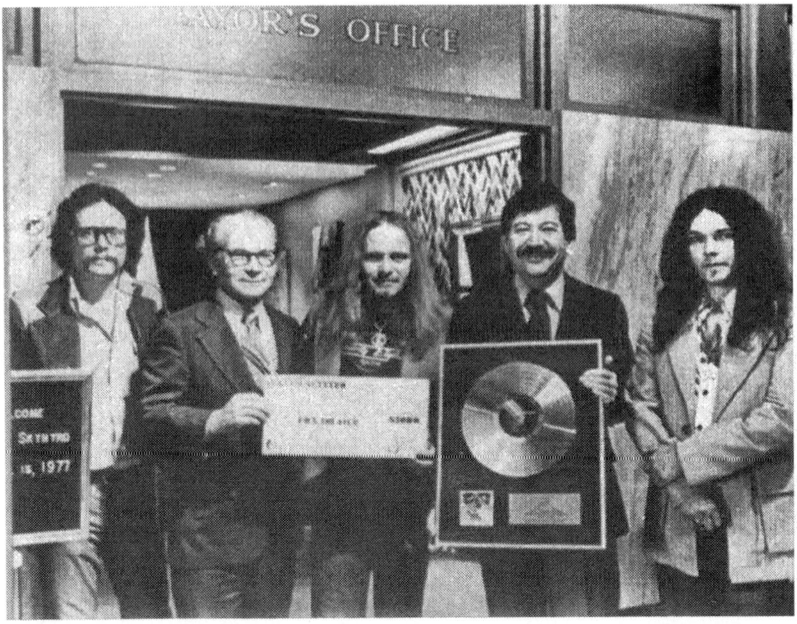

OR'S OFFICE

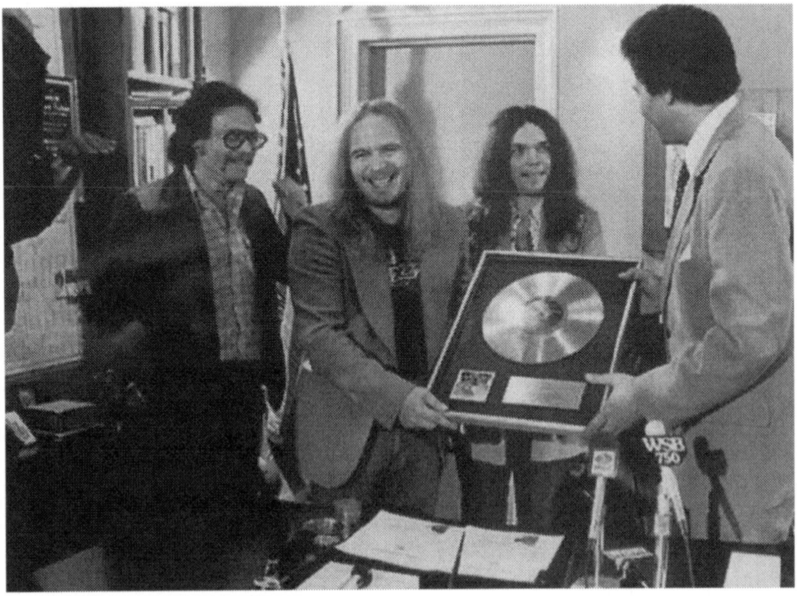

WSB
750

CHAPTER 14

Everyone was sitting in the crash position: everyone's heads between their knees. There was no movement in the cabin at all. No talking. No screaming. Nothing but the faint sound of air rushing by the windows. I turned back and strained to see out the window over the frame of Mark Howard, who was maintaining his safety crouch. I could barely see anything out the window. The gray tint had overcome everything, both inside and out, and it felt like a thick blanket had been thrown over the plane, encompassing us in a death-hold. The words of our former pilot, Les, came to my head: "This plane can make it down anywhere, it's one of the safest ever made, unless you're faced with a mountain... or maybe a forest." I kept hearing his words over and over as I gazed out the window at the rapidly approaching trees.

April 1977

On April 21st the Convair was waiting at the airport in Jacksonville when the group arrived. It flew in prepped with the band's logo on the nose, ice and soft drinks in the coolers, and magazines and newspapers on every table. It was ready to go, complete with brand new VCRs I had purchased in New York during our time off. I selected the Sony betamax, as my research indicated that the betamax format was of superior quality to VHS, so I figured it was sure to win the format wars. I also had one at home, purchased at the same time and place as the ones obtained for the plane. The only problem was material, but the guy at the electronics store copied a few movies for me so we'd have something to watch, and I had taped a few off the air at home. We had *Monty Python and the Holy Grail*, *Deep Throat*, and a few others. *Monty Python* was watched a few dozen times. *Deep Throat* was never watched, at least as far as I know.

We drove right up to the hangar in Jacksonville where

the plane had parked and everyone had their cameras out and were shooting pics as we loaded. It was a joy not to have to deal with airports and security, but Dean had just become aware of the luggage detail, which was a far cry from what he was used to. Normally everything went to a skycap and he could forget about it until they tumbled down the luggage belt on the other end, where another team of skycaps would be waiting. Since Dean wasn't shy about tipping, they'd gladly take care of us so it was a fairly simple procedure.

Now the luggage actually had to be loaded into the cargo hold and no one had even considered this part of the routine. The bags had to be loaded onto the plane by us, which meant Dean, whomever he could draft to assist, and the pilots. Luckily the pilots didn't mind, as they had to be aware of and supervise the pack anyway since weight had to be balanced for efficient and safe flights. There wasn't a whole lot of science to it – they simply guessed at the weights they were handling and adjusted the placement: heavier bags in the center, lighter ones on the periphery, resulting in a surprisingly well balanced plane.

It didn't take very much time to load, and everyone was anxious to fly in the comfort of our own plane. We entered through the galley, using the plane's own stairs, the type that folded into the door.

As we filled the cabin you could feel the excitement, the anticipation. It was hanging in the air. This was a very big deal for the band and crew.

There were smiles everywhere that day and a lot of excited conversations as seats were claimed. It was an interesting boarding process. I watched from the galley as people tried out a seat, then moved to another, until everyone had inspected the plane and tried most of the seats, at which point they would finally settle into one and strap in.

Dean, Robert, and I huddled with Les, our pilot, to hear how we should proceed with the safety lecture required before every flight. It was a regulation, and Les flew by the rules, but it didn't take long for him to forget about that one. As soon as we had run the routine a dozen times, we abandoned it unless we had new passengers, at which time we would run through it with precision, just in case a guest may comment to the authorities. We never got it right anyway, as the hand waving, the indication of the exits, would soon deteriorate to crotch-grabbing or some other ridiculous pantomime. And the announcer would mangle the procedures so badly it was better off to never hear it at all.

Everyone took part in the announcements at first, rotating to whomever was in the closest seat to the microphone, but after every comedic gesture that could be imagined had been used, and every derivative of the original instructions exhausted, it got boring and was discontinued.

Once we were all in the plane and the doors were sealed, the engines came to life, the left one first. We heard, and if there was a window open, watched, as the engine started to rotate. The propeller blades turned in jerks at first, but after a short moment the engine sputtered, blew out a thick cloud of black smoke, and chugged along on its own until, seconds later, it smoothed out and purred, or at least quieted down. I don't think turbo-props ever actually purr. But the engine was running smoothly and a moment later the right one was awakened as well, and we were under our own power for the first time.

It was a little bit nerve racking, as the smoke was alarming, but once I had thought about it, it was no different from watching a bus crank up. Every bus I had ever seen behaved very similarly to the plane – a few chug-chugs, some black smoke, and then it all smoothed out and you were off.

I sat in the rear of the plane, a habit of mine even on commercial flights unless I'm lucky enough to be in first class. It was safety I was concerned with really, as I reasoned that planes never back into anything. I also took the last swivel seat in the rear, which afforded an excellent view of the rest of the cabin. Les opened the flight deck door and made a quick inspection to make sure everyone was seated and strapped in, and then made an announcement over the P.A.

"I need everyone to be seated and strapped in. We're about to start moving. Ron, could you have someone check and let me know when we're ready to go?"

I didn't have to do a thing. There was a group answer, yelled out by almost everyone.

"We're ready."

A moment later we felt a shudder run through the cabin as Les put the power to the craft and then we were rolling. It seemed to take a great deal of power to get the plane moving, as the engines were roaring by the time we picked up any speed, but then Les pulled them back and the plane's momentum kept us moving at a decent pace. I glanced around the cabin and noticed a lot of people were doing the same, and I assumed we were all looking around for the same reason: we were trying to gauge one another's fear level. I tried to look confident and cool, but there were definitely a few butterflies in my stomach. We were in uncharted territory. It seemed like it may be a common feeling from what I saw, and there were more than a couple of people holding hands... white knuckling it, so to speak, and we had yet to taxi to the runway.

We approached the runway slowly, sandwiched between commercial jets that dwarfed us in size. We were too big for a lot of the smaller airports, yet too small, from our perspective, for the commercial airports. It had nothing to do with technical requirements except for the small airports, which simply didn't have a long enough runway. It was really a matter of perspective. Those jets looked huge in comparison to us, and in all actuality, the smallest of them carried three times the amount of passengers we did. At any rate, it did make the pulse quicken when you stared out the window at the whales ahead of you and thought about the minnow we were in.

After about fifteen minutes we had reached the runway and were cleared for take-off. Les aligned the plane and put the power to the beast. We could hear the roar of the engines but the pressure of velocity, the feeling you get during a take-off in a commercial jet when you're pushed back into your seat, was absent. We started much more slowly. Instead of bolting through the gate, we were tiptoeing through the tulips, but we were slowly building up speed.

Finally, after what seemed like forever, the craft lifted from the runway, shaking as it did, until we were in free air a few hundred feet off the ground. I had watched out the side window as we took off and was more than satisfied when I saw that we had plenty of runway left. Once airborne, the craft settled into a relaxing flight, engines audible but low pitched and smooth. Maybe you could call them purring after all, they just had to be in their zone.

Once we had trimmed to our cruising altitude, Les came on the intercom and told us we were free to move about in the cabin, but he added that he preferred for everyone to stay seated throughout the flight. We did, and talked amongst ourselves until we felt the engines being trimmed and our altitude falling. We were already preparing for landing less than two hours later. It was like being in a limo, only we had a lot more room and had covered a lot more distance.

Spirits were high when we landed smoothly in Johnson City, especially when we climbed directly into limos at the charter facility. The crew, including the six lighting and sound techs from Showco, the sound/light company that was hired last September, rode in a couple of station wagons directly to the gig. We had to leave Dean with the pilots and baggage. They would all be riding back in the luggage van. So far, so good.

We were fast approaching Johnson City proper from the airport and the atmosphere turned to one of depression as we neared the city. You could see the soot in the air the moment we dropped into the basin. Johnson City had an inflammatory history, known as the second Chicago. It was one of the major distribution points and producers of white lightning, the popular substitute for brand alcohol during the prohibition. The stuff could take the chrome off your bumper in minutes, and separate the lining from your stomach in months. It had certainly taken the shine off the city, and I felt a little twinge of sympathy for the residents as we continued into the downtown area.

We were back in the land of Holiday Inns and Howard Johnson's - none of the more elaborate hotel chains operated here, because there's just no money. Thankfully though, residents had no trouble digging up the six or seven bucks to attend a Lynyrd Skynyrd show – we were in prime Skynyrd country. Their songs could be heard on the radio constantly, and it had been that way for several years.

Like many states in the south, *Free Bird* had been adopted as a sort of national anthem, no doubt a carryover from the years in the Confederacy. And, like everywhere else in the States, in the world, really, when that confederate flag dropped during *Sweet Home Alabama*, a whole new Confederate army was created.

The flag was the subject of controversy everywhere the band played. The more sophisticated individuals claimed the flag was a symbol of the band, so it therefore must be a symbol of the attitudes of the people in the band, leading to claims of racism. Nothing could be further from the truth. The flag came about in much the same way as the song *Sweet Home Alabama* did. It was all a joke - an inflammatory one, granted, but still a joke. A joke Ronnie took very seriously. Ronnie wrote the lyrics for the tune to get a rise out of people and he was overwhelmingly successful at it, and the flag, too, was in the same vain. It was a joke – a little punch at the Yankees. The band was far from racism and had nothing at all against blacks.

The band's history wasn't exactly conducive to understanding all this. After all, they had spent years developing their redneck image. It wasn't intentional, either, but happened due to their life style and tempers, which went out of control on a regular basis dependent on their consumption and habits.

Those surrounding the band and the media had a hand in it as well. They propagated all of the tales: the street fighting, the drinking, the drugs, and the hard life. If they had drilled a little deeper they would have known the truth. Ronnie had been actively pursuing a new road, a tamer one, as he was getting tired of the fighting and destruction, and especially tired of the damages, which was severely curtailing their income. The other problem was cancellations.

Cancellations had become a real problem over the last year. Promoters had become nervous about booking the band as we had developed a reputation for cancelling due to Ronnie's sore throat and the accidents that seemed to occur every time the boys had a few days off. It was a very big deal: refunds were issued, replacement shows had to be booked, and so on – it was tremendously expensive. It also added a huge amount of work to my load, and the crew's. They would become irritated – they would set up the gear in the hope of a show at every venue – and we always cancelled at the last minute, usually after everything was set up. Then they'd tear it all down and repack the truck, all for nothing.

Several times when they knew Ronnie wasn't feeling well they asked if they could just skip the whole ordeal. I couldn't let them. I never knew when Ronnie was going to cancel, or when we'd get into some other trouble… and I never knew if it was really his throat or not, since he had expressed some animosity to some of the cities in which we were scheduled. I never fully understood why, but I could guess – previous experiences.

The band started off the tour with a bang, selling out Johnson City, followed by sell outs in Louisville, Dayton, and Wheeling, West Virginia. Yes, we were hitting all of the hot spots on the white lightnin' circuit. And in Wheeling we actually managed to taste the stuff. A fan of the band talked his way backstage with a large mayonnaise jar full of the clear liquid. It looked harmless, it was completely clear, but when you took a shot – well, your eyes would tear and your nose would sting as soon as your glass was within a half foot of your face. It tasted like lighter fluid to me... or what I imagined lighter fluid would taste like. The jar was passed around the dressing room once so everyone could have a taste. It didn't go around a second time. We'd stick to the safety of Jack Daniels and Dom Perignon.

Gene Odom finally joined us toward the end of April, and he was quite a bit different than what I had expected. Ronnie wanted him out for security, to replace Big Robert, yet the guy was smaller than anyone that had been out yet. He was fairly clean cut as well and had never smoked, drugged, or drank. How he had remained one of Ronnie's best friends over the years was a mystery.

Gene was one of the most likeable fellows I had ever met, always cracking jokes, always keeping spirits high. He was a welcome addition to the crew. Big Robert left in a good mood after I explained the situation. He understood, so there was no foul there.

We were getting used to the plane, and the pilots were getting used to us. Adjusting their schedule, they were taking a cab so they could get to the plane early and have it warmed up and ready to go by the time we got there. Everyone had settled into a regular seating pattern, but it would change slightly each day depending on interaction of the band and crew. We had also begun a non-stop poker game in the back of the cabin where there was a fold-up table. I usually played, as I discovered I could reinforce my salary with poker winnings, dependent on who else was in the game.

It didn't take too long to figure out who the poker players were, and I always tried to load the table with the worst players ensuring I received my road bonus each week. Some of the guys were absolute suckers. I always invited

Billy and Leon to play, neither of them had much experience but both were always willing. They'd join in until they became frustrated, then I'd let them win a hand or two to keep them in the game, and they'd play until they were cleaned out. Although it seemed smart, I sure had to pay out a lot of per diem advances.

Dean and the pilots, Les and Walt, made sure that the plane was always stocked with soft drinks, beer, and snacks, and if there was a long flight, we'd pick up some pizza or sandwiches. We took turns riding up front with the pilots, and Les was good about explaining things and relaying stories from the Jerry Lee Lewis days. He told me the plane had been through the worst weather you could imagine and always pulled through without a hitch. He seemed very comfortable in it and he should have been - he'd been flying it for years. It was his second office. It didn't take us long to make it our second office as well. It beat the hell out of buses and commercial flights.

By the time we hit Richmond, Virginia the band was in the zone. They were unstoppable, reinvigorated by Steve and the new material they had recorded, and playing with a fury I had not yet witnessed. Steve had gained confidence and had taken a leading role in the band, much to the delight of Ronnie and the boys. There was a new competition in the band, a friendly one that fired each of the players to new heights. It wasn't often an artist captures the "magic" necessary to hit it big, but Lynyrd Skynyrd captured it consistently. The band also had this unique connection with their fans, which they constantly cultivated. Here in Richmond, for example, as the guys powered their way through the show, Ronnie noticed a guy in a wheelchair getting crushed near the front of the stage. He pulled Gene to the side and pointed him out, and moments later the chair was hoisted from the floor by security and put on the stage. He was then wheeled to one of the sound wings where he could watch the show in comfort. It was a magical moment. Like I said, it's rare when the magic appears. They had it...

consistently.

We completed the jaunt with shows in Charlotte on April 29th and Fayetteville, N.C. on the 30th, and then flew back to Jacksonville for more studio work.

I flew to my new home in New York. Linda and Mona picked me up at the airport and we drove straight home. I was overjoyed to be home with my new family. We had adjusted well, and although Linda was suffering from depression due to the move, my constant touring, and the weather, she brightened up when I was home, and I finally felt I had a home rather than a house. My whole outlook was beginning to change, as my desire for a home life had finally overtaken my desire to be on the road.

CHAPTER 15

There was a shudder in the plane... it quickly became repetitive, a horrendous vibration that shook every inch of the vessel. It was followed by a series of impacts, loud explosions that sounded like gunshots, machine gunshots, and they were rapidly increasing in both speed and force. It had grown quite dark in the last few minutes, but I could make out shadows in the window, strobe-like ribbons of darkness were crossing the windows at a rapidly increasing rate. They were trees. I suddenly realized, as most of us surely did, we were clipping the tops of trees. And just as suddenly I realized we were crashing in the forest. It was our worst nightmare. The plane that couldn't crash "unless we were in a forest or mountains" was crashing. I couldn't hold the crash position... I had to sit up.

May 1977

We began May with a stop in Colombia, South Carolina on the 11th, not far from where we had wound up when we completed the first leg of this jaunt, in Fayetteville, which is why we left the plane in the Carolinas and took commercial flights to and from home. It didn't make sense for the plane to return to Addison, Texas.

The guys were in good spirits and ready to go when they arrived, and the pranks had already begun. Unlike me, they were itching for the road life after a week off. Evidently, Leon had been picking on Allen, one of his favorite subjects, on the flight up. He had managed to sit directly behind Allen, and Allen had been napping on the plane, so Leon decided his hair needed some decorations. When Allen awoke from his nap he was wearing a beautiful crown fashioned out of toothpicks, straws, and a variety of other ornaments fashioned out of snacks, wrappers, and anything else Leon could find. Allen wasn't even aware of it until he stood up and banged his head on the overhead compartment, knocking about half the junk into the aisle. Leon knew what was coming and had managed to "jump the gate" standing before the plane had stopped, and running down the aisle so he had about twenty individuals between Allen and him. I heard about the whole thing from Billy, who couldn't quit laughing about it. Allen, in mock anger, was on the hunt for Leon, claiming he hadn't seen nuthin' yet – the payback would be huge. By the time they got to the hotel everything had blown over, but Leon was still checking over his shoulder every few minutes.

It was as if we'd never taken any time off. The band was hitting their stride from the first show on, and still experimenting with their new songs, gauging audience reactions. Steve was singing one number, *Ain't No Good Life*, by himself, while Ronnie laid back by the drum riser cheering... no, ordering him on like he did during guitar solos. It was a very unique situation, seeing the response to brand new songs. Other bands lost a little ground when they did unfamiliar material. Not Skynyrd - the fans were eating it up. They loved the new, unfamiliar tunes. It was like they were discovering dark secrets, or the band was sharing these secrets with them.

Like I said, it was unique, this intimacy the band had with their fans. It was all things Skynyrd, didn't matter what it was, if it was related to the band, the audience loved it.

A couple of days later on May 14th we checked into the Sheraton Inn in Savannah, Georgia, a city for which I cared very little – a disappointing place to spend an evening off. The Sheraton was really a motor hotel, one of those two story brick jobs with the little air conditioners in the window. The furniture was worn, the carpet faded, but it was the best we could find near the gig. At least it had a bar.

We were late arriving so everyone threw their bags in their rooms, freshened up, and hit the bar. Everyone but me, because I was swamped with paperwork. Like the band, the paperwork kept growing. Everyone had started putting room charges on their hotel bills and not clearing them. So now I had to keep records of everyone's hotel charges, deduct them from the hotel bill, and run tabs on each person's account so the charges could be deducted from their paychecks.

Quite a few of our entourage were also starting to ask for advances on their per diem, too, which I granted. It was awfully hard not to when someone tells you they don't have any money to eat, regardless of how they spent their last issue. So I had to keep records on that front as well.

In spite of my good intentions of catching up on my records, I became wrapped up watching TV. Other than the news I never watched TV on the road, since there wasn't enough time, but it was *One Flew Over the Cuckoo's Nest*, so I had no choice.

I heard the commotion before anyone beckoned me. Knowing it must be an internal band fight I paid little attention, preferring to wait for a call. Sometimes these things blew over. Instead, it intensified, and then I realized it wasn't my troupe, or at least I didn't hear any of them. When the phone rang, I was quick to answer. Seems that some of the band were squaring off with a few locals in the bar. People were getting loud enough to hear them from two flights up on the opposite side of the building. I ran out the door and Billy, who was rushing in the direction of the bar, yelled to me that the band was getting the shit beaten out of them. Grabbing a shirt, I threw my briefcase into a dresser drawer, then proceeded to the bar, heart racing and adrenaline pumping... ready for trouble.

By the time I was on the scene our whole entourage had assembled and they were all standing around baffled, as I was. There was no trouble. In fact, no one had even been to the bar.

I turned to Billy, "Why'd you tell me the band was in trouble?"

"That's what this guy told me. He knocked on my door and ran off as I answered. But he told me Lynyrd Skynyrd was in the bar, and *he* was getting beaten up bad."

"What about the rest of you?" I asked.

"Ronnie grabbed me," Gary said.

"Leon told me," Ronnie answered.

It didn't take long to figure out that we'd been set up so we quickly returned to our rooms. Within seconds my phone was ringing.

First Leslie, "Someone broke into my room. They stole my money... and some jewelry."

One by one each and every member of the entourage reported a break-in. In the meantime I was frantically searching my room for my briefcase. I opened and reopened the drawers, thinking it would somehow magically appear if I kept looking.

We had been hit, every one of us. I immediately went to the hotel office and called the police. The rest of our evening was occupied by reports and interviews, and I had become convinced it had to be an inside job there at the hotel. How else could they hit every single room within the five or ten minutes we were out of them?

I found out later that Mick Brigden and Montrose had also been hit in the same hotel... in the same way. Since I was sure it was an inside job I demanded the staff take lie detector tests. That didn't go over well with anyone, but we came to an agreement: if I take the test so would they. We arranged to do it in 30 days, when I had a day or two off.

The next day we struggled through interviews and a night off. We were in Dothan, Alabama, and it was a tough one, the fourth show in five days, and the third in a row. The crowd wasn't as large as they'd been lately and was less than enthusiastic. It caught us off guard. There was no explanation for it, other than a weak market. It happens, but when it does it can really throw things off kilter. The band picks it up from the audience and their energy wanes, and then the audience picks it up from the band, and you have this self-supporting feedback loop. That's how shows go bad - it's happened many times before. But with Skynyrd, it's

Lynyrd Skynyrd Rock Band Loses $38,520 to Burglars

Constitution State News Service

SAVANNAH — Members of the Lynyrd Skynyrd rock band told police they were burglarized of $38,520 in cash, checks and jewelry Saturday night in a ten-minute job that apparently occurred while its motel rooms were watched by the group's own security guard.

Ron Eckerman, tour manager for the rock group, told Savannah police his briefcase, containing $5,000 in cash and $25,000 in checks, was stolen from his room while he was downstairs at the Howard Johnson's motel making check-out arrangements.

Other members of the band reported jewelry and cash taken from five of their rooms during the same period, about 11:40 p.m., after the group's return from a Savannah Civic Center concert. The group's security guard was in the hallway near the rooms at the time of the burglaries, Eckerman told police.

Savannah police said none of the group's doors had been forced. The only pass key was in the possession of the night manager, who was with a policeman at the time the burglaries were reported to have occurred.

"If the theft actually happened, it had to be someone inside ... right with them, in my opinion," said Savannah police Detective Robert Scott.

According to Scott, 24 persons associated with the band and 14 band guests were occupying 11 single and five double rooms at the downtown motel.

The items reported stolen included a custom-made $2,000 diamond ring inscribed with "I love you," he said.

The group, whose songs include "'T' for Texas, 'T' for Tennessee," is on a three-week Southern tour.

---

really unexpected – their audiences are always over the top.

In the end, though, they turned it around: Free Bird finally woke up the crowd, and the show ended the same as they all did, a frenzied band playing a rock and roll anthem to a frenzied audience.

After the show the guys blew off some steam in the dressing room and decided a night out was in order, so we did our research and ended up at a little club not far from the hotel. Artimus, Gary, Leon, and Steve ended up doing a set, perhaps to make up for the concert. Once they got going, they ran through half a dozen old blues numbers: songs by Lightnin' Hopkins, Howlin' Wolf, and Jr. Walker's

Road Runner. It was a blast, the main reason being the guys didn't care one bit how things went – they were just having fun.

From there it was on to Athens, Georgia, followed by appearances in Lexington and a return to Knoxville, and every show was a sell-out. Apparently Dothan was just a fluke.

The band had calmed down quite a bit, spurred on by Ronnie. Ronnie was on his new kick – the clean-up, and he wasn't putting up with any horseplay. He was staying relatively straight himself, so he expected everyone else to do the same. I suppose he had taken me up on my "lead by example" challenge and it seemed to be working. We'll see how long it lasts.

When we got to Mobile, Alabama, with only one more stop in Columbus to go, the mob I was charged with finally got too restless and broke from their run of good behavior.

"Mr. Eckerman, there's been an incident," the hotel manager told me. One of my maids was just in here, and she was in tears. It seems you have a practical joker in your group... that's gone too far."

"What happened?"

"You have a Leon Wilkeson in your group. He sat off some fireworks in one of the rooms."

I expected much worse.

"Are there damages?" I asked.

"Just an additional clean-up fee. And an apology and tip for the maid. He scared her to death."

We settled on $100 and $20 for the maid - nothing really, and I went to Leon's room to find out what happened.

"You should have seen it, Roneckerman," Leon began, "Billy was asleep in his room, you see, and the maid's in the hall. So I get her to let me in, I showed her my ID and key, and told her my key wasn't working. Anyway, Billy's sleeping through all this and the maid lets me in and I light this string of firecrackers."

I couldn't help but laugh – this one was too good.

"Then I throw the firecrackers in his room and close the door and start running down the hall. When I got to the maid, I yelled out 'He's got a gun!' and the firecrackers go off and she freaks out and starts screaming and goes running down the hall. It was hysterical."

Now I had to admit, it was hysterical, but I couldn't let him get away with it.

"That will cost you $100 for clean-up, $20 for the maid, and a $100 fine that will go into the kitty. You could have given that woman a heart attack."

I had just come up with the idea of putting all the fines into a "kitty". That way if the band acted badly enough that we would have plenty of funds to provide for the band's cocaine. I know the logic was twisted, but I had to cover that cost.

In Columbus the band performed to another sold out audience. That night after the show, Artimus gave me a call, inviting me to his room to hear share some music. It was rare that Artimus called to share something with me, and I really liked him so I took him up on his offer.

I entered his wonderland of a room, looking around in the dim light. He had done his usual redecorating job and had thrown colorful scarves bearing an Indian motif over all the lamps, and had candles burning everywhere. There were scarves pinned to the walls, effectively transforming his room into the "hippie" pad my own room was like at home... several years ago. It had a mystic quality to it. His boom-box was fairly loud, and the haunting music of Holtz's "Planets" was playing... again. He had left the Mars orbit and moved on to Venus.

I took a seat on the side of his bed while Artimus settled to the floor, legs crossed. It looked like a classic Yoga position to me, but I knew nothing about Yoga – he could just as easily been a Native American praying to Buffalo.

"This is sheer genius, man," he said.

"Hmmmm," I muttered back, listening to what truly was a fascinating bit of music. I understood why he was listening to it again.

"I love the way the drums come pounding in over the horns."

Artimus seemed to be traveling in a journey... of his mind. I sat with him until the side played out.

"Thanks, Artimus. I really appreciate it."

"I can make you a copy of that if you want."

"That'd be great," I said, studying his face. Something wasn't right. His eyes were much, more wild than normal. "Are you okay?"

"I'm great, man. Great!" he exclaimed, a big smile breaking across his face. Then he got dead serious and leaned into me, whispering, "I just took some acid. Want some?"

"No, thanks. I've got a lot to do."

"Ah, come on. You have to release once in a while. Acid will clear your mind... and your spirit."

"I'm pretty clear, Artimus, and we fly tomorrow."

"Okay, just trying to share..." he said as he closed his eyes, "I try to keep my mind active and alive, man. It can get so boring on the road, you've got to allow yourself to enhance your mind..."

As he continued talking, I eased out the door to allow him and his mind a little privacy.

In the middle of the night, Gary came to my room with a sleepy grin on his face.

"Hey, I think ya better come with me."

"What's going on?" I asked as I pulled on a t-shirt.

"It's Artimus."

"He was fine a little while ago," I said, following Gary down the hall.

"Oh, sure. He's fine, that's for sure. He ate some acid."

"Yeah, I know. But he looked okay last time I saw him."

"I guess it hadn't kicked in yet," Gary replied, his narrow, bloodshot eyes focused straight ahead. Gary was always somewhat mysterious and quiet - it appeared he was always in deep thought... until you looked a bit closer, about fifty percent of the time he was in a deep stone. His eyes gave him away every time.

It was quiet as we approached Artimus' room... and wet. The hallway floor was soaked, and it got wetter as you got closer to Artimus' room.

Gary knocked softly, "Artimus, you in there?"

We heard some shuffling noises from inside, but he didn't answer. Gary tried again, and then one more time. I stood at his side patiently.

"Now what?" I asked.

Gary looked at me, grinned widely, and pulled out a key-waving it in the air like he was performing some sort of magic trick. I didn't know how he got Artimus' key, but he unlocked the door and we opened in time to see Artimus slide his patio door open. He looked back at us, his eyes blazing, frightened, then we watched as he slipped through the door and blasted across the well-manicured motel lawn.

We stood and watched, both of our jaws agape, as Artimus, shirtless and shoeless, only wearing a pair of cut-offs, fled into an overgrown field of weeds and disappeared into the night. His floor was a mess – there was about a quarter inch of water, and when we looked into the bathroom we saw the full tub. It had apparently overflowed.

Gary turned to me, "You know what? That there is what happened to our last drummer."

Gary and I sat in Artimus' room, talking, waiting, and watching for a sign of our wild-eyed bear of a friend, then gave up. We had done the last show for this stint.

Now we had two weeks off – plenty of time to find Artimus. The next day Artimus found his way back, and damages were $4,500.00.

CHAPTER 16

I glanced out the window once again, then turned in my seat toward the front of the cabin. Everyone was still tucked into their crash positions as instructed. Everyone was bouncing up and down, shifting in their seats with the movement of the plane. It was all so well-choreographed. Everything was timed perfectly to the sound. It was like being trapped in an amusement park ride, or in the middle of a special effects scene in a movie, but there was no way to stop it... no "cut" was going to be cried out by a director, and no ride operator to shut the ride down. There was no control, and the feeling I had was beyond helpless... way beyond. No, it wasn't helplessness I was feeling at all... it had turned into hopelessness, and it was the first time I had ever experienced it. Hopelessness – a gut emotion that can rip your soul apart. If you've never felt it it's difficult to explain. It's a primordial feeling, an instinct, and it pervades your being far past the "flight or fight" syndrome that's so well taught in Psych101. It's past panic, past any emotion I've ever felt. It's a feeling that can't, or shouldn't, be thought about. It will grab your mind and twist it until you're incapable of reasoning or thought. It is, without a doubt, the emotion on which religion was born and exists today.

June 1977

We had all been flying in the cockpit, each one of us allowed a little air time behind the controls. Les was right there, guiding us along, showing us all the instruments, the radar, and making sure we didn't do anything foolish. During my short stint as pilot we were threading our way through some ominous looking thunderclouds and he had to grab the controls back at one point due to turbulence. I moved to the jump seat to watch as Walt got behind the co-pilot's wheel and Les poked through the thunderclouds a half hour later, after winding through holes he found using radar. It was quite educational and provided some entertainment as well.

I'm not exactly sure when it all started, but Chuck got into a fight with Raymond Watkins, one of the latest additions to the crew. They were best friends, but had managed to get stinking drunk during the flight, and were now in a heated argument. We were on them, pulling them apart as they rolled on the floor, but it was touch and go for a second. It started off with a punch and quickly escalated into a wrestling match, and they fell against the cabin door at one point. After they were separated, they were placed on opposite ends of the plane and I told each of them that this was it – they were both gone. There was no way I could tolerate something like that - it endangered all of us.

The next day they met with Rudge in his office, and as I understood it, he was going to let them stay on, but when they asked for more money, he too, blew a fuse and sacked them. They were on the next flight home and I never saw them again, in or outside of Jacksonville.

Poor Craig was covering the whole band damn near single-handedly now, covering both Chuck's and Raymond's jobs, so he was always running on empty.

As we felt the engines lighten up, we began our descent into Philadelphia, where we were performing with Peter Frampton, J. Geils, and Dickie Betts and Great Southern in front of about 100,000 fans on June 11th.

My brother, Rodney, would be there, and our Clearlight crew, Steve, Mark, and Jim. Linda and Mona were driving down from New York, and her sister, Judy, was coming in from Washington. It was like Houston on the east coast for me. Peter Rudge and Mary Beth would be down from New York, as well as my office-mate, Chris Ehring. If Terry Rhodes made it down, we'd have the whole crew.

The stadium was packed shoulder to shoulder everywhere you looked, from the grounds to the highest seat in the bleachers. Clair Brothers had installed a massive sound system, with the sound columns extending forty feet high on each side of the stage. Clearlight had a substantial lighting system out on the Frampton tour, but if everything ran on schedule Skynyrd would be finished and off the stage by the time lighting would be required. Once again, lighting by God. He'd done us right so far; I had little concern.

Dickie Betts started the show late, stubbornly refusing to go on until the stadium was full, which was ridiculous. Craig Reed and Clayton Johnson, our new production manager, had told me that the place had been packed all morning. Dickie got the crowd moving when he finally took the stage, although I heard it wasn't the most exciting performance, and the set change ran long again. By the time we arrived at the gig, the show was running an hour behind. Not too bad, really, as most of these stadium shows usually ran an hour or two late. The band was a bit nervous and were drinking more than usual, even though Ronnie was on the wagon, so to speak. Ronnie was into the champagne as soon as he walked into the room, and Gene was pulling his hair out, whispering to me,

"Just get me a gun so I can blow my brains out."

That was one of Gene's favorite expressions, I came to find out, and he used it often, especially when dealing with the band. Ronnie had gotten Gene hyped up with his quest to clean up the band, so Gene had a mission, one that would frustrate him to the end.

The dressing rooms were full thanks to our wide assortment of family and friends, but we had some side rooms blocked off, and turned the main dressing room into a hospitality room. The band sneaked off to one of the side rooms for privacy and warm-ups.

Peter Wolf from The J. Geils Band stomped his way through their set, and had done a great job getting the audience to their feet, especially when they performed *Surrender*, their current hit.

When I returned from the stage to monitor the set change, I gave the band a fifteen minute warning. Gene and I then made one last trip to the stage to lock down security. Since Rudge was there and there were a lot of guests, we were locking it down tight.

As I looked around I had a flashback of Knebworth – it was the crowd, a rippling, waving, sea of people. Finally we were set. Gene and I returned to fetch the band as Clayton and Craig finished the stage prep.

The band exploded once again, shaking all 100,000 people to the bone. Ronnie was at his best and had his foot soldiers firing their rounds with gusto. Allen was doing some of his best cheerleading, waving the stage to Billy for the piano solos and then launching into a solo of his own, twirling around until he handed it over to Gary. Gary would take the lead, arching his back as he held a note, then march over to Steve, who would boogie with the best of 'em. Leon had one of his silk top hats on, and roamed around from player to player, finally tucking in with Artimus, who was flailing wildly on his drums.

It was always a moving experience to see the crowd's emotions during *Free Bird*, and this time was no different. The crowd would start swaying back and forth in time to the ballad, and then explode into a frenzy as the song started rocking.

The guys came off the stage satisfied and sweat soaked. I gravitated to Ronnie in the dressing room, who was wiping down with a clean towel, and he gave me a big grin as soon as he saw me.

"Man, that was a hot one," he said, cupping his face in the towel.

We were flying to Charleston, West Virginia that night. Charleston was where we were doing one last show in the deep south before changing direction and heading to Portland, Maine, followed by a run of eastern seaboard gigs until we crossed the country again to the west coast where more stadiums awaited.

We were booked in coliseums, arenas, and stadiums now – no more small theaters, and we would even be headlining Anaheim Stadium at the end of the summer. Up to this point we'd played it safe, opening the stadium shows for larger performers and then blowing them off the stage, but this would be the last summer for that. Anaheim Stadium marked the first of the Skynyrd stadium shows, and by next summer we were planning our own series of stadium shows, starting with Atlanta Stadium.

Charleston was one of those grand old southern towns, famous for the confederacy, thus perfect for Skynyrd. The fans there were rabid for anything Skynyrd, and when they did the unreleased *That Smell*, the place came apart – it was like a new *Sweet Home Alabama*.

The guys had loosened up slightly after Philadelphia, prompting Gene to look much, much harder for that gun to blow his brains out. I had to laugh at the escapades involved in keeping the band dry. You had Gene on one side, arriving at the gigs early, confiscating the alcohol, hiding it from the band, and you had Dean on the other, who collects the confiscated liquor from Gene and moves it into the bar... where it eventually gets dispensed back to the band. But Gene had managed to get the Jack Daniels under control, only to be replaced by Dom Perignon, Ronnie's new favorite beverage. I have to admit it was a giant step up, as the Dom is smooth, but all in all, the only thing that had changed was the brand... and the cost. Gene had been successful, however, at significantly retarding the rate of consumption, and Ronnie had lowered the alcohol content of their beverages, so there was some progress in our clean-up program. Obviously this was going to take some time.

By the 15th we were in Springfield, Ma, having just performed in Portland. Portland was a treat – they served lobster for lunch, and not those scrawny things you get in the south, but full-fledged, meaty lobsters, with huge claws. It was a welcome break from our traditional dinners, which typically consisted of roast beef, potatoes, and beans. The entire band stayed for dinner, where we ate on picnic tables with red checkered tablecloths sat up backstage, and the crew joined us so it turned into quite an event. I found myself checking for cover in case a food fight broke out.

We were following Springfield with a gig in Hempstead, N.Y, where Linda and Mona were driving down to see me. I missed them terribly these days, especially with Linda feeling so blue, it worried me. I'd have a few days off soon, but five days later I'd be heading back across the country, to San Francisco, and I wouldn't be back to the New York area until mid-July.

Linda and Mona had already arrived in Hempstead by the time we did and had checked into my room. I turned check-in duties for the band over to Gene and rushed to my room to see them.

"Ronnie!" Mona shouted as she threw her little arms around my neck. I was hoping one day she would start calling me Daddy, but I never pushed it. She had no relationship at all with her natural father, so I hoped that one day, if Linda and I ended up getting married, that I would be able to adopt her.

I took Mona down the hallway to get some ice and some sodas while Linda said she was going to take a shower and freshen up. I was going to ask Leslie or Cassie to watch Mona for an hour or so while Linda and I had some alone time.

That was the original plan, but when we got down the hall Ronnie's door was open, his TV was blaring, and he yelled at us as we passed by the door. We went into his room.

"I didn't know you were here," Ronnie told Mona.

Mona smiled shyly, holding my hand and waving it back and forth, and then hid her face behind me.

"What are you up to?" Ronnie asked me.

"I was just going for some ice and drinks. The girls just got here."

"I've got an idea," Ronnie replied. "Why don't you leave Mona here with me? I'll babysit for a while so you and Linda can have some time to yourselves. We'll order some food and I'll see if I can find some cartoons or something on TV." Ronnie said to Mona. "How does that sound? I'll bet there's something on TV you might like to watch. You hungry?"

Mona didn't answer, preferring to nod her head up and down instead.

I jumped at the chance. "Okay, you know where I am if you need me. I'll see you guys later."

"Don't do anything I wouldn't do!" he shouted, laughing as I ran out the door.

When I went back a little while later to Ronnie's room, Ronnie smiled widely, looked at his watch, and chuckled.

"That sure didn't take long," he said, winking. "I figured you'd be gone longer than that. I guess I gave you too much credit..."

"You're such a smart ass," I said, shaking my head and laughing.

They were finishing up fried chicken that Ronnie had ordered, and they had managed to find Bugs Bunny on TV. I think Ronnie was maybe substituting Mona for his girls - it had to be hard on him to be away from them... that, and he just loved Mona.

After a swing through Hyannis and Buffalo we were off for seven days, more than enough time to get to Denver. Being so close to the city I flew home, where I split my time between the office and my house. I had to fly to Denver on the 26th. It was June, and it seemed like it had gone from freezing and snow bound to hot and humid overnight. I had been home enough to see the seasons change, but my visits were so sporadic and so short that none of it flowed together the way it should, so my perception of the seasons was seriously distorted. Everything just blends together after a while, and all the cities start looking the same, as do the hotels, and the venues.

I decided to move back to Houston. I had done so well promoting recent concerts I was going to give that a go, so we'd be moving back to Houston after the next tour. It was the only logical thing to do.

Arriving in Denver from New York, I made my way to

the hotel, where I'd take advantage of my early arrival and check our entourage in. It was a big day tomorrow, another stadium show, and Lynyrd Skynyrd was second billed to The Marshall Tucker Band - just one more mismatched show we would take advantage of. At least this one continued a theme, even though Heart and Foreigner were a bit out of place. The rest of the acts on the bill included old friends Atlanta Rhythm Section, The Outlaws, and good old Dickie Betts.

The gates were opening early the day of the show, so we had arrived one day early in order to get a sound check. We had our sound check, a rushed one but a sound check just the same, and returned to the hotel. The next day it was packed, another sea of people, and, just as I thought, the boys blew the pants off Marshall Tucker, and another act learns their lesson. Skynyrd's a tough act to follow. Only fools try.

We returned to the Salt Palace in Salt Lake City the day after Denver, and Bear had loaded the plane with his famous ribs. They were the last things rushed on-board as Bear just reached the plane before we were due to take off for the lengthy flight. Everything went fine for the most part. The plane was running smoothly, the weather was great, spirits were high, and we were settling in to a very enjoyable flight, when Artimus worked his way to the back of the plane and sat cross legged in the luggage area, half laughing, half crying. I watched him until I couldn't take it anymore, and I unstrapped and made my way back to sit down beside him.

"What's up with you, Artimus?" I asked, peering into a pair of wild eyes.

"It's the ribs, man. The ribs."

"The ribs?" I asked. "Yeah. Did you get some? They're the best I've ever had, and that's saying a lot coming from Texas."

Artimus burst out laughing. I waited for him to stop. And waited some more. Finally he recovered enough to answer.

"No, man. You don't understand," he said.

"What don't I understand?"

"I can't stand it anymore. I can't watch all these people gnawing on those bones. It's freaking me out."

I knew Artimus was an on-again off-again vegetarian. His favorite saying was "You are what you eat" but this was ridiculous.

"What is it? The smell?" I asked.

"No, it looks like a bunch of cavemen... everyone's chewing on bones – I can't stand it."

Ahhh, the truth comes out. I looked down the cabin and saw for myself. We did look like quite the carnivores. Everyone was hunched over in their seats gnawing on those bones like cavemen, just like Artimus had described. I could see where he was coming from.

"Listen Artimus, there's nothing anyone can do if you're going to keep dropping acid. You're going to have to calm down... and quit taking that shit." Then I decided to fight fire with fire and hit him with his own expression, adding "You are what you eat, you know."

"Yeah, yeah... I know. I'll just hang out here until everybody gets through."

And he did, and he calmed down, and we continued our flight to Salt Lake City where we landed without further incident.

We were late getting into the show in spite of our early take-off and had to rush to make sound check, where Steve did most of the vocals to give Ronnie's voice a rest. And old Steve did a damned good job, singing a soulful version of *Sweet Home Alabama* before we returned to the hotel for a short rest before the gig. The show was so close to selling out we went ahead and called it that, and when you looked out from the stage, it was full to the brim.

Our entire entourage was in good spirit, and had been that way ever since Steve had joined them, and they were back in the clean-up routine, reinforced by Gene. Most of the Jack Daniels was absent from the dressing room although there was a stash of several bottles somewhere in the road cases. There was also champagne and beer, but a limited supply of that. Of course we had all the usual backstage treats: breads, multiple deli trays, hot appetizers, nuts, sweets, etc., and plenty of coffee and soft drinks so no one could complain... or shouldn't, but I think that acid Artimus took still had some teeth left.

"Damn, can't we get something better than this? It's the same food everywhere we go. This meat is more than I can take. Gross, man," he complained to me.

"I'll see what I can do – we'll have something different in San Francisco. That's Bill Graham's gig. And get me a list of things you'd like. Just don't get carried away."

Artimus was satisfied with that.

Once the band was onstage, I began my rounds, starting with the sound board, where I could listen to the show, and see how it looked. Kevin didn't even look up he was so focused on the sound. He was bent over the board making an adjustment when I first climbed on the sound platform. Then, when he did see me, he just raised his eyebrows in welcome – there was no sense trying to talk - it was far too loud. I remained for a couple of songs, just listening, watching, and then I wandered through the audience to see how the crowd was reacting.

It was the same across the world. Fans studied every move, listened to every word, and sang along with every song

About the time I positioned myself behind the speakers on the right of the stage, some clown had clawed his way on stage and was heading towards Ronnie. Within a split second Gene had crossed the stage and had the guy in a bear hug. There was a moment of confusion and then it looked like punches were thrown, and then Gene must have connected because the guy went back first into the audience. The show continued as normal from there, but after the show, we saw the guy handcuffed and on his knees in the corner of the backstage area.

In the meantime, in the dressing room, Billy was jumping all over Gene, telling him that he'd been too rough out there, and Allen was supporting Billy and adding fuel to the fire. You could tell Gene was steaming, but before he could blow his top, someone noticed that Gene's right sleeve was turning red. When he pulled off his shirt there was a deep gash just above the elbow.

"I told you that bastard had a knife," Gene exclaimed, looking down at the wound. Billy and Allen shut up in a hurry and Billy even apologized a few minutes later. I have no idea what happened to the overzealous fan... or rather, the incompetent assassin.

CHAPTER 17

We felt a huge impact while I watched the cabin twist apart in the middle. Light blue sky was streaking in, then the gap widened as the plane separated further. It was like it was being unscrewed by giant hands... it seemed to come apart so easily. All of a sudden, it wasn't dark anymore. It was, in fact, quite light, as the early evening twilight streaked in. It was the most beautiful color of blue, with splashes of rose and magenta, mimicking a sunset. Then everything went black. All thought ceased - I slipped into unconsciousness. There was no flood of memories, no bright light in the tunnel, no friends appearing from my past, no dead ancestors greeting me. There was nothing. No thought at all. I was simply in deep sleep. I knew nothing, I saw nothing, and I heard nothing... just sleep, wonderful, glorious, and welcome sleep... and total darkness.

July 1977

We arrived in San Francisco, back in the capable hands of Bill Graham and company, and I couldn't wait for this show. It was Peter Frampton, Lynyrd Skynyrd, Santana, and The Outlaws, and we were doing two performances.

It was going to be quite an ordeal, the next few days, as we were doing the show on the 2nd with Frampton, then packing up and flying to Tulsa for Willie Nelson's 4th of July picnic, which was on the 3rd, then back out to Oakland to do the second and final date with Frampton on the 4th. We had a couple of days off immediately afterwards, so we thought we were on safe grounds booking such a tight schedule.

The band was well behaved, back on the wagon, so to speak, which certainly made Gene breathe easier. It was the usual mob scene backstage, with all sorts of celebrities and musicians present, and the usual side shows Bill arranged for the events. I've got to give him credit – he provided the best conditions for the artists possible and no one treated us better anywhere in the world, and every single group that played for him felt the same way.

In the dressing room, Ronnie was sipping champagne and relaxing, just joking around with his troupe while the rest of the guys drank beer. It was great to see them out from under the influence of Jack Daniels, but I knew Jack, and he could rear his head the moment our guard was down. I also knew Dean had an emergency stash consisting of four or five bottles of the stuff somewhere in one of the road cases. Rudge was running around the dressing rooms, visiting with each of the band members, but seemed to be still avoiding me. It was awkward, but I was getting used to it and didn't let it bother me. After Santana finished, I grabbed Gene and we visited the stage to see how the set change was going.

It was a huge stage and it was packed with gear, roadies, and bystanders. Gene and I looked at each other, both knowing that it was going to be next to impossible to clear it, but we started in anyway, promptly locating half a dozen people that didn't need to be there and throwing them off. Bill Graham's crew saw what we were doing and came to our aid. Fifteen minutes later the stage was clear of everyone other than working personnel. We let all of Frampton's people have total access, out of professional courtesy and also because half the crew were my own employees. When it was down to fifteen minutes I returned to the dressing room and gave them the heads up, then Dean helped us clear the room. Bill Graham came in right before the performance and escorted the band, with Rudge and me, to the stage.

Mary Beth had come up with the idea to play *The Magnificent Seven* as intro music. As soon as it started, the audience caught on, and when the band hit the stage, they went nuts. Rudge held the entire band up in front of the piano that day, their backs to the audience, and they all turned around and posed, some 60,000 cheering fans in the background.

The band lit the audience up on the first number and kept them burning through the whole set, finally climaxing with *Free Bird* as usual. The stadium responded, and that San Francisco crowd was one of the best I'd seen – every time I think I saw the best performance, they'd do one even better. Rudge was crouching down between speakers, as was his custom, cheering the band on, and the wings were full – every crew member on the grounds was trying to catch the set. Ronnie would look at me from the stage on occasion, making faces, and came over during one of the solos, asking me "Can you believe this shit?" to which I just laughed, then he returned to stage center without missing a beat. He was so comfortable on that stage. He commanded the crowd... and the band, and he remained in complete control until he left, waving at the crowd as he did.

Dean, Gene, and I began gathering everyone for an overnight air lift. Barry Fey, the promoter from Denver, was doing Willie Nelson's 4th of July Picnic in Tulsa and had chartered a 727 for us and Waylon Jennings. We would be leaving Oakland and flying to Los Angeles to pick up Waylon and crew, and then on to Tulsa. It was going to be wham- bam-thank-you-mam, and then back to Oakland, a reverse of the whole process inside 48 hours. Dean, Gene, and I were really hustling to ensure it all happened, and as smoothly as possible.

We loaded the plane, the crew having to tear down all the equipment and load it in the belly of the plane while the band enjoyed themselves in the cabin. No one was into a party - we were all well aware of the journey ahead and knew strength must be conserved if we wanted to pull this off successfully. There were a few drinks being consumed, that was for sure, but it was more for medicinal purposes, to help us get some sleep in these uncomfortable seats – it was a commercial plane.

By the time we were on the runway, everyone had a mild buzz and were settled into small groups, all quietly talking amongst themselves. It appeared this was going to work out okay but as we got closer and closer to Burbank airport, where Waylon's bunch were joining us, the liquor was starting to flow a bit faster, and conversations got wilder, and it continued to escalate until we rolled to a stop at a private terminal. That's when we decided to be courteous and move to the back of the plane – Waylon's bunch could have the front.

Waylon was accompanied by a local chapter of Hell's Angels and they had come to see him off, riding a huge assortment of bikes, all Harleys. Steve and a local DJ who was tagging along with us were outside smoking a cigarette when they showed up, and they scampered back on the plane and were strapped into their seats before you could blink an eye. It wasn't surprising, all those Angels. Killer had been working for Waylon for years – I had met him at a bar once while doing one of their shows. Killer was very appropriately named and had done some time. He actually was still doing time really, only now it was with Waylon, as his bodyguard. And he always wore his colors and had a cane that he walked with due to an accident years ago. The cane had a nifty little knife that came out the end when he pushed a button.

So these guys said their goodbyes to their cohorts, and then one of the most ominous looking crews we had ever seen boarded the plane. It was Killer, a couple of other color-bearing Angels, and Waylon's band and crew. While they were loading, I noticed quite a hush come over my entourage and when I looked back at them they were in their angel mode – all of them sat there perfectly silent, somewhat awed by Waylon's entourage. If there would have been desks in front of them I'm sure their hands would be neatly folded and sitting square in the middle of them – they were that subdued. Waylon's gang was the real thing, bona fide outlaws, and they were practicing outlaw-ism all the way: snorting speed, drinking, and generally having a good time.

In contrast, the Skynyrd bunch were practicing some surprisingly good behavior, curtailing their consumption and saving their blow for later in the day when they'd really need it. We used the remainder of the flight to catch up on sleep.

We flew into Tulsa, arriving well before the sun rose, and went directly to the hotel to catch naps. The poor crew had to wrestle the gear out of the plane, transport it, set it up, and repeat the whole thing again when we got back to Oakland. It was a roadie's nightmare and our crew was shining. That was one thing about the entire entourage - when the going gets tough, they got tougher. Same with the band, this kind of pressure always made them shine as long as it wasn't in Jacksonville.

By the time I rolled into the gig with the band, the crew had everything set and prepped, so there wasn't much to do but wait. The gig itself was a nightmare. It was held in the state fairgrounds, a venue more suited to rodeos than rock and roll, and the stench of manure and sweat from the beer guzzling crowd of tens of thousands proved it. We were in the middle of the dust bowl, and in spite of a shoulder to shoulder crowd the dust still swirled, coating sweat soaked bodies, including our own, and generally making it miserable for both performer and spectator. This crowd didn't mind much though, as it was full of cowboys and outlaws, and they were there to consume as much beer as possible before the day was over. Damn the heat, damn the dust.

Lynyrd Skynyrd had the perfect spot, right before the Willie Nelson/Waylon Jennings sets. I'm not exactly sure who was on before Skynyrd, I wasn't paying much attention and was worn out, having to continue with my bookkeeping duties in every spare minute, and there were few spare minutes these days. All I really know is that when Skynyrd took the stage and blew up the joint, it took the cowboys by surprise. No one expected this crowd to get on their feet and shake their asses off, but that's just what they did. It was quite a sight, all those middle aged folks rocking to Skynyrd. There were plenty of kids, too, but it was the elderly portion of the crowd that stood out in my mind – they were rocking with the best of them.

By the time Skynyrd was finished, they had whipped that crowd into a frenzy, and poor Waylon and Willie had to learn the hard way about booking Skynyrd – you didn't want to go on after them, it would thin your crowd in a hurry.

After the show we moved to the hotel to clean up and repack. We were returning to Oakland in a couple of hours. Same plane, same crew – everyone minus Waylon's mob, since they were going elsewhere.

Things couldn't have gone more smoothly on the return trip. We picked up an hour thanks to the time zones, and the crew had the stage reset in record time at the gig thanks to the Graham crew, who had bent over backwards to help. They had an uncanny memory of how we had set up for the previous show.

It was July 4th and Oakland stadium was completely sold out, packed to the rim. It was a redo of the first concert, complete with decent sets by the opening acts, Santana blazed as usual and the crowd was well primed when Skynyrd hit the stage. The band should have been the walking dead with all they'd been through in the last couple of days, but it was no different than usual.

You could almost see the energy pouring off the stage, being soaked up by the audience. I was watching from the side of the stage with other onlookers and noticed Gary was wearing a Clearlight t-shirt, so I was prouder than usual. I had made everyone t-shirts when I promoted the Houston show with Cooley, and Gary was the first one to wear it on stage. Our Frampton crew most likely noticed it as well. They were all Clearlight guys, so it was a good day for the company. The guys ran through a blistering set, and set the whole stadium on fire, the audience even more enthused then at the last show there and the excitement kept escalating until it peaked. My brother Rodney decided to stay on stage and watch the set, and as they neared the end, he grabbed me and pulled me close so I could hear.

"Are you fucking crazy?" he asked. "You're really thinking about leaving this?"

I didn't answer, just turned my full attention back to the stage. He had a point.

We used our day off the next day wisely, sleeping, at least until the late afternoon at which time I grabbed Ronnie and Gary for an interview at a local radio station. I didn't usually get involved in this, as I had accidently sat on a turntable in a station the year before, creating "dead" air, scratching a record, and damn near ruining an expensive broadcast turntable. It was no one's decision but my own - nobody banned me from interviews, I just never wanted to go through that embarrassment again, so I quit going.

The next day we re-boarded our own plane and moved on to Madison, Wisconsin. Les Long, our old pilot, had just retired, so the co-pilot, Walt, moved to the pilot's position and John Gray, our new pilot, took over as our new co-pilot.

Having a new pilot was a little unsettling to all of us, as we felt so safe with Les. Les was such an outstanding man, and he was older, so it gave us a heightened sense of security. We had nothing against the new arrangements in particular, we just missed Les. I tried to reach Les and get him back out, but the leasing company insisted that he had retired and was through with flying.

Madison is a college town and there's nothing like playing college towns. The crowds were always good, and young, so there were always a greater number of good looking girls in the audience than usual. None of us ever minded that - it usually meant there would be plenty of flashing and we weren't disappointed. Ronnie was hilarious that night. Every time he looked over at the side of the stage, he made a face or stuck out his tongue, pointing at some girl in the front row.

From Madison we flew to Springfield, Missouri, where

the boys chalked up another winner and proceeded to another stadium in Chicago. They were headlining at Soldier's Field in front of 80,000 people with Ted Nugent and .38 Special. Journey and REO Speedwagon were also on the bill, so it was jam-packed with talent and an all-day affair.

The band, back on the wagon, did their thing, blowing all the other bands out of the water. They were becoming rock and roll assassins, only with guitars instead of guns, and they spent their professional time knocking off one band at a time as they climbed their way to the top.

All we had to do was one more show, in Poughkeepsie, New York on the 12th, before I'd see Linda and Mona in Asbury Park, followed by a long month off which we could use to paste our lives back together.

We wouldn't be using the plane again until we started our October tour. It was too expensive to keep it, since we only had three shows in August, and the whole month of September off.

In Poughkeepsie I had spent most of the morning on the phone trying to keep our plane in service. I was worried that we'd lose it during our time off. Gene was in my room while I was on the phone with them. The company couldn't give me an outright guarantee that they'd still have the aircraft when we went out on our winter tour. During the conversation I asked if I would get a commission if I found a suitor for the plane while we were off. I figured if I was going to go to the trouble and take the time to place our plane with another group, I should get paid for it. It was work. Gene overheard the conversation and jumped to a conclusion: he decided that I was getting a kickback from the plane for *our* use.

This misunderstanding spread quickly, and I had to straighten out this rumor. It didn't make sense. I had only known Gene a few months, since he was hired in late April, but he knew me well enough by then to simply ask me if he didn't understand something I was talking about on the phone. If I had been getting any kickbacks or doing anything unethical or backhanded, why in the world would I be having conversations about it right in front of Ronnie's lifelong friend? It was unnecessary drama, but I didn't hang on to any bad feelings.

I was thrilled to get to Asbury Park for a number of reasons. I'd be seeing my family, and I'd always wanted to see where Bruce Springsteen got his start. It wasn't that long of a flight for us, so we all got some rest, and it was the last show for almost a month, so the band was in some of the best spirits I had seen. It probably didn't hurt that they had been relatively drug and alcohol free for a few days.

As soon as we arrived in Asbury Park we were hitting the boardwalk. It was a fun place to visit but it was almost a ghost town compared to what it had been, and many of the old games and fortune machines from the old days still remained. The general flavor of the place too, remained intact.

As I approached the convention center I was taken back in time, as the building had been kept true to its architecture. It was a grand old building, with spires at all the corners and amazing craftwork in the details - it brought you right back to another time, one that was much grander, back when Asbury Park ruled.

Once we were inside the building our opinions couldn't help but change... performing there was another thing entirely. The building had been built in the twenties and had a small stage and smaller backstage area. It certainly wasn't designed to hold rock and roll productions.

It was July 13th, the height of the summer, and we had a sold out crowd once again. It was also hot and muggy so we knew it would get super-heated inside the building before the night was over. Ronnie's brother was on the show, singing for .38 Special, so we were also amidst family and friends.

At the time I had no idea what I'd be doing in a month, but I'd been very careful not to let the cat out of the bag.

Only Linda and my brother Rodney knew of my plans. This could be the last gig with Skynyrd, although I supposed that the three shows in August certainly weren't out of the question.

I hated the thought of leaving, but my home situation was unmanageable, so I really hadn't paid that much attention to the upcoming schedule.

We got through sound check quickly. Everyone had grown impatient and looked forward to some time off the road, mainly because they had a lot of tunes in the can that needed finishing. There was a celebratory mood in the air, everyone had caught it, and there was nothing but smiling faces everywhere I looked.

I had finally taken a good look at the band's schedule and it was ridiculous: three shows in the next seventy six days. That didn't mean that there wasn't a lot of work to do, though... just no touring work. And I was a tour manager. And that fact probably had a lot to do with the decisions I was making.

At show time, there were a few minor difficulties: one being the power in New York City – they didn't have any. So all the visitors coming in from New York were tied up in traffic and people here in Asbury Park were close to a panic even though the power seemed to be perfectly normal. There was also a problem with the limos: Gene had to go rent a station wagon so we had enough room, because the power outage in New York affected our limos in Asbury Park. That's another mystery I never figured out.

We were never affected by the power outage other than the cars and arrived at the gig in time to see .38 Special perform. Ronnie even sneaked onstage and watched for a while. You could tell he was so proud of his younger brother.

Skynyrd had two new songs in the set, *I Know a Little* and *That Smell*, and the crowd cheered loudly for both of them. It was always interesting to me to watch the interaction between the crowd and the band. It was fascinating, the stage presence they all enjoyed, which was part of that band magic that happens to certain groups, where the group as a whole is far superior to the solo efforts of any one individual. Nearing the end of the set, the band was getting fairly loose, so I had one of the soundmen put up an extra "dummy" microphone on the back-up singer's riser. Then, when they launched into *Sweet Home Alabama* and Ronnie's brother Donnie joined him on the song, we helped Mona, only six years old, up to the back-up singer's riser. Mona joined right in, dancing in unison with the girls. It was Jo-Jo, Cassie, Leslie, and our Mona. She was so cute, and she really thought she was singing with them onstage, although afterwards she asked why she couldn't hear herself in the monitors. She caught on quickly.

We closed out that tour with a bang, and almost rocked the building off its foundation as everyone got frantic during *Free Bird*, and when it was all over, there was a little sense of sadness in the air. Everyone knew we had gone through some magic moments in the last few months, and no one really wanted to see it end.

CHAPTER 18

I awoke in total darkness. I don't know where I was or how long I'd been here. I felt a warm, thick liquid dripping down my face, and when I tried to lick my lips I got a salty metallic taste. I tried to move, but couldn't. Nothing responded. As much as I wanted to move my limbs, it was out of the question – they had ceased functioning. There was some sound, it sounded like rustling grass, and there were footsteps and voices, but I couldn't make anything out. It was all muffled. I couldn't feel anything, and I knew I had little time left before the darkness would envelope me again, so I tried to call out. I couldn't hear my voice, I don't know if I was successful, and then a wave of darkness washed back over me and I returned to a wonderfully deep sleep.

August 1977

Linda, Mona, and I drove home from Asbury Park the next day. I was trying to settle back into the swing of things and commute to the office, while at the same time making plans to move back to Houston. The guys were taking about going back to Doraville, just outside of Atlanta, to finish the album. The project was taking longer than anticipated to complete... much longer.

There wasn't much of a tour - three shows in eight days, but we were hitting stadiums while we were out and doing new photos and an album cover, so it was worth the trouble. The plane sat in Addison, where it was presumably under maintenance and inspection.

I continued to work on the few shows that were booked and was coordinating the bookings of the next tour, beginning in October, with Terry Rhodes over at ICM. The new record still wasn't complete, and we couldn't afford to jeopardize or rush it, so we couldn't book anything in the near future. At this point in their career it was of the upmost importance, and it had to be killer, so the pressure was on.

I was doing the commute on a daily basis, settling into the office again, and had also dug into the books from the last few months. I had all the spread sheets from the shows but I still had to do the last leg's books, so I was also buried in accounting duties.

I was curious after my conversations with Judy and wanted to be able to give her a full accounting of the tour books. By everything I had seen so far, we were into fairly good money, but I also had to throw in all the salaries that would continue to be paid while the band was off the road and all the expenses for rehearsals, the warehouse, and other assorted items. It was a bit intimidating at first, but after a few days I had made good progress.

It was obvious the overhead to support the band's operation was enormous, over $15,000 a week, so the band had to pull in at least $60,000 a month, and that didn't include any road expenses. If I include per diem, and only per diem, we were looking at another $3,500 a week, and once hotels and transportation are thrown in we had a tough nut to crack. It was becoming much clearer to me – the band had to stay on the road. A single month off still cost the band over $60,000. I had gone along with the band in my beliefs - that they should be making good money on the road. But, after examining their expenses and looking at their grosses, which had to be reduced by management and booking agency fees, the pie wasn't that big. Next step was looking at the road expenses; that would take a while.

Finally it was time to hit the road again, and in spite of my love for the home life, I found myself itching to go back out. It was something in my blood, difficult to overcome. Linda wasn't pleased. We had been getting along so well that she was actually overcoming the depression and alcoholism but was fearful that she'd fall into it again. I did my best to console her, and talked to her friend Magda, who promised me she'd keep an eye on her while I was gone for two weeks.

On August 21st, with most of the album complete and in the can, we flew to Los Angeles to do new promo pictures and the new album cover. Then it would be off to Fresno on the 24th to make up for an earlier cancellation. We were playing Selland Arena, a mid-sized sports arena seating 6,500 that the city had built for their professional sports teams, none of which ever made it to the big leagues.

I left on the 20th, a day ahead of the band, to meet with Steve Wolf, the Anaheim Stadium promoter. Then to MCA, insuring all arrangements for the photo shoots had been made.

The next day I grabbed the limos and met the band at the airport, and as soon as I got them checked into their rooms, my phone was ringing. First Leon, then Allen, followed by Steve, Cassie, and Leslie - they all made calls, and for what? Money, cars, and good times. They had decided it was early for L.A., which it was, and wanted to go to the Strip in spite of the eight hour flight they just made. Since I was rested and wise enough to pick up cash before I left New York, I arranged a car and told them I'd meet them downstairs.

We went the Rainbow Room and tossed back Jack and Cokes. We hung 'til closing, saw a really crappy punk band, then returned to the hotel. It wasn't the good time we were expecting – I think it was the punk band.

The next morning we were up and rolling into Reservation Rehearsal Studios, as the band was going to get in a few hours of rehearsal and some "behind the scenes" photographs. I was shocked. The band, all of them, were awake and ready to go when I started calling around at 9:30. Maybe they had turned over a new leaf. Who knows, but I certainly wasn't counting on it. I didn't attend the rehearsals; they had Dean and Gene with them. Unless you're active in them, which I wasn't, they were about as exciting as a snail race.

Soon after they returned, I heard the oddest noise in the hall. I listened carefully and heard this swoosh of rushing air and then a thunk, like someone had dropped a small book, and then I thought I heard some laughter. I turned down the TV and listened again. Whoosh... Thunk! It was much louder, followed by distant laughter that sounded suspiciously like Gary and Leon.

I crawled off the bed where I'd been relaxing in front of the TV to look into the hallway, where I saw something streak by at eye level with a whoosh, and then heard a thunk on the other end of the hall. Since the sounds seemed to be happening a few minutes apart, I carefully stuck my head out the door (at the right time) and caught a glimpse of Gary, Billy, and Leon on the far side of the hall. Gary was just pulling back on a bow so I quickly pulled my head back into the room - I didn't know where the arrow would go. Seconds later I heard the whoosh – thunk and raced into the hallway.

"What the hell are you guys doing?" I yelled.

They froze. All laughter ceased. Busted!

"Roneckerman! Come on down here. You gotta try this," Leon shouted.

I walked towards them but I had no intention of participating, I'd leave that to the wilder of these natives. As soon as I started down the hall towards them, their expressions changed. I swear, it was like raising a bunch of teenagers

"You guys don't like this hotel?" I asked.

"No, we love this hotel," Billy said. "They have targets in the hallways."

Gary said nothing; he was looking at the floor trying to hide the smile on his face.

"And how much are you willing to pay for this target?' I asked.

"I don't want to buy it, I just want to shoot at it." Leon stated.

At this point I could hear Gary, still looking at the ground, but letting a chuckle escape. I had to admit I was suppressing my own laughter. Those pictures did look like targets.

"You guys know better than this. Fill those holes in the pictures with toothpaste or something, put the glass back on them, and hide those bows and arrows. Maybe we can get out of this place clean."

The next day we were asked to leave, but somehow I talked them into letting us stay. I knew I overpaid for those pictures - there's no way they were worth $1,000 each. I had to promise there would be no more incidents. I had my fingers crossed.

Once I was done with the hotel management, we went back to the rehearsal studios for more rehearsals and more pictures. Then it was off to Universal Studios to shoot the album cover.

George Osaki, the art director for MCA, met us at the studios and guided us onto the back lots where the photo would be shot. It looked like your typical city street, one from the East Coast, possibly the Bronx, or Baltimore.

David, the photographer, was already set up at one end, and there were a small army of technicians and stagehands running around as well as a couple of firemen. David asked the band to stand in a line about twenty feet in front of the city street. There was piping running across the ground only a few feet in front of the band's line-up, and more piping running about twenty feet on either side of the street, running the length of the building facades. And at the very end of the street, right before it dead ended into what appeared a five story stone building, there was a small chamber of some sort sitting on the ground with another pipe leading off from it. It looked like we were in the middle of a construction zone, where all the pipes are laid out right before they begin to excavate the streets.

Once the band was lined up in the right position, I cringed. It was Artimus' clothes, but when I compared him to Leon and Steve it actually wasn't that bad. These guys needed a makeover in the worst way. They were, however, in their stage clothes, so it would be what their fans are used to. Ronnie, Gary, Allen, and Billy looked good, really, same as on stage, and Steve had yet to figure out stage clothing at all – he just wore street clothes. Leon did have his grey top hat on, though, so he was a little bit closer to what I'd consider appropriate for the stage, but they had a long, long way to go. I made another mental note – get these guys to a stylist.

Once everyone was in a line, David began on the instructions:

"Here's the thing, guys: you need to concentrate on keeping your eyes open and standing perfectly still. We're going to light fires that will blaze out of the pipes – we'll have to set the right level so it could get a little hot before we're ready. We also have fires along each side of the street, and in some of the building windows behind you."

I could see the band squirming a bit as he continued, "When we get to the shot we're going to release a large fireball behind you. Remember, you're in no danger - we've got plenty of firemen around to take care of the fire. So when this explosion goes off you're going to want to flinch... and blink. Just hold yourself rigid. Any questions?"

"Yeah," Ronnie said. "If we're standing here all rigid it's not gonna look too natural, is it?"

David smiled, replying, "Just do the best you can."

With that, we were set. Moments later the fires were all set and the technicians adjusted them up and down according to David's instructions. As David started the countdown, Artimus and Steve really froze – you could tell they were expecting the blast. "3, 2, 1..."

The blast was huge - a fireball perhaps thirty feet in diameter went off, and all of us could feel the intense heat. It was blistering and produced a thirty degree change in temperature in a split second. If it hadn't dissipated quickly it would have certainly singed the hair right off our heads. Steve flinched... and blinked, so his shot wasn't quite as good as the rest of them, and Artimus was so rigid he looked like iron man, but all in all we felt we had it. It was a one take deal. After we were done, technicians and firemen appeared everywhere and quickly extinguished a dozen or so fires that were burning throughout.

That night MCA took us all out to dinner to celebrate. George Osaki was there, and David Alexander, the photographer, as well as Leon Tsillis, our champion over at MCA. They showed us a great evening and the band was on their best behavior, a refreshing break from our usual cataclysmic dinner parties.

We were on our way to Fresno the next day where we were doing a remake of the show we had cancelled the previous month. REO Speedwagon was opening for us, and the show was about 90% sold out. Kevin was also recording the concert off the board, and was doing a secondary mix for the recording, thus capturing a "live" show, as the band had shifted into a set that included a good mix of their new tunes.

The band was surprisingly straight during the performance as well, thanks to Gene's efforts. He had managed to cut the dressing room beverages down to beer and soft drinks, although Dean was still sneaking shots of JD to band members when Gene wasn't around. Still, it curbed the drinking considerably.

We flew the friendly skies of United the next day, Fresno to Los Angeles, and we would ride on to Anaheim and meet with Pepsi. I don't know how I had missed this in our schedule but there was no way we'd make it to the meeting in time. As soon as we hit the airport I hit the phones and called the hotel, asking them to explain to our guests we'd be late. I figured they'd understand – after all, this was rock and roll.

I was surprised at the Pepsi meeting. In the past, at least one band member would show up to such an affair loaded, especially on a day off. Even Allen, known for his belligerence in meetings, was calm and cool, hardly opening his mouth as we dined with our possible future business partner.

I've got to give it to Rudge - he was ahead of the game. Having a corporate sponsor to help us with tour promotion and expenses was brilliant.

When the meeting wrapped, it was hard to say how successful it was. They certainly had interest, but it was the mountain of details that came up that could derail it. We'd see how it played out. If we were successful, we were looking at a substantial amount of money for the next tour to help with promotion and tour expenses. It could make the difference - we could tour at a profit for a change.

I actually got a full night's sleep with no interruptions, and the next morning I was up early so I could visit the Stadium. It was our largest headlining stadium show yet and I wanted to make sure it went off without a hitch – this was Los Angeles… rock and roll heaven.

The next morning, I located Gene and Dean and sat down with them for breakfast, where we discussed a variety of subjects, all unrelated to the band. Gene and I were trading fishing stories, and Dean was adding fishing stories he had heard. It was a nice change.

After that, it was wonderfully quiet the entire day. Everyone wandered the hotel, visiting each other from time to time, smoking a few joints, and generally taking it easy. Steve and Cassie dropped by my room - Steve had some good pot, so we smoked and joked and I finally got to know him. He had been so shy and reserved, and so quiet, that I really knew little about him other than he was a really nice guy who could sing and play his ass off. He really didn't fit into this band of outlaws, but he hung with Allen so he was learning. It wasn't much to worry about though, Steve's inherent personality wouldn't change, and he'd always be his easygoing self, which I was sure of after our visit. He kept thanking me for being out here, which Cassie and I laughed about, as Cassie had much more to do with it than I did.

After a quiet evening in Anaheim, I wandered to Ronnie's room, where we had room service and ate dinner together, and then stared at the TV until Ronnie turned it down.

"Twenty six percent. Can you believe that?" Ronnie stated, scrunching up his face for emphasis.

I looked at him curiously. I had no idea what he was talking about.

"Twenty six percent," He repeated. "That's what Rudge gets."

"It could be higher," I said. "I know acts that pay their managers a lot more than that."

"Twenty six percent." Ronnie repeated, shaking his head. "No wonder we can't make any money. What do you think we ought to be makin'?"

"I don't know Ronnie. Here's the deal, we make a good bit of money on the road now, but as soon as we get off the road, we're losing close to sixty grand a month, maybe more."

"How much do we make while we're on the road?"

"It depends on where we're playing."

"On average, then. What do we make?"

"We could pull in a $100,000 a week."

"$100,000 a week?" Ronnie asked, surprised.

"Yeah, but once you take out commissions, it's $74,000. And we have to pay road expenses out of that."

"How much is that?" he asked.

"Doesn't Peter give you this info?"

"He does – I don't know if it's on the level, though."

"Okay, it varies, but we pay out about $40,000, or maybe $50,000 a week."

"So we make $30,000 a week… $35,000?"

"Give or take. Sometimes less, sometimes more. But that's only when we're touring heavy – at least five shows a week. And that doesn't include the damage bills, or the overhead – that's another $15,000 to $20,000. All in all, we break even at best."

Ronnie shook his head. "I always thought we were losing money most of the time."

"I don't know, Ronnie. I've only been with you a couple of years."

"You think that's fair?"

"What?"

"That Peter gets that much money. I know we can't do anything about the agents, they're all the same."

"I don't know. Like I said, there are other managers that charge a lot more."

"It seems like you do most of the work."

"Yeah, well, I get a lot of support from that office. Peter has a lot of people on staff, and he puts in his work - he knows a lot of people."

He went silent again. This time I restarted the conversation,

"I'm moving back from New York."

"What? I thought you loved it up there."

"I do, but Linda hates it. Too much snow, too few friends."

"Sounds like it's cold all around."

"Yeah, I guess you could say that."

"You going back to Houston?" he asked. He was watching me closely, most likely looking at my body language. I tried to sit still.

"Yeah, our families are there."

He turned his attention back to the TV for a minute, and then asked, "Houston's hot and muggy, ain't it?"

"Yeah." I replied. "100% humidity and 100 degree temperature in the summer. Not much better in the winter."

"You like Houston?" Ronnie asked, his eyes back on me.

"It's okay."

"You know, Jacksonville has the same weather."

He returned his attention to the TV. A few minutes later, I did too, but my thoughts were elsewhere. Then Ronnie started changing channels until he landed on a NASCAR race. That's when Gary walked in, just saying hi, and seating himself in front of the television where we all three sat in silence. The cars were racing around the track noisily, the announcer trying to up the ante with his dramatics. Gary finally broke the silence.

"You know, we ought to be sponsoring one of those cars."

Ronnie and I looked over at him; he had our attention.

"Imagine that car going around the track five hundred times, and all those people watching. There's our name, Lynyrd Skynyrd, going round and round."

"That's a great idea," I exclaimed.

"It'd probably crash," Ronnie said, a big grin on his face.

We talked about it some more, trying to guess what it would cost, and Gary asked me to look into it. I tucked it in the high priority section of my brain, and we watched the rest of the race, or at least until we saw a minor crash, then I left, leaving Gary and Ronnie to watch the rest.

I was up early the next morning, having rested well, and

went to the stadium early. By noon the stadium was a little better than half full and the temperature was north of 90 degrees. I was beginning to think we'd have a very late crowd that they were waiting for the temperature to cool instead of spending all day shoulder to shoulder in the heat. It depended on how much they wanted to see the rest of the bill, which included REO Speedwagon, Foreigner, and Ted Nugent.

At 1:00, the stadium was still short of full and the promoters and I decided to delay the show a half hour. That's all the time that could be spared, as we didn't have any lighting – it was something we cut from the budget.

At 1:30, I didn't hear any music. I gave it until 1:45 and then proceeded to the stage, looking for Clayton. The show should have started by then. Clayton told me he was trying to get it going, but Rex's managers had delayed the show, refusing to let the band go on until the stadium was fuller, and the promoters went along with it. Clayton and I took off in separate directions, Clayton looking for the promoter and me looking for Rex's tour manager. They were going on stage now or not at all. It took about fifteen minutes for our efforts to pay off, and by then the show was running an entire hour late. I returned to the production office after that, avoiding the heat. And there I would stay for the rest of the day, venturing out only to check the stage, the schedule, and the crowd. All three were disappointing.

At about 3:30 I became concerned. REO Speedwagon had yet to go on, and the schedule was slipping. If REO did forty five minutes and I allowed a half hour for set change Foreigner wouldn't be on until after 5:00, maybe as late as 5:30. That left forty five minutes for Foreigner, two set changes at a half hour each, and an hour for Ted Nugent; Skynyrd wouldn't be on until the sun was setting... or later. I huddled with the promoters and started the calls – I had to get a lighting system out here by sunset. Not only did it have to be here, it had to be set up and ready to go, and that had to be done during set changes. I had a sinking feeling that I had made the largest blunder of my career.

As the show continued the schedule slipped even further. I had finally reached Dave Oberman, and he was able to get some film lighting out for us – it was way too late to try to assemble a traditional lighting system and we'd never get it up. I gave it no thought and ordered the system. There was no time to waste.

I also called Dean and told him to delay the band an hour. Then I located Clayton and gave him the news, which he reacted to with both relief and concern. We would have lights, but it was going to be late in the day and they were going to suck; they weren't concert lights. But at least the audience would be able to see the stage. Otherwise it would be almost totally dark. And the show went on.

At 6:00 the band arrived, much earlier than I would have wished. I was both embarrassed and ashamed to tell the band. It was a horrendous mistake, not having lighting for this show, and the impact could be huge. After all, we were in Anaheim, part of the Los Angeles area. I found myself wishing we were second billed so I wouldn't be in this trouble. When I went to the dressing room and told the band, I was shocked. They didn't seem to care. I guess it was all those gigs they played in broad daylight. They didn't even hesitate to think about it – just went about their normal pre-show tasks. When I told them they wouldn't be going on until around eight was when they started getting pissed. They didn't want to be here that long. I took a bit of bashing from them and made myself scarce, retreating to the production trailer.

The lighting arrived at around 7:00 and Nugent was just beginning his set, so we'd have to wait until he finished to set up. That was cutting it extremely close. The set change was mad, with all of the band's gear being interchanged and the lighting being moved in at the same time. They had brought out some big guns, 5 and 10K Fresnels, which were used extensively in film. They illuminated a lot with a small amount of fixtures. It was definitely the best thing for us given the situation. Because of the lighting and the insane set change the delay grew longer, and it was apparent lighting was crucial.

After about an hour we were almost ready, but before we could even power the main lights up Dean and the band showed up at the rear of the stage, and the band was the drunkest I'd seen them in ages. Evidently the pressure of this show had enticed them to drink, and drink they did. I assume Gene had done his best, but figured Dean was slipping in the back door as Gene was going through the front. At any rate, it looked like a disaster waiting to happen. The band stood at the back of the stage, guitars already strapped on and ready to go, where they had to wait another fifteen minutes before they could go on. My temper was short and I lit into Dean harshly, scolding him for bringing the band to the stage before they were summoned. He claimed he was overpowered; that they were going to go out with or without him so he went ahead and brought them out. The band, of course, had a full view of this, but when I glanced back at them they didn't seem to be paying attention.

Finally the massive lights were fired up and aimed and the band took the stage. The crowd roared as usual, and there was well over 50,000 in attendance, so it was a mighty roar.

Skynyrd took the stage with their usual ferocity and launched into their set. About midway through the second song, I decided to wander through the audience to see how it looked. It wasn't good. I fought my way through a lively crowd that was dancing with the music, thoroughly entertained and enjoying themselves. The stage looked okay, but just barely. Those giant white lights on the band were creating these weird shadows behind them, and there was no definition, everything was washed out. It was definitely a different concert experience.

"I knew there weren't going to be the usual lights, but damn those things were hot," Ronnie told me, then added, "and they never went off, that's what really surprised me. We just charged through the set with no breaks. Those damn lights just never went off."

I never said another word about it and no one ever mentioned that particular show afterwards. It was an odd one... almost as if it didn't happen. It was one I'd never forget.

We flew to Las Vegas the next day - it was a travel day, so we all got to sleep in. I had to return to the stadium after the show to settle the box office, so I was quite a bit later getting back to the hotel the night before. We did about 57,000 tickets, 2,000 more than The Who sold the year before, and a stadium record. And from all accounts, all 57,000 fans loved every minute of it. I woke up a bit later than normal. The stadium had taken a lot out of me. I started the phone routine while packing my briefcase, which seemed to have exploded the night before - papers were scattered about the table and dresser, and there were even some on the floor. There was no hurry really, but I wanted to relax a bit as it was Sunday and I had few phone calls to make. I called and confirmed our limos, then pre-registered us at the hotel in Vegas, called Linda before I finished packing, then went downstairs for brunch.

Everyone had paid attention to the tent card in their room, and the dining room was full of the Skynyrd crew, all taking advantage of the Sunday Brunch special. I joined Cassie, Leslie, Steve, and Gary at a large round table where we gorged on crab legs, roast beef, shrimp – all the usual buffet fare. We hadn't put much thought into the fact that tonight we'd be in the buffet capital of the Universe.

The flight took us an extra two hours in travel time since we were flying commercial. It was a major hassle after traveling in our own plane.

After we checked into the Aladdin, I unpacked a few things, locked our cash in the safe, and searched the tables, finding Billy, Allen, and Jo-Jo at a five dollar blackjack table. I broke a hundred and joined the game. Billy was insane and

I began to wonder if he knew the point of the game, or if he just couldn't add the cards up. He was splitting tens and hitting nineteens, it made no sense at all, and he would win a hand on occasion, but mostly he was just feeding his money to the casino. Allen and Jo-Jo were doing a little better but their chips were dwindling as well, just not as fast as Billy's. When I saw Billy pull a second hundred out of his wallet I left and began roaming the casino, wondering where the rest of our gang had gone. I roamed around the long line of black jack tables, crossed over a couple of craps tables, and then circled the next row of blackjack tables. Finally I found Gary, Leon, Ronnie, and Steve at a table, all with small stacks of chips. It didn't appear anyone was winning. I returned to my room to watch TV.

I slept in the next day, as did the rest of our gang. My phone started ringing, it was Gene, and his call was followed by a half dozen more. The troops were on the move. The trick, I figured, was keeping them out of the casino long enough to make sound check, and then keeping everyone under wraps until show time. I'd been through this before - you don't want to lose band members in casinos. When I'd been here with Fleetwood Mac, I did lose the band, every one of them, and I had to enlist security to help find everyone. We used the cameras, and I got to visit the security office where we panned from area to area until I located everyone, then sent security to fetch them. They did the show, but we were a half hour late going on. Casinos don't stand for that nonsense – I found out the hard way, but I managed to make amends and was welcome back.

Styx opened the show promptly at 8:30 that night and Skynyrd was finished with their powerhouse set by 11:00, so it was party on. This was probably the end of my time with the band, not by choice, actually, but out of my new sense of duty to my family. I'd also be leaving SIR and New York, so I was looking at a lot of hopes and dreams dashed and I was depressed and confused. What I desired was a way to have both my career and family, and it seemed impossible.

Actually it wasn't the job, it was the family. I had two, and both were equally important. I had come to love the Skynyrd mob, at least most of them, as much as my own blood family. And I had fallen in love with Linda... and there was our girl, Mona. Giving up any of them was a stake through my heart.

Ronnie crept up and took a seat beside me at the casino bar.

"Ron, how could you do this to me?" he asked. "I have to find out from Allen? After I told you you'd always have a place here? How could you do this?"

I knew immediately what he was talking about. I had had a fight with Allen a few days before and told him I didn't give a shit, because I was going to leave soon anyway.

"It's my family, Ronnie. Linda can't take it anymore. You know I'm moving back to Houston.."

"Yeah, it's gotta be New York, man. Get 'em outta New York and everything will be just fine."

He was studying me closely. It made me uncomfortable.

"It's not just New York. I can't make any money doing this. As the band climbs to the top, I'm working my way to the bottom."

"You get paid the same as Gary and Allen, the same as all the guys."

"Maybe so, but I don't get royalties to supplement it."

"You got Clearlight, don't you?"

"I don't draw any money from that. Everything we make, we put back into the company. But that shouldn't have anything to do with what I get paid from you guys."

Ronnie ordered a drink, and we both watched in silence as the bartender mixed it. Ronnie took a sip of his drink, then asked,

"What'll it take?"

"What do you mean?"

"What will it take to keep you on? I'm open to anything."

I turned, looked him square in the eye, sucked in my breath, and let it fly.

"I want management. Why else would I have signed on to SIR and moved to New York?"

Ronnie smiled and had another sip of his drink, "We gotta talk about this. I've got some ideas…"

About that time, we were interrupted. Here came Allen.

"There you fuckin' bitches are!" he shouted.

We had to finish our conversation later that night in Ronnie's room.

"So… you want to be our manager?" he asked.

"It's like this, Ronnie. When I moved to New York after Rudge recruited me, I figured I would be handling management for him. And I have… but now he's avoiding me like the plague. We don't even talk anymore."

"Yeah. We've having our own problems. He's been good for us, no doubt about it. He's taken us a long way, we owe him credit for that."

"You know I've never had anything against Peter," I told him.

"I know that. Look, things are sticky all over. Our biggest problem – we're on the road too much. I can't even see my girls grow up. And we're about to start another one – it's going to be a marathon."

"It doesn't have to be."

Ronnie looked at me curiously. "What are you talking about?"

"We do these markets – these shitholes, and get paid pennies for it. If we only do the largest gigs in the strongest markets – take the money and run."

"What about the small markets, though? We want to play for all our fans. We have to play those shitholes."

"We cover them with stadiums, festivals… in the summer."

"Might work."

"Of course it will work. This is going to be your biggest record yet, I'm sure of it. And it's not Southern Rock. Sure, you guys have your southern theme intact, but this record will transform you from the best Southern Rock band in the world to the best rock and roll band in the world, or one of them, anyway. It's going to be huge, and we'll be doing all stadiums next year. I'm sure of it."

"Yeah, well. Don't count your chickens…"

"Ronnie, we both know this is going to happen."

I waited for a response. Ronnie just smiled and sipped his drink. I continued, I was just buzzed enough to let it all out.

"You guys should get 90% of the door on some of these gigs. Not 60%."

"We'll never get that," Ronnie countered.

"Sure you will. I learned that from promoting Houston. In some markets, you hardly need any promotion, they're guaranteed sell-outs. And anywhere we have those, the promoters aren't at risk. So we take back the risk premium."

Ronnie just sat there, thinking, so I nudged him,

"What are these ideas you have?"

"You think you could live in Jacksonville?" he asked.

"Maybe."

"You know, if you lived in Jacksonville, we could set up our own management."

"Yeah?"

"I wouldn't want to kick Rudge outta the picture – not yet, anyway. He's done too much for us, but his contract is comin' up."

I was listening attentively, this was interesting, and I had no idea it was coming or where it was going.

"If you moved down to Jacksonville you could run our company, and if we could renegotiate our contract with Rudge, you could split management with him, and it would be a joint venture thing – SIR and Lynyrd Skynyrd Productions would share management. If he thought we were leavin' him he'd do it, we'd get a better deal, and you'd get paid outta commissions so we wouldn't have to keep you on payroll. That way we could start promotin' our own shows like ya said. Everybody wins, I think."

"I'm in," I said. I didn't have to think about it.

"We'll have to run it by the Prez, of course. Let me work

on Gary, then you can fly down to Jacksonville. And Ron, this is gonna take some time, ya understand?"

"Yeah. I can hang in there."

"And we can't tell anyone," he added, "and I mean anyone. If this gets out, we're gonna have all kinds o' trouble."

"Double trouble," I added. "One more thing."

"Yeah?"

"I signed on with you guys for three weeks. We're closing in on two years now. And one of the reasons I'm still here, working for nothing, basically, is that Peter promised me you guys would start using my lighting company on your tours."

"Yeah, I heard."

"He promised. And I'll give you a bigger and better production for less money."

"Done. I'll have to run that by the Prez, too. But Gary will go along with it. We both know he will."

CHAPTER 19

My eyes opened for a moment and I realized I was being helped along by a couple of men, their shoulders under my arms, and my feet were dragging along in the mud. I had no idea where I was or what had happened. My face and clothing, my whole body, was dripping with a thick dark fluid, it felt like molasses. I saw Dean lying on the ground, just visible in the darkness, although there were sporadic beams of light flickering around and some spotlights were illuminating the scene from above, the sun gone crazy. The lights were creating weird shadows that moved about in slow sweeps, and then they'd jump erratically to another spot and start sweeping again. I was furious at Dean, and I remember thinking "Here we are in trouble, in some kind of Twilight Zone, and Dean's over there sleeping." Then things went grey... and proceeded to black, and I once again faded into the comfort of nothingness.

September 1977

I took a day off before going into the office. I wasn't as exhausted as I'd normally be, since I had only been gone a couple of weeks and we didn't do any one-nighters. The next day I commuted in, knowing that Peter was out of the office, and I planned to gather as much information as possible while continuing my normal duties. I hated this espionage stuff, but I had promised Judy I'd provide a full disclosure and Ronnie and I had made plans.

Within a week I had finished my spreadsheets and checked the figures, so I called Ronnie to see how the album was going. They were nearing completion and Kevin had taken the helm, along with Rodney Mills, and he was delighted with it, which was a good thing, it was overdue and MCA was anxious.

I finally broke the news that I was moving to everyone at

SIR and got a mixed response. Those closest to me knew what I was going through at home and were sympathetic, wishing me the best of luck. Those that weren't couldn't understand it at all and thought I was nuts. Calls were put in to Peter but he didn't call back, at least not that day. A few days later I finally heard from him.

"I hear you're leaving."

"Yeah Peter, I'm afraid I have to."

"You could have given me some notice."

"I was on the fence. We just decided."

"Okay, then. I'll talk to you next week."

That was it. He had little to say, further supporting my thesis that our relationship was on the rocks. We didn't talk again for a couple of weeks.

On Monday, we were on our way back to Houston. I didn't do a whole lot with the band in that first week of September, which was good, as Linda and I had moved into her mother's house while we looked for a new place in Houston. It was uncomfortable at her mom's house and I had no place I could spread out and work. It wasn't conducive to work in the first place, the household operated in chaos mode twenty four hours a day. Once Linda and I made the move to Clear Lake, a community on the outskirts of Houston where we found a comfortable temp apartment in a nice area, I set up a home office and dug in.

That's when things got fast and furious. SIR was sending me all kinds of material on the new tour and record, and I was on the phone twelve hours a day, juggling Clearlight and the band.

The album was going to be called *Street Survivors*, one of a handful of names that had been considered over the last year, so everything that was done in connection with the tour was themed to that "Survivor" message. The tour was named "Tour of the Survivors" and I had even started calling the crew survivors. It was fitting with this band, there had been a high turnover in the last year or two, and the only ones that were left were the survivors. The final cuts on the record; all of them juggled in and out ever since the recording process began, consisted of works from all over the spectrum. They were using a track from Criteria that Tom recorded, one dug out of the can from the old Muscle Shoals sessions from years back, and the rest from the Doraville sessions, which Kevin and Rodney Mills had produced with the aid of Dowd's associate, Barry Rudolph. It was unusual for the band, as it had two songs written by Gary and Ronnie and only one written by Allen and Ronnie. Two more were written by Steve and Ronnie, and Steve had two songs on it he had written without Ronnie, one of which, *I Know a Little*, was written long before he joined the band. And one song co-written with Ronnie, *Ain't No Good Life*, was sung entirely by Steve. It also had a song written by Merle Haggard, *Honky Tonk Night Time Man.*

 I hadn't heard the album assembled, but I'd heard all the individual songs at one time or another and the resulting record, in my opinion, was the best thing they'd ever done and would change the course of the band to the better. It had such mass appeal their audience should grow multifold. The three guitar assault was put to good use and Steve had introduced this jazzy – bluesy feel.

 The last couple of weeks before the tour I moved into the Clearlight office so I could get my staff to help me assemble the tour packages. We had backstage passes to make up, documents to produce and print, itineraries to produce, and a lighting system to package and document. The lighting system had been under prep for a while and I had even talked the group into some production with a new stage configuration. So we were building new fast-fold risers for the girls, the piano, and drums, and a beautiful portable bar with built in coolers and drawers for Dean – a gift from Clearlight,

 Linda was delighted to be back in Houston and spent a lot of her time visiting family and friends making up for lost time. We enrolled Mona in a new school and she was getting her first taste of real education, 1st grade. I still spent most of my time working, but now that Linda was happy, I no longer had to spend so much time at home which led, inevitably, to my longing for my larger family, and for the road.

CHAPTER 20

I awoke at some point. It was like coming up for air, and when I opened my eyes, I saw Linda. There was nothing else there – everything was grey around her, but she was there, glowing and smiling, and she was holding something large and white in her hand on the bed. I didn't know where I was, but I knew something really bad had happened. I looked at Linda, trying to focus, and asked, "Ronnie?" She teared up, and with a brave smile told me he was gone. The grayness quickly washed over me and turned black. I slipped back into my comfortable world of nothing. My eyes opened again at some point... it could have been hours, or days, or weeks. Linda was there, and I saw my father behind her. And there were flowers all around the room. I felt myself slipping and quickly asked, "Cassie?" Linda was shaking her head back and forth as I slipped back into my cocoon. It was safe there – safe, and quiet, and warm... and full of nothing. Sometime later I awoke yet again, and again there was no sense of time, but my brother Rodney was with Linda and my father. I had nothing to say, but heard my lips utter a name, "Steve?" I awoke from my coma one last time, and managed to whisper "Dean?" before I collapsed into my world of comfort... of blackness.

October 1977

Steve, Jim, Mark, and I were just buckling in; the engines started and were running smoothly when Jim Griswold, one of the owners of the aircraft, came running to the plane from his office. The pilots cut the engines, opened the door, and lowered the stairs. Jim had the contract for the plane.

"I thought that was taken care of," I told him.

"I sent it to your office, no one ever sent it back. You have to sign this."

"Can't you just re-send it?"

"I can't let that plane go up without papers. You have to sign this."

I grabbed the papers out of his hand and glanced over them,

"Is this the same contract we signed last time?"

Since no one from the office ever questioned the document, I trusted it, and since Jim claimed this was an exact duplicate, I went ahead and signed it.

Jim glanced at the signature, wished us well, and resealed the aircraft. The pilots, Walt and John, same as the last leg, started the engines and let them warm a few minutes. They were obviously going through their final check list, then we felt the engines surge and we started for the runway.

When we landed in Jacksonville the entire entourage was already there, waiting and ready to go. Spirits were as high as I'd ever seen them and all the wives, friends, and families were there to see us off. I made the rounds, giving Judy a hug and holding little Melody as long as she'd let me, then giving Teresa Gaines a little kiss. I hugged Kathy, Allen's wife, and his two girls, and met a few of their friends. Steve, Jim, and Mark were introduced to everyone, and then the goodbyes started. Needless to say it took a while, but the plane slowly filled and we were finally able to secure the door.

Dean took over the steward details, giving everyone some abbreviated flight instructions and while I reminded everyone of my own rules, the engines sputtered to life and began warming up. It didn't take long for them to smooth out as we had just come from Houston and they were still warm. In moments we were on the runway waiting for clearance to take off.

It was a short flight to Statesboro, Georgia, where we were playing in a sunken basketball arena. It was a decent sized arena but the architects had never even considered holding any event outside of basketball there. The load in was through the same doors through which the crowd exited, and then everything had to be transported to the arena floor to be prepped and set up. All we had were student stagehands, so we were handicapped from the start. The beefy union stagehands were always preferable – they knew what they were doing.

Since this was the first show for Clearlight I was at the load in from the get go and witnessed the problem with our gear as soon as it appeared. We had twenty foot long lighting trusses, and due to the way the building entrance was designed, the trusses lacked about an inch of making it around the corner of a wall that obstructed the stage entrance. We were baffled. There didn't seem to be a way to load them into the building. I huddled with my crew and we were all standing there, scratching our heads, when an enterprising student on the crew told us it was no problem.

He disappeared for a short time, telling us he'd be right back, and he returned carrying a small sledge hammer. I looked at Steve, he looked back at me, and we both started walking away. We returned about ten minutes later. Lo and behold, somehow a corner of the wall had been damaged; there was enough clearance to get the rig in. As we were loading the remainder of the lighting gear I asked Steve, "Aren't you glad we have student stagehands?"

That advanced us to the next problem. There were no riggers. Riggers were required at every gig to hang our systems from the building's ceiling. It was a dangerous job, crawling along four inch beams a hundred feet or more above the floor, which is why we required these specialists at each show. You certainly didn't want someone that didn't know what they were doing suspending a two ton lighting rig over the stage. Mark Howard, one of the Clearlight crew members, was a rigger, but it was a two man job. That's when I climbed into the ceiling. I knew enough about rigging and had enough experience to hang the show and there were no other options. A few hours later the show was up, I was dusting myself off, and Clayton was giving me a hard time.

"I saw you up there doing the rigging."

"So?" I answered, still dusting. The ceiling and beams

were filthy.

"So, are you going to do that every day?"

"What the hell are you talking about?" I asked.

"Well, you had to come down and do the system rig. I just want to know if you're going to be here every day to do that."

I don't know why, but Clayton wanted to see us fail so badly it hurt. I think he might have been threatened by Steve Lawler, who was Frampton's production manager, or it could have just been a dislike for me, he knew I was slowly moving more and more of my own assets into the Skynyrd operation and knew little about the business end of the deal. Perhaps if he knew what a deal I'd given the band he would have changed his mind. At any rate, he was venomous.

The crew rolled out the thick brown carpet I had purchased for the stage and assembled the various platforms. The stage was now configured with the drums slightly offset from the center, with the girls on the left on a slightly lower riser, and the piano on the opposite side of the drums on yet a lower riser. It was certainly different from their previous configurations and the band seemed excited about it. It was their first venture into any production at all other than the mirror ball and flag... and *The Magnificent Seven* intro.

When they arrived at sound check, they seemed pleased and experimented a little bit, but mostly they fussed over the monitors. It was a long sound check, typical of first shows, as there were lights being adjusted, sound problems, etc. – all the usual stuff. It was the very reason I couldn't understand why they refused to do stage rehearsals. I'd been harping on it for months. Finally we returned to the hotel with just enough time to clean up, grab a snack, and return for the show.

When we returned, everyone was relaxed and sipped on beer and juice, the only beverages we were allowing. Dean had the liquor already locked up in his new bar and he had filled the coolers with ice so he was ready to go for the show. Of course these days he was only serving beer and soft drinks but after the show he was allowed to open it to full service. He had even made a little tip cup, which was placed on the side of the door and was always empty. I was wandering the building, as was my habit, gauging the audience and checking security with Gene. It looked like a sold-out show - I couldn't find an empty seat in the house. In fact, I was almost certain they had oversold, but being a college there were probably a lot of college staff and crew sneaking their friends in.

The guys seemed to struggle a bit during the show, regularly complaining about the monitors, with Ronnie turning to Kenny every few minutes, pointing to his monitors when he did.

The band played a 50/50 mix of material, half new material, half old, and the response was phenomenal. When I was out at the sound board it sounded a bit rushed and Kevin agreed that something was off, but we had chalked it off to typical first show problems.

After settling with the promoter, I went back to the dressing room and the band launched in to me immediately. I wouldn't say I was attacked, not a bit, but the band certainly voiced their complaints:

"Man, there was no fucking sound on that stage, it was like being in a studio," Allen told me.

"Yeah," Gary added, "I couldn't even hear myself half the time."

Steve just sat to the side and monitored the situation. He knew the boys would address his own concerns.

"It was that carpet," Allen said. "It sucked all the sound off the stage."

Ronnie pulled me to the side at that point. Everyone could still hear, but he wanted it between me and him.

"Ron, remember when you told me the carpet you got would make it feel like I was walkin' on clouds?"

"Yeah"

Ronnie grinned one of his best. "Well it does, so send it down to Jacksonville. I'm gonna have it installed in my house. I like that wood under my feet – it heats up, it keeps me movin'.'"

Allen then added his comment, "And put the stage back like it was. I can't hear right like it is now."

And so we went back to the old set-up - Lynyrd Skynyrd, the non-production band. Give us a mirror ball, a confederate flag, and an intro song, and we're good to go.

I should have known actually. I'd seen it all over the world. They didn't need production, they just needed a stage – the music did all the rest... and Ronnie's magic. He commanded that stage and even when your eyes were drawn to a soloist they went right back to Ronnie. It was the strangest thing I'd ever seen and never ceased to amaze me.

We had a quiet night in Statesboro that night, which surprised me. Three months ago, things would have come unglued. But they weren't drinking anything until after the show, and weren't drinking that much then, and everyone was so excited about this simple fact that it fed back on itself, reinforcing the whole thing. It appears Gene had finally succeeded. There was the usual migration from room to room by almost everyone, but the parties were small and involved a glass of wine or a beer at most. Usually they'd just smoke a joint or two.

We flew to Miami the next day, a long haul for our aircraft, three and a half hours. We had adapted to the aircraft fairly well and after the take-offs and landings, which we white knuckled, same as in a commercial plane, we enjoyed ourselves quite a bit. And we definitely spent less time traveling if the time in and out of airports were added. We weren't saving a whole lot of money, but it was enough to offset the plane's cost.

During the flight I lost about $40 in the poker game. I didn't catch a single card and my bluffs quit working after the third win. $40 was about my limit, so I got up and wandered the plane for a while, and Ronnie had taken my seat. When he saw me coming, he motioned me over and showed me his hand with a big grin. He had a pair of 3s, and I raised my eyebrows when I saw them, pretending it was a powerhouse hand. He held all five cards when it was his time for new cards, they were playing five card draw, and bet his ass off, raising to the limit every time it went around. He won the pot as soon as the draw cards were dealt, everyone threw in their hands. It was a good bluff. I patted him on the back and returned to the mid-section of the craft where there was a seat open on the sofa, falling asleep a short time later. When I awoke, we were descending to Miami.

We had almost 18,000 people squeezed into the sorry excuse for a building known as the Hollywood Sportatorium. Hollywood, Florida looked like a pretty rough place when you drove through it, but not spending any time there I didn't really know. It certainly wasn't too rough for Skynyrd or their fans, although the comfort level in the place was off the scale... the lower scale.

We buzzed in and noticed a huge amount of kids wandering about the grounds looking for tickets. It was sold out, yet hundreds remained outside. The band performed one hell of a show, and we raced out as quickly as we could, almost beating the fans out of the parking lot. Those same kids, the ones that couldn't get in, were still roaming. We found out the next day those wanderers caused some $10,000 in damages, mostly broken windows in the building, but when they broke most of those they turned to cars and smashed out windows all over the lot. It was obviously time to find a larger venue.

I visited Ronnie after the show. We sat there in his room, sipping a glass of Dom Perignon, toasting another show under our belts.

"You know Ron. I still hate some of these guys."

"I know. I've got some problems with a few of them too."

"Not always. But most of the time," Ronnie said, taking off his hat.

"I know, believe me."

"I'm not worrying about it as much, not that I ever did. I just got used to it. And with all the shit I did? I can't say too much. But these guys still ain't grown up."

"They're trying. You got to give 'em credit."

Ronnie refilled our glasses. Another couple of sips of Dom, and away we go.

"You know I wanna sing country."

It was my turn to grin now, "Why do you keep telling me this stuff I already know?"

He ignored me. "Maybe do a solo project next year."

"You're best off sticking with it. Skynyrd's magic. It's not the individuals, man, it's the group. It's you and the group. Take either part out and it doesn't work."

We sat there a moment in silence; I think Ronnie was digesting what I had said.

"You know what you've got, don't you?" I asked. When Ronnie didn't answer I continued. "You've got a band and a brand! You know what I mean? It's already there. And I know you've heard this before: you guys are the American version of the Stones. And you're Mick... with a little weight."

Ronnie just stared out the window, not really looking at anything in particular. "Someday, though. Country."

"Take those boys with you when you go that route, Ronnie. Just guide them along, they'll follow you. Here's the deal: if you stick with this band and hang on – it's gonna be a wilder ride yet, but then you can do anything you want in a few years. You want to do country? Do country. But take the band country - just wait until Skynyrd makes it to the top. Then you'll take all those fuckers with you."

"Who, the band?"

"No! The audience – take those fuckers with you. And the band, of course, at least some of them."

"That just might work," Ronnie stated, wiping the sweat from his brow. "I'd just about given up on those boys. It seems like every time we had something goin' they'd run off and bang themselves up. Now that we got Steve... and Gene, they calm everyone down."

"Yeah, I never thought I'd see the day."

"So... how'd we do?"

"Sold out – and then some."

Ronnie tugged his hat down a little and leaned in, almost whispering, "Ya gonna move?"

"I think so. But I haven't talked to Linda yet."

"She'll love it. You know that."

"I'll have to pull her away from family."

"Just into her new one," he said, grinning.

And so I committed, and was going to be a Floridian, and I prayed that Linda would accept it. I really loved the idea, not that I loved Florida that much, but I did love Ronnie and most of the band, and it was the opportunity of a lifetime.

We moved on down the road the next day – to St. Petersburg. Our old plane purred like a kitten – a kitten with an occasional cough, but it was purring and we were comfortable.

We were playing the Bayfront Center there in St. Pete, and it was sold out... it only took 2 hours once the tickets were released.

The new album, *Street Survivors*, was to be released the following day, but the radio stations had already gotten their hands on it, and were already playing the hell out of *That Smell*. Deciding to watch most of the show from the sound board, I was sitting out front with Kevin for a good half hour. It was the first time I watched Steve sing Ain't No Good Life all the way through. He was so laid back, yet attacked the song with such gusto. Ronnie roamed the stage behind him, never giving up an inch of it to Steve, instead, he leant it to him for the song. At the same time he was directing the whole audience's attention to Steve, and had assumed the role of inspector general, still pushing the guys up front for solos. Then he'd wander around spending a few minutes with everyone, watching them play.

Ron Eckerman and a fan backstage October 19, 1977
(Since it was "The Tour of the Survivors" I had T-shirts made up with the band's name on the back and "Travel at your own risk" on the front.)

It was a fantastic bit of showmanship – only Ronnie could pull something like that off. Most performers would have simply left the stage for a break. The show was typical – the audience was in the kill zone – and the band... the killers.

The evening seemed relatively tame – we had this new, mellow band... but it was only a matter of time, I knew these guys wouldn't lie low for long; it simply wasn't in their nature. I'd spent a year with the new mellow and it exploded every two or three days so, even though we were really playing it cool for a change it felt like it was the calm before the storm. All we needed was a few days off, a misplaced bottle or two of Jack, and some rowdy friends to drop by – I had no doubt that things would revert to the norm in spite of the good intentions.

I answered the call relaxed, things were going smoothly, and I had just about accepted the new gentle Lynyrd Skynyrd, at least for the time. It was Ronnie.

"Ron, get down here now. We have something to settle."

I braced myself for the worst and proceeded to Ronnie's room. Gary was there, and Gene, and Cassie and Leslie. I was invited in.

"Okay, Ron," Ronnie started, pulling up his shorts, "who's got the best legs?"

"Mine are the best. Just ask Cassie," Gary stated.

What the hell? I was called down here to judge these guys' legs? The guys really had changed. I threw out a leg.

"What about mine?"

Cassie spoke up. "Your skinny legs aren't even in the competition." She draped her arm around my waist when she said it, easing my discomfort.

"I can't help it - it's hereditary."

Gene jumped into the fray. "Looky here. No one can beat mine."

"So whose is best, Ron?" asked Ronnie.

"Yeah Ron, which ones are the best?" Gary chimed in.

"I ain't no judge of your legs. And I could give a shit. Now if you want me to judge the girls' legs, that's another story."

The contest ended in a three way draw, they were all equal, and I escaped back to my room, thoroughly amused... and quite amazed. They had turned to beauty contests.

We woke early for the flight to Greenville, about 400 miles - a two and a half hour flight, and we piled into the plane and made ourselves comfortable quickly. Seating arrangements had become somewhat fixed: poker in the aft lounge, where the card table folded out of the wall, sleeping in the mid-section, and, in the forward lounge, lounging... and talk.

I was sitting in the back in my usual seat, an aisle seat, the last one in the cabin, and I had my whole Clearlight crew to play cards: Jim Brace, Mark Howard, and Steve Lawler... and I was doing fairly well, winning every second or third hand.

Once we were really settled into the game and our attention was completely focused, the right engine decided to hiccup, and it sounded like a friggin' bomb.

Gene said he saw a huge flame shoot out of the engine. I missed it due to the card game. It was just one loud pop, like a backfire, and then we seemed to be running fairly smoothly again. It was upsetting to all of us. Backfires aren't good at 15,000 feet, and so the balance of the flight was difficult. It was hard to keep your concentration. Jim Brace was a pilot himself. He was only certified for small planes, Cessnas, but he was knowledgeable about flying. Since he didn't appear that concerned, I wasn't either. I'd talk to the pilots and get it straightened out once we landed; there was nothing that could be done while in the air anyway. The plane landed in Greenville a short time later and we all boarded the waiting limos to transport us to the hotel.

There was a lot of talk that day. Some of us were scared shitless, others not so much. The backfire was troublesome. Discussions about the plane waned as it grew near sound check, but continued as soon as we returned to the hotel. I was in my room on the phone where I'd remain for hours as I searched for alternate transportation.

The performance that evening went smoothly. There was no sign of trouble and the band performed with their usual fire, the audience soaking it up and giving it back, and we left them in their usual state – whipped into a mass of writhing, twisting bodies with air guitars everywhere, each male in the audience imagining they're on stage and in the thick of it. Each girl... well, I don't know about them, they probably wanted a shot in bed with their favorite of the band, or perhaps to be up there singing back-up vocals.

Most everyone abandoned their no drinking vows that night. It must have been the anticipation about the plane. Dean's bar was raided, and there were a couple of bottles of Jack Daniels floating around. People were moving from room to room as usual, but tonight every discussion concerned the plane. Our trusty craft wasn't appearing so trusty.

I was up early the next morning. Even if it was just a backfire, it was unacceptable. Gene had even gone to the airport already, and the pilots were both there as well. The plane was certainly comfortable enough but the mental anguish we were suffering just wasn't worth it. I found the leasing company was well aware of the situation once I got through to them. The pilots must have been doing their job as I was told that the problem was a faulty magneto in one of the engines. They were flying out a new magneto and a mechanic to the next stop. I pressed them,

"What's a magneto? Is there any chance we'd have a failure?" I was told that we were safe, and that the aircraft could run on one engine if needed. And there was very little chance of that happening, both engines had two magnetos each. By the end of the call I was breathing easier, but not by much.

Next stop – Ronnie's room. He wasn't too happy about it. I explained the situation and asked him what he wanted to do.

"Ron, let's keep the plane. Look, if your number's up, your number's up. Doesn't matter if we're in a plane or a bus." It was still a decision I had to make regardless of what Ronnie said.

It was a rough morning. It took a while to load up and some had hangovers so severe they wouldn't answer their phones. I called Dean and told him to physically go to Allen's and Billy's rooms and get them up, as everyone that had behaved and were on time were getting angry.

Allen had said that he had gotten a call from JoJo, who had not been out with us during the leg of the tour, but was headed out to meet us in Baton Rouge and continue touring with us. She told him not to get on the plane, because she had a dream that the plane had crashed.

A short time later, transported by taxi due to missing limos, everyone was seated in the plane. Everyone warming up for the day, hitting the bar, rolling the joints, and generally preparing for the daily grind, but I wasn't seeing the cheery faces I normally would, hangover or not. The excitement in the plane had turned to fear. But at least the plane would be repaired at the next stop. From there it would be smooth sailing. After all, we were survivors.

PLANE CRASH KILLS 3 BAND MEMBERS
10/21/1977

MCCOMB, Miss. (AP) -- A twin-engine airplane apparently low on fuel crashed Thursday night while attempting an emergency landing, killing three members of the rock band Lynyrd Skynyrd and three other persons and injuring 20.

The propeller-driven Convair 240 skidded across tree tops for about 100 yards, then slammed into a swampy area and split open about eight miles short of the McComb airport after reporting it was "having fuel trouble or was running low on fuel," an air traffic controller reported.

The dead included lead singer **RONNIE VAN ZANT**, guitarist **STEVE GAINES** and vocalist **CASSIE GAINES**, GAINES' sister, medical authorities said.

Pilot WALTER WILEY McCREARY and co-pilot WILLIAM JOHN GRAY, both of Dallas, Tex., and DEAN KILPATRICK, assistant road manager for the group, also died, officials said. A breakdown provided by officials listed 10 of the injured in critical condition and 10 in stable condition.

Authorities suggested that the pilot may have been trying to land the plane in one of several open fields near the trees where the crash occurred.

The chartered plane came down on its nose southwest of McComb, twisting the cockpit to the left, and threw seven or eight persons to the ground when it split open at about the middle of the fuselage, witnesses said. The impact, which triggered no fire, tossed other passengers toward the front of the aircraft.

"They were all in front of the plane and they were all shouting. 'Get me out, get me, get me," said Constable Gerald Wall. "We were actually standing on top of some people to get the others out."

Johnny Mote, who lives near the crash site close to the Mississippi - Louisiana border, said the plane "sounded like a car skidding in gravel" as it clipped the trees.

"When it hit ground it was a deep rumble, like it was underground. It sounded like thin wrinkling metal," he said.
The group was en route from a Wednesday night performance in Greenville, S. C., to a Friday night concert before an expected crowd of 10,000 persons at Louisiana State University in Baton Rouge.

The plane had passed McComb when it reported that it was having fuel trouble and was told by the Houston, Tex., flight center to turn around and land at McComb, said Everett Fairly, an air traffic controller at McComb. "I tried to call them, but we couldn't raise them and Houston reported it had lost radar and radio contact," Fairly said.

A spokesman for the Federal Aviation Administration in Atlanta, Ga., said the pilot had reported being low on fuel.

The group was formed in Jacksonville, Fla., producing its first album in 1973 and then earning its first $1 million gold album with "Second Helping" in 1974. Later albums sold a million copies each for the group noted for its hard-driving rock and unrestrained performances.

The band's fifth and latest album was "Street Survivors." It had just completed visits to four cities on a lengthy tour.
Thick undergrowth hampered rescue operations and some emergency vehicles became stuck in the mud when they tried to drive through the woods to get

close to the aircraft. Rescue crews also were hindered by a 25-foot wide, waist-deep creek they had to cross to reach the plane and then return with the injured and dead on stretchers.

A helicopter hovered over the plane with floodlights to help rescuers.

Pickup trucks and vans were used along with ambulances to carry the dead and injured to hospitals.

A Southwest Medical Center spokesman said identification of victims was complicated because passengers apparently were playing poker before the plane went down and had their wallets with identification papers out.

Fairly said a small jet was landing at McComb at the time the plane was reported in difficulty and he asked the jet pilot to fly over the area.

"But it was very dark and the pilot said he could see nothing from the air," Fairly said.

The plane came down near open pasture land, tearing off one of the wings and twisting the other. Rescuers had to rip open the nose to get to victims. Bulldozers were used to cut a path through the woods and brush from nearby Mississippi 568.
Donald Chase, who lives about five miles from the area, said he heard that "that the plane was having engine trouble because it was sputtering."

Mote said he was putting some hay out when three bloody survivors who had made their way through the woods called to him for help.

Fatalities:
WALTER McCREARY, pilot.
WILLIAM GRAY, co-pilot.
RONNIE VAN ZANT, singer/songwriter.
STEVE GAINES, guitarist/vocalist.
CASSIE GAINES, vocalist.
DEAN KILPATRICK, assistant road manager.

Survivors of the Crash:
LEON WILKESON, bass guitarist.
GARY ROSSINGTON, guitarist.
LARKEN ALLEN COLLINS, guitarist.
BILL POWELL, pianist.
ARTIMUS PYLE, drummer.
LESLIE HAWKINS, vocalist.
RON ECKERMAN, road manager.
GENE ODOM, security manager.
JAMES BRACE, road crew member.
MARK FRANK, road crew member.
MARK HOWARD, road crew member.
CLAYTON JOHNSON, road crew member.
DON KRETZECHMAN, road crew member.
JOE OSBORN, road crew member.
KENNETH PEDEN, road crew member.
CRAIG REED, road crew member.
PAUL WELCH, road crew member.
STEVE LAWLER, lighting technician.
KEVIN ELSON, sound engineer.
BILL SYKES, television film crewman.

CHAPTER 21

If anyone is responsible for the crash and the demise of Lynyrd Skynyrd, it is me ... shared in part with Peter Rudge. I was the one who initiated the desire to travel by private plane, I chose the aircraft, and I signed the lease. Peter Rudge should have been reviewing the contracts with the attorneys and checking the plane's history and maintenance, although I, too, could have done the same.

Rudge was an excellent manager, and I was more than pleased to work with him. Although I believe that we would have been safe to fly if the plane had been adequately fueled, I now would have grounded the plane for any mechanical problem whatsoever.

One engine had a faulty magneto and caused the engine to run rich, and the pilots miscalculated the fuel requirements to get to our destination with a safe surplus; we simply ran out of fuel. The National Transportation Safety Board said it was a miracle that there were any survivors.

Ronnie repeatedly told me and others that he wouldn't live to the age of thirty. His birthday was less than three months away. The most popular song on the last album was *That Smell*, a song about death. The album was named *Street Survivors* and the tour was named *Tour of the Survivors*. I had made a T-shirt the day before with the encryption, "Travel at your Own Risk." We were also given a warning shot – the previous day's backfire.

Ronnie Van Zant, Steve Gaines, Cassie Gaines, Dean Kilpatrick, and the two co-pilots, Walter McCreary and John Gray, lost their lives on that fateful day, October 20, 1977.

Allen Collins passed away in January 1990 due to complications of pneumonia after being paralyzed from a car accident.

Leon Wilkeson passed away in 2001 due to complications resulting from liver disease.

Billy Powell passed away from heart failure in 2009.

Jo-Jo Billingsly passed away in 2010 after a battle with cancer.

In 2006, Lynyrd Skynyrd was inducted into the Rock and Roll Hall of Fame. Gary Rossington, Ed King, Bob Burns, Artimus Pyle, and Billy Powell were the band members there to accept the honor.

I never saw Alice again after separated, and I continued my life with Linda and Mona. Three years after the plane crash, my divorce from Alice was finalized, and I married Linda and I was finally able to legally adopt Mona and raised her as my own. After 30 years of marriage, Linda left on our anniversary. We went our separate ways and divorced, but we remain friends. Mona is an accomplished musician and fronts a band called *Mona's Vices*.

About six months after Linda and I separated, I met and fell in love with my sweetheart Carolyn in the fall of 2011, when she took on the role of editing this book.

Artimus Pyle continues to travel and play with a band that plays Skynyrd material.

Gary Rossington tours and plays original Skynyrd music as well as records new music with the greatest Lynyrd Skynyrd tribute band in the world. Technically, they're as good as the original band, perhaps even better. Ronnie's youngest brother Johnny is the singer, and he does an amazing job. They still tour as *Lynyrd Skynyrd*.

The band and all the passengers aboard filed a class action lawsuit against me after the crash. The lawsuit was against me as well as the airplane leasing company, and the estates of the pilots. After many months of litigation, the judge did, in fact, release me from any and all responsibility for the crash. I continued to work with Gary and the surviving members with their new band, Rossington-Collins band, but after a falling out, we went our separate ways.

I lost four friends on that flight whom I loved dearly. I think about them every day of my life, and will be haunted by this unfortunate incident to my death. But I do believe, like Ronnie, however, that we are in the hands of destiny, and when your number's up, your number is indeed up, so it might have happened regardless of the circumstances.

The release of responsibility by the judge did not change the fact that I still felt responsible for the loss of the lives of people I cared so much about. After all, I was the tour manager. It was my responsibility to make sure the band got from city to city safely. I was never able to truly put it behind me.

Ron and Carolyn in February 2014

About the Author:

    This book was a labor of love, and is dedicated to furthering the legacy of Lynyrd Skynyrd and Ronnie Van Zant.

    After recovering from the crash, Ron spent a few more years in the concert industry, working with Foreigner, Waylon Jennings, and a few other groups.

    He produced in television and film, and taught at Santa Monica College for five years.

    In May of 2013, Ron was diagnosed with acute myeloid leukemia, AML, a fast growing form of bone marrow cancer.

He fought a very courageous battle. His journey ended on May 11, 2014.

During his illness, he began writing his second book with his wife, Carolyn, also a writer. He wanted the book to be about surviving 3 things: a plane crash, heart surgery, and leukemia. Since Ron's health took a turn for the worse, they were unable to finish the book together.

After Ron's passing, Carolyn decided to complete the project she and Ron started, and write a book in his honor to let everyone know how courageous he was and how he remained optimistic until his very last day. It is a heartfelt testament that the phrase "laughter is the best medicine" is absolutely true.

"The Last Tour: Love, Laughter, and Tears," by Carolyn Day is not only about Ron's battle with leukemia, but also his story of finding love, facing destiny, and his amazing ability to stay strong and keep a sense of humor no matter how he felt, or how bleak his future seemed. It chronicles the last two and a half years of his life.

It is also a story of mending broken relationships before leaving the world. It is about finding out who *you* really are and who your true friends are.

Available on Amazon in paperback, Kindle, and Audiobook.

The proceeds go to leukemia research.

PREVIEW
of

"The Last Tour: Love, Laughter, and Tears. In memory of Ron Eckerman"
By Carolyn Day

Chapter 1
December 6, 2012

Christmas was just around the corner, and I had really made Ronnie upset by telling him I didn't want to spend the holidays with him. As much as I adored him, I was mentally drained from hearing about the book he had written and his new ideas of how to promote it. I wanted to spend Christmas with my mom, my daughter, and my family. Ronnie and I had argued a little in November, and I didn't want to spend the holidays listening to him talk about his book the whole time. It had gone on for more than a year, and I was really losing my patience. I wasn't nice about it at all.

"I feel like I haven't seen you in forever," he told me. "We didn't spend Thanksgiving together, and now you don't want to see me for Christmas, either?"

"It hasn't been *forever*," I snapped. "You just spent 12 days here in October. You need to spend Christmas with your mom, anyway. She's 80 years old. She might not have a lot of time left."

"I've told you this a million times," he said angrily, enunciating every syllable in his deep, serious tone, "this is probably my last Christmas. *I'm* the one who doesn't have much time left!"

He hung up on me.

He had told me for over a year that he didn't have much time left to live. He had recurring dreams that he was going to die from heart failure on May 23, 2013. He was convinced that he had less than two years left, and he wanted to spend every second with me. He fell in love with me so quickly it was almost scary, at least at the time. Looking back now, it wasn't scary at all. He just knew what he wanted and what was meant to be. He was right about a lot of things. He was just wrong about the date.

There we were, three weeks before Christmas, the time of year when couples are supposed to be looking forward to the holiday together, but we were arguing on the phone instead. We continued the argument on Skype, and I was the rudest I had ever been to him. I told him that I'm done: done with him, done with our relationship, just plain done.

"Fine! I'm done, too!" he shouted, and quickly turned off his computer.

I went to bed and tossed and turned for several hours and couldn't get to sleep. I hated fighting with him. I got up to go to the bathroom and realized that I had left my phone downstairs. Since I used the alarm clock feature, I thought I'd better get it and plug it in next to my bed so I wouldn't oversleep and be late for work the next day.

When I plugged my phone in and it started charging, I saw that I had quite a number of text messages from Ronnie.

The first one read, "Goodbye."

The second one read, "My will is in a folder on the pool table. You'll have the rights to the book. Maybe it will sell better after I'm dead. Thank you for everything you did for me. I love you."

The third one read, "Maybe it will make the news. Lynyrd Skynyrd plane crash survivor commits suicide. Maybe then the book will be a big seller."

The fourth one read, "You aren't even answering! You don't even care! Please tell my mom I did this because I can't deal with the headaches anymore. I don't want her to blame you."

At that point, I didn't take the time to read any more

texts. I called him, but it went straight to voicemail. I called his daughter and left a message, and then texted her. Since I had only known him a little over a year, I wanted to find out if he had made any previous suicide threats to get attention, or if he had a history of actual suicide attempts I didn't know about. I didn't hear back from her. It was late, so she didn't get the messages until the next morning. After no response from him or his daughter, I became very nervous and decided not to take any chances.

I called the Houston police to report his suicide threat and to give his address. I was in Annapolis, Maryland. We had been living separately since May. We had lived together six months in Tennessee, but I had decided we needed to live apart for a while when I decided to make a career change, so I went to Maryland where my family was, and he went temporarily to Houston, his hometown. We had hoped to move back in together before this, but we were getting finances situated, and trying to decide if we were going to settle down in Texas, Maryland, or maybe even go back to Tennessee. I still had my house in Nashville with renters living in it, so there was always the option of going back there.

The Houston police officer told me that an officer in Annapolis would come over shortly and take a report.

"It's not that I don't believe you," he explained, "it's just that you're calling from Maryland to report a suicide threat in Houston, but you're calling from a Tennessee area code. We have to make sure this is a legitimate call. We get a lot of crazy calls. I'm going to send a local officer to talk to you."

An Annapolis officer arrived and started taking down the report, which included Ronnie's information and address, and he looked at the text messages on my phone. He got the strangest look on his face when he saw Text #3.

"What's this about the Lynyrd Skynyrd plane crash? Selling books? What's he talking about?" he asked, shaking his head, looking quite confused.

"Well, he was their tour manager back in the 70's-"

"For Skynyrd?" he interrupted.

I nodded, and he continued, "Oh, wow... so he survived that plane crash? This guy we're talking about?"

"Yes," I answered.

"I wasn't even born yet," he said, "but I've heard all about that. I thought everyone died in that crash. Are you sure this guy's for real?"

"Yes. You can Google him. Ron Eckerman. I call him Ronnie. He's talking about a book he wrote last year. He still has horrible headaches because of the crash, and he's had one for about 4 days now. He was drinking tonight, so I don't know if he's not thinking clearly and just trying to upset me or if this is legit. I didn't want to take any chances."

"It looks legit to me," he said, still holding my phone. "I'm going to take this out to the car and read these texts to the officer in Houston. Is that ok?"

"Of course," I told him.

He went out to the cop car. For a few minutes I sat in the kitchen, stressing out and biting my nails. The officer came back to the door, quickly handed me my phone and said the Houston police were with Ronnie now, and an officer would be calling me shortly. He said everything's going to be okay, and he left without giving me any more details.

I thought, *Good. He's not really suicidal. He's just trying to get attention. I guess I showed him... embarrassing him in front of the neighbors like this. I hope he learned a lesson.*

A few minutes later, my cell phone rang. It was a Houston policeman.

"Miss Day? We're so glad you called. Five more minutes, and he would have been gone. He's in an ambulance right now on the way to the hospital."

I started trembling so much I could barely speak. I didn't know if he shot himself, or took a bunch of pills, or what. I had no idea.

"What happened? What did he do?" I asked.

"Carbon monoxide poisoning, ma'am. We got to the address and we heard a car running in the garage. The place was locked up tighter than a jug. We got over the fence at the back and got into the garage, but we had to break the door. I think he's gonna be alright. It sure was a close call."

"Is he coherent? Can he talk?"

"He was unconscious when we pulled him out of the car. He sort of woke up while we were putting him into the ambulance. He knew his name, but when we asked him what year it is, he said 1977, and he thought he was in Baton Rouge for some reason. He grabbed my arm and kept asking if Ronnie is okay. Ronnie is *his* name, right? So I kept saying, *'Yeah, buddy, you're gonna be alright.'* Then he kept asking if anyone else is hurt. He kept saying, *'It's all my fault'* over and over. He was really confused. Didn't make any sense."

"Sounds like he's having flashbacks," I told the officer. "He has PTSD from a plane crash a long time ago… nevermind. It's a long story. Did he ever come around?"

"When I told him you called to get him some help, he seemed to remember who you are, and then he suddenly was aware of his surroundings and what year it is. I think he'll be okay. Just a few more minutes, though, and he would have been gone. After they check him out at the hospital, they'll send him to the psychiatric unit. It's state law that when there's a suicide attempt, they put you in the psych ward for 72 hours for observation. We sure are glad you called! You saved his life!"

I *SAVED* his life? All I could do was think of all the hurtful things I said that made him not want to live anymore. How could I take credit for saving him, when I felt like I caused this?

Life is so strange sometimes. It's so hard to imagine how a man can want to die so much that he tries to commit suicide, then only four months later, all he wants to do is… LIVE.

How quickly life can change.

Thank you for your interest in the story of Ron's last and most important "tour" of his lifetime – his one year battle against acute myeloid leukemia.

Available on Amazon in paperback, Kindle, and audiobook. All proceeds go to leukemia research.

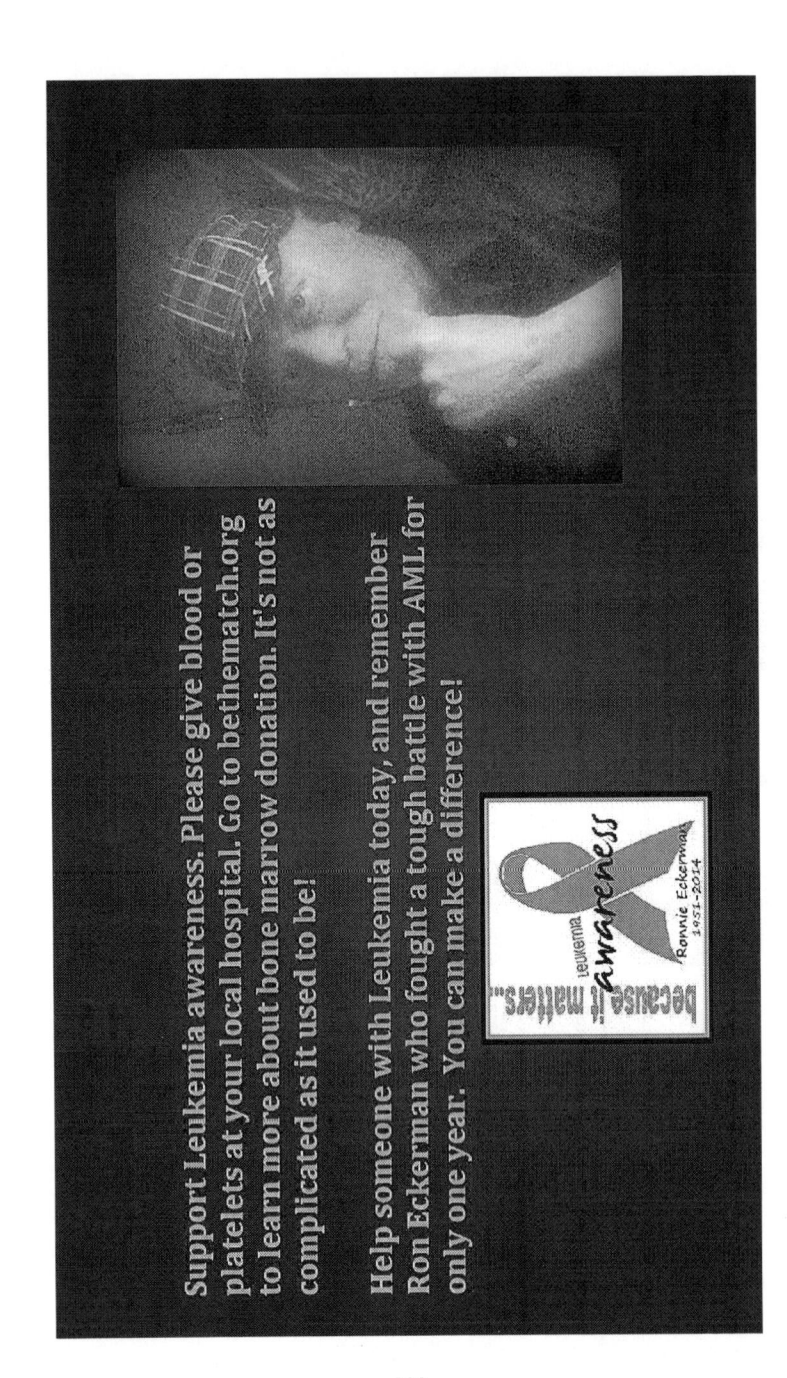

Support Leukemia awareness. Please give blood or platelets at your local hospital. Go to bethematch.org to learn more about bone marrow donation. It's not as complicated as it used to be!

Help someone with Leukemia today, and remember Ron Eckerman who fought a tough battle with AML for only one year. You can make a difference!

Printed in Great Britain
by Amazon